THE HOUSE OF LORDS

HOUSE
of
LORDS

Donald Shell

University of Bristol

Philip Allan/Barnes & Noble Books

First published 1988 by

PHILIP ALLAN PUBLISHERS
MARKET PLACE
DEDDINGTON
OXFORD OX5 4SE

First published in the USA 1988 by

BARNES & NOBLE BOOKS
81 ADAMS DRIVE
TOTOWA
NEW JERSEY 07512

British Library Cataloguing in Publication Data

Shell, Donald
   The House of Lords.
   1. Great Britain. Parliament. House of
   Lords.
   I. Title
   328.41′071

   ISBN 0–86003–402–X
   ISBN 0–86003–702–9 Pbk

Library of Congress Cataloging-in-Publication Data

Shell, Donald.
   The House of Lords / by Donald Shell.
     p. cm.
   Includes index.
   ISBN 0–389–20794–2
   1. Great Britain. Parliament. House of Lords. I. Title.
   JN6231988
   328.41′071--dc19   88–3957
                                           CIP

ISBN 0–389–20794–2

Typeset by Photoprint, Torquay
Printed and bound in Great Britain
by the Oxford University Press, Oxford

CONTENTS

PREFACE

The House of Lords is a paradox. Predictions of its decay and collapse have been made frequently for over a hundred years, yet in the 1980s it not only survives, but appears in rather rude good health. Popular mythology has viewed the House as troublesome to Labour but co-operative to the Conservatives. Yet since 1983 the House has been widely described as more effective than the Commons in obliging the Thatcher Government to adjust and modify its legislation. As long ago as 1911 the preamble to the Parliament Act clearly embodied the widely held expectation that the House would soon be subject to comprehensive reform, indeed replacement. But the seventy years since have seen no such change. Late twentieth-century Britain retains a 'House of Lords' which is still, as far as nominal membership is concerned, composed predominantly of hereditary members.

Schemes for reform of the House have regularly been brought forward, but no substantial agreement about an alternative House has yet been attained. In default of this, the present House remains. Yet it is by no means an unchanged House. Throughout the past thirty years, ever since the 1957 Life Peerages Act, the activity of the House has steadily increased. Procedural adaptation and innovation have occurred. The party balance has shifted, and the character of the active membership has altered. This book seeks to describe, analyse and evaluate these facts. Who are the active members? How pronounced is the rôle of party within the House? What influence does the House have within the whole business of government? What changes have taken place within the House, and what further changes are contemplated? Such questions as these are the focus of this book. The possible reform of the House, or the implications of its removal, are not entirely overlooked, but these matters are considered incidentally rather than as the major theme.

This is neither an historical nor a comparative study. The introductory chapter briefly considers the 'bicameral' (or two-chamber) principle and glances back at the development of the British Parliament. But this is really only to set the scene, as it were. The reader who wants to know more about the history of Parliament, or the comparative study of parliaments or second chambers, must be directed elsewhere.

Not since Professor Peter Bromhead's book *The House of Lords and Contemporary Politics* appeared in 1958 has a work similar in scope to this been published. Janet Morgan's *The House of Lords and the Labour Government 1964–70* provided an excellent discussion of the attempt to reform the House in 1968–69, and ably set this in the context of an analysis of the work of the House in that period. But the period since then has seen no publication of a systematic study of the House. Undergraduates studying British politics, as well as all who teach the subject at various levels will, I hope, benefit from this book. Those who work in and around Westminster, in parliament, government or journalism — and who want to develop a clearer understanding of the House of Lords — will also, I trust, find this work of some value.

The main sources for this book are listed on p. 221. Few scholars have conducted research on the contemporary House of Lords, but those few sources have been culled in the preparation of this work. I have over a number of years tried to keep a close eye on the House, and have frequently researched various aspects of its activities, and this study does of course draw on that work. I am indebted to many peers who over the years have given time to answer my questions and have furthered my understanding of the House. Several clerks have also been kind and generous in sharing with me their knowledge and insight concerning the House, as have a number of academic colleagues, particularly fellow members of the Study of Parliament Group. Particular mention must be made of David Beamish, now principal clerk in the Committee Office, and Gavin Drewry, reader in politics at the combined Bedford and Royal Holloway Colleges — both of whom have read and commented on my manuscript. Their help has been of great value, both in prompting attention to matters overlooked and in enabling me to avoid errors. Notwithstanding their efforts some errors no doubt remain and for these I alone am responsible, as also for all opinions expressed.

I am grateful to the Oxford University Press, publishers of *Parliamentary Affairs*, for permission to include here material which first appeared in that journal in 1985 (Vol. 38, No. 1).

Philip Cross, of Philip Allan Publishers, has been a steady source of encouragement throughout this enterprise and I am grateful for all his expert assistance. Finally, I am deeply indebted to Mary Woods for taking upon herself so cheerfully the main burden of typing and retyping successive drafts of this book. At various stages help was also given by Anne Dempsey and by my wife Tina, to whom I also express my gratitude.

Donald Shell
Bristol
January 1988

1

THE HOUSE OF LORDS
AND CONSTITUTIONAL DEVELOPMENT

Parliaments are frequently classified according to the number of chambers they possess. Those with a single chamber are termed unicameral, and those with two chambers bicameral. Most countries which have recognisable legislatures have unicameral bodies. But, if attention is focused on liberal democracies, most are bicameral, and the minority with one-chamber legislatures are without exception comparatively small in population. They include a number whose switch from bicameralism to unicameralism has been made in the post-war era, for example, New Zealand in 1950, Denmark in 1953, and Sweden in 1973, none of which have populations above ten million. We may generalise by saying that all large liberal democratic countries continue to have bicameral legislatures and that elsewhere bicameralism remains by no means uncommon, especially in liberal democracies. Why is this?

Bicameralism

The underlying justifications for bicameralism have changed as prevailing ideas about legitimate forms of government have altered. In the pre-democratic period parliamentary assemblies were generally two-chamber because this reflected the view that some sort of separate representation for aristocrats, or 'elders', or people of property, must be provided. As the acceptability of such notions of distinct class-based representation diminished, so the language in which second chambers were justified tended to alter. Instead of recognising the desirability of providing distinct representation for aristocracy and property, the need for a body to provide some restraint upon directly elected popular chambers came to be emphasised. J. S. Mill spoke of the corrupting influence of undivided power. Others argued that a second chamber was desirable in order to impose delay upon what a first chamber might rashly decide. For some this became a defence of second chambers grounded in the principles of democracy itself, as entailing the over-riding importance of a popular will. In 1918 the Bryce Commission justified the retention by the House of Lords of a power to

1

delay legislation so as 'to enable the opinion of the nation to be adequately expressed'. Second chambers were considered desirable to limit potential excesses of first chambers and to ensure that they did not run too far ahead of public opinion.

But the argument for delay was never securely based. As democratic values became more widely accepted, it was an argument which lost credibility. A directly elected first chamber was always likely to be more sensitive to public opinion, and a more faithful interpreter of that opinion, than a second chamber constituted by appointment, heredity, or even indirect election. In more recent years the justification for second chambers based on a delaying power has tended to give way to a justification based on the need to revise legislation after it has been dealt with by the first chamber. The greater complexity of legislation is frequently cited in support of this view. The need for a different kind of body to have a 'second look' at legislation, quite distinct from the examination given to it by the first chamber, is stressed. To do this properly, or at least to ensure that whatever alterations proposed by the second chamber are taken seriously by the first, it may be necessary to retain a power to delay. But it is less a delay intended to enable public opinion to be expressed than a delay intended to oblige genuine attention to be given by the Government and Lower House to changes proposed by the second chamber.

If one theme in contemporary discussion about second chambers is the need for bodies capable of revising legislation, another is their value in providing 'checks and balances' within a constitution. This is not so much a matter of delaying controversial legislation passed by a first chamber, as providing a means by which a first chamber acting alone can be prevented from carrying through changes which are thought to have important constitutional implications. This may be particularly well illustrated in relation to federal systems, which provide an obvious rationale for second chambers. This rationale may be said to have been invented by the founding fathers of the USA, even if it was by no means the only reason why a bicameral structure was preferred at the Philadelphia Convention. Almost without exception, wherever a federal system has been embodied, a bicameral national legislature has been established. Second chambers are a convenience in such situations: they can be composed in such a way as to provide a measure of reassurance to the constituent parts of a federation, and they can be given powers to fulfil the same purpose.

In practice, of course, they may scarcely fulfil this role. The German Bundesrat consists of members appointed by the Länder (or State) governments, and its functions are closely related to the federal structure in regard to which its formal powers are actually superior to the Bundestag. But in other matters its powers are very weak, and in political terms it has become a very marginal body. The Canadian Senate represents the

Table 1.1 Second Chambers in Seven Democracies

Country	Date of constitution	Federal	Directly elected president	Size of upper house	Method of appointment to upper house	Length of term of upper house
USA	1787	Yes	Yes	100	Direct election by simple majority	6 years (⅓ re-elected every 2 years)
France	1958	No	Yes	319	Indirect election by electoral college	9 years (⅓ re-elected every 3 years)
W. Germany	1947	Yes	No	41 (plus 4 non-voting)	Appointed by Land governments	4 years
Italy	1948	No	No	315 (plus ex officio)	Direct election PR	5 years
Canada	1867	Yes	No	104	Appointed by Governor-General	To retirement at 75
Australia	1901	Yes	No	64	Direct election by STV	6 years (½ re-elected every 3 years)
Ireland	1937	No	No	60	Elected from electoral colleges and co-opted	5 years

provinces in a formal sense, but unevenly, with twenty-four members from both of the largest two provinces and six members from each of the five smallest. In its activity, however, the Canadian Senate does not defend provincial interests; but neither has it any clear political role: rather, it has become a very quiescent, if not moribund, body. By contrast, the US Senate, the composition of which is also linked to the federal structure, with two senators per state irrespective of population, has become in political terms the senior house within Congress. And in its operation the US Senate has been by no means restricted to the role of defendant of states' rights (see Table 1.1).

If the role of providing 'checks and balances' within a constitution is most easily illustrated within federal systems, it is not necessarily confined to such systems. Second chambers frequently have particular powers in respect of ensuring the continuity of constitutional arrangements. Significantly, when the Parliament Act of 1911, limiting the powers of the House of Lords, was passed, an exception was made for any bill to extend the life of a parliament. On such a measure the House of Lords retains an absolute veto. This is intended to ensure that the House of Commons does not have the sole power to postpone a general election beyond a five-year interval. Such postponement was possible in wartime (from 1940–5), but only because both Houses agreed on the matter.

Second chambers, therefore, have diverse roles. They may help to safeguard the interests, even the integrity, of units within a federation. They may be of value because of their work in revising the details of legislation. They may be a means by which checks and balances within a constitution can be maintained. In a more general and less easily definable way, they may afford points of access to government which help to keep the executive in a modern state responsive to the interests and needs of different sections of the community. Any or all of these factors may seem important within a particular country, and as the needs of state and society develop so the functions of second chambers will change.

Wherever they exist, second chambers have invariably been subject to attack from the political left. The historical legacy they carry in the popular mind as being bodies representing propertied or aristocractic classes is one reason for this. But more modern arguments for second chambers, focusing on their restraining and revising roles, or their responsibilities as constitutional watchdogs, do not endear them to the radically minded. Their composition, too, usually ensures that they contain a high proportion of senior public figures. The average age of their members is invariably older than that of first chambers, and age and radicalism rarely combine. Second chambers, if elected at all, are usually elected less frequently and by less direct methods than first chambers. Not surprisingly the principle of bicameralism finds less general support on the left than on the right in politics.

Wherever a bicameral legislature exists, there is the possibility of conflict between the two chambers. That this can be damaging to the interests of a society is not to be doubted. But it need not be so. After all, conflict is inherent in the whole political enterprise. The real need is for institutions to be arranged in such a way as to ensure that processes for conciliation exist. A bicameral legislature may be part of such a process. The oft-quoted remark of Sièyes that, if the second chamber disagreed with the first it was obnoxious and that if it agreed it was superfluous, may have a certain logic about it, but in real political life agreement and disagreement are rarely so clear-cut. Rather, there tend to be both formal rules and informal understandings that shape the pattern of relations between two chambers. For example, the primacy of first chambers in regard to finance and taxation is general. Where a cabinet system of government exists, with the executive responsible to parliament in the sense of being removable by parliament, it is necessary clearly to establish that responsibility is to one chamber rather than to both. The Australian crisis of 1975 arose because this principle was not clear; the Australian Senate used its power to withhold supply in such a way as to bring about the downfall of the Whitlam Government at a time when that Government still retained the confidence of the Lower House (see Butler, 1976). In the USA the President is not responsible to either house of Congress, and differences between the two houses as well as differences between Congress and President are resolved according to rules stipulated in the Constitution and by various conventions. In the UK, as the notion of government responsible to parliament developed in the eighteenth century, it became established, though not without difficulty, that it was to the Commons and not to the Lords that governments were responsible.

Any discussion of the reasons underlying bicameralism runs the risk of implying a degree of deliberate self-conscious intent in the design of constitutions. This would be false to the reality of constitution making. The UK may be a rather extreme case in this regard, but all constitutions which have survived for any length of time show signs of adaptation. The consequences of this are that particular institutions operate in practice in such a way as to belie, to some extent, their original purpose. It may well be argued that the retention of second chambers has more to do with inertia and the force of tradition than any clear or widely accepted rationale. Second chambers exist because they always have existed. Where a second chamber is present it requires a considerable act of political will to abolish such a body. Even where entirely new constitutional arrangements are introduced, as in Germany after the war or France in 1958, the continuation of a bicameral structure of some kind may be due largely to the force of tradition and the sense of what is appropriate for a legislature, feelings and sentiments derived from the past.

Apart from reasons of constitutional principle which may offer some justification for second chambers, a practical point of considerable importance may be that such bodies do afford membership, status, and offices to individuals whose aspirations in this regard need to be satisfied. (Significantly, the way to abolition of the Kenyan Senate in 1966 was eased by securing seats for all incumbent senators in an expanded lower house.) In Britain the House of Lords undoubtedly has a value in providing a dignified home for rather senior political figures who might otherwise, through their continued occupancy of Commons seats, block the entrance of new blood.

   If the reasons underlying the widespread continuation of bicameralism are varied, so are the ways in which second chambers are composed. Most are elected, but frequently election is indirect, and may effectively amount to nomination. The West German Bundesrat has forty-one voting members, who are members of the Länder (or State) Cabinets. Where election to a second chamber is direct, this is usually from larger units and for longer terms than is the case for the lower house. In the USA senators are elected for six-year terms, with partial re-election every two years. An implication of senior status is hard to resist even if formally the powers of both chambers are equal. A significant minority of second chambers contain members appointed by the executive, and some are entirely composed in this way, though a formula may constrain the choice to ensure a degree of representation (as in the case of the Canadian Senate). Such a method of appointment almost inevitably carries with it the notion of award or honour, as for example with peerages in Britain. To do away with a second chamber may well involve the abolition of positions very highly valued by a minority, while being regarded with indifference by the vast majority. Britain alone retains heredity as a basis of membership. Why is this? For an answer we must look more specifically at the way the British Constitution has developed.

Development of the British Parliament

The British Parliament may reasonably claim to be the oldest continuing parliament in the world. Its origins lie in the Witans consulted by Saxon kings over a thousand years ago. Sometime in the fourteenth century two distinct houses emerged, with the representatives of the shires and boroughs becoming known as the Commons and beginning to meet separately from the magnates or great men of England, the Lords. Over the next two centuries the right of an individual to receive a writ of summons, as opposed to the right of the monarch to choose whom he summoned, became established. Thus the basis for membership of the Upper House became more clearly defined. The emergence of various ranks within the peerage also took place (Powell and Wallis, 1968).

In the Tudor period there arose the classical theory of the English constitution, a mixed form of government in which, following Aristotle, 'the King represented the monarchic element; the House of Lords the aristocractic; and the House of Commons the democratic' (Weston, 1965, p. 2). This provided a theoretical justification for the institutional arrangements which had emerged. It was a justification which outlived the seventeenth-century Puritan revolution. During that period, for eleven years, the throne was vacant and the House of Lords did not meet. But the Cromwellian era was an interlude. In 1660 separate sittings of the Upper House resumed. A Restoration took place, the monarchy was brought back, and the classical theory of the constitution became ascendant throughout the eighteenth century. Important changes had of course taken place, involving limitations on the power of the monarch and alterations in the relationship between Lords and Commons. But these were accomplished through the modification of ancient institutions rather than through their abolition or replacement. For this reason no formal or written constitution ever became necessary. The House of Lords, like the monarchy and other institutions, gradually evolved. No authoritative document ever defined its role, though commentators propounded various doctrines to explain and justify the pattern of relationships which existed.

Because the House of Lords acquiesced in change — if with great reluctance at times — it survived, a point the truth of which has been demonstrated right down to the present day. For example, immediately after the Restoration the House of Lords attempted to involve itself in matters of finance. The Commons' privilege here had been implicit in the emergence of two separate houses, but in response to the Lords' action, the Commons resolved in 1671 that 'in all aids given the King by the Commons the rate of tax ought not to be altered by the Lords', and in 1678 after a further attempt by the Lords to amend a financial bill, the Commons passed a stronger resolution stating that it alone possessed the right to grant aids and supplies and to determine the purposes for which they were used.

The eighteenth century saw confirmation of the idea that the King's Government was responsible to Parliament, but it was responsibility to the Lower House which became recognised as fundamental. This may seem strange because most of the great offices of state were still held by members of the Lords. But it was the Commons which had insisted on a Bill of Rights in 1689 — establishing the authority of Parliament *vis-à-vis* the King — and it was the Commons which had successfully asserted its primacy over taxation matters and the control of supply, an area of ever-growing importance. But of the need for reform of the Lords, or argument for its abolition, very little was heard in the eighteenth century. Discussion of reform for the Commons could proceed apace, the more so as the century ebbed away, but that was in order to improve the quality of the democratic element within what was thought to be a perfectly balanced constitution, rather than in obedience to any doctrine of democratic supremacy. A further reason why no serious conflict between the two Houses emerged lay in the extent to which Commons membership was still controlled by peers through their powers of patronage.

In the event the great Reform Act of 1832 not only brought an extension of the franchise but also, in effect, brought about the collapse of the theory of mixed government. During debates on the bill Whig leaders declared that it would constitute a permanent settlement of what had become a great constitutional question. But as soon as the bill was passed, and this, be it noted, against the intentions of monarch and Lords, the democratic element within the Constitution had been recognised as pre-eminent. From then on the House of Lords was talked of as a revising chamber, and schemes for its reform abounded. In 1836 James Mill called for the Lords' veto over legislation to become suspensive only, a proposal eventually adopted in 1911. In 1867 Bagehot first published his *English Constitution* which firmly relegated the House of Lords to the status of a dignified rather than an efficient part of the Constitution; earlier (in the eighteenth century) the House of Lords, if not a 'directing chamber', had at least been 'a chamber of directors', but by the mid-nineteenth century its value lay in the fact that it inspired reverence in the people, and while clearly subordinate to the Commons, could yet revise and possibly suspend bills (Bagehot, 1963, Ch. 3).

For fifty years after 1832 the 'two Houses lived together in general harmony, quarrelling about privilege rather than about policy' (Le May, 1979, p. 127). One reason for this lay in the continued influence of aristocratic families in the House of Commons though this gradually diminished, more markedly after the second Reform Act of 1867. More significant was the rise of the modern notion of party. In the latter part of the century government became first and foremost party government, with power more heavily concentrated among the few who forced their way into the front ranks of the parties. Talk of the decline of parliament began — and has continued ever since. Within the House of Lords Conservative peers under the influence of the third Marquess of Salisbury developed the 'Referendal Theory'. According to this doctrine it could be right for the Lords to delay legislation about which the opinion of the nation was not clear until a 'higher authority than the House of Lords' (the phrase was Salisbury's) had spoken. The problem with this theory lay in the impossibility most of the time of deriving from an election result any clear view of what national opinion was on a specific issue. Nevertheless it was a doctrine which emboldened Conservative peers in their opposition to the measures promoted by Liberal governments. In particular the events of

1893 to 1895, with the Lords defeating home rule for Ireland, and the Liberal Government being itself convincingly defeated at the polls, encouraged Conservative peers to see the Lords as once again a decisive factor in government.

The Pre-World War I Constitutional Crisis and Its Effects

When the election of 1906 gave the Liberals 400 seats in a Commons of 670 members, conflict with the Conservative-dominated Lords was inevitable. The new government's reforming legislation was soon being mutilated or rejected by the Upper House. The Conservative leader, Balfour, declared in 1907 that the Lords had a duty to see that the laws of the country were not 'the hasty and ill-considered offspring of one passionate election'. In the same year the Commons approved a resolution emphasising that the will of the Lower House must prevail. The parties were set on a collision course. But what would be the best issue on which the government should take a stand against the peers? And what constitutional adjustment should then take place? Opinion within Liberal Party circles was divided. Some argued for a suspensory veto, others for a plan which would have allowed 100 peers to join with MPs to vote jointly on disputed issues, a proposal which would have meant that the legislation of any non-Conservative government lacking a comfortable Commons majority would be at risk. While social reform was an obvious area of controversy, the spectre of Irish home rule haunted British politics throughout this period.

In 1909 the Lords rejected outright the Finance Bill embodying that year's budget proposals. This was a challenge the Government had to take up. Throughout 1910 the argument raged; two general elections were fought, with Liberals losing ground in the first but holding their position in the second. A constitutional conference between party leaders met for several months (Blewett, 1972). Eventually the Parliament Act of 1911 was passed, but only because Conservative peers knew that if they didn't acquiesce, enough Liberals would be given peerages to swamp their majority. This major constitutional measure removed the Lords' right of veto, replacing it with a power to delay ordinary legislation for approximately two years; bills certified by the Speaker of the Commons as 'money' bills could only be held up for one month. The Parliament Act dealt with the most urgent question, which was the power of the Lords, but its preamble made clear that it was only intended as an interim measure before the composition of the Upper House was fundamentally altered. Schemes for reform abounded, with peers themselves, in 1910, accepting by 175 votes to 17 a resolution endorsing the view that possession of a peerage should no longer automatically carry with it the right to sit and vote in the Lords. In 1917 a Commission was set up under Lord Bryce to consider both the powers and composition of the Upper House.

Meanwhile, the constitutional crisis, though ameliorated by the 1911 Act, was not exhausted. In 1912 the Government brought forward its home rule bill for Ireland; the Conservatives objected violently to this measure and it was rejected repeatedly by the Lords. The new Parliament Act procedure was invoked. Not until 1914 did the bill reach the statute book, only to be immediately suspended because of the arrival of war, by which time the Government had become convinced of the need to exclude Ulster. Between 1911 and 1914 the House of Lords delayed three other bills, thus showing that Conservative peers, notwithstanding their defeat over the Parliament Act, were still quite prepared to make vigorous use of the remaining powers of the House.

War brought an interlude, and by the time normal peacetime policies had started up again, the Conservative Party was once again dominant within government. The Bryce Commission, which consisted of thirty-two of the leading political figures of the day, produced its report in 1918 (Cd. 9038). As to powers, its members agreed that the 1911 Parliament Act did not provide a suitable permanent solution. Instead it recommended arrangements by which members of both Houses would meet jointly to resolve differences, having also carefully considered but rejected proposals for referenda in such circumstances. As to composition it proposed an Upper House partly elected by MPs and partly chosen by a joint committee of both Houses in such a way as to ensure that some hereditary peers remained as members. But on this some members of the Bryce Commission dissented.

Most subsequent references to the Bryce Commission have been to its definition of the functions of the Lords, which remains worth citing despite the passage of the years. Four functions for a second chamber received general endorsement: first, the examination and revision of bills brought from the Commons; second, the initiation of bills of a non-controversial character, which may have an easier passage through the Commons if they have been fully discussed and put into a well-considered shape before being submitted to it; third, the interposition of so much delay (and no more) in the passing of a bill into law as may be needed to enable the opinion of the nation to be adequately expressed upon it (this would be especially desirable on bills affecting the Constitution); and fourth, the full and free discussion of large and important questions, especially when the Commons is otherwise occupied, and possibly with the advantage that in a second chamber such discussions can take place without the constraint that the fate of the Government might depend on the outcome of any divisions which may take place.

Subsequent discussion of the functions of the Upper House has invariably endorsed three of the four above points (for example, the Labour Government White Paper in 1969 did so), but controversy has surrounded the delaying function. It has always seemed artificial to entrust to an unelected chamber the task of deciding when delay should be imposed in order to enable public opinion to be expressed on a matter. Inevitably any exercise of this function would be selective, and it has never seemed likely — at least until the 1980s — that Conservative governments would run any serious risk of having delay imposed on measures they considered important. At the same time the possibility of leaving the second chamber totally without powers of any kind has seemed inappropriate to most Labour, as well as Conservative, governments.

After the Bryce Commission report, a general expectation that reform of the House would take place continued. Government proposals, not unlike those of the Bryce Commission itself, were put forward in 1922 and again in 1927. On both occasions the proposals received substantial parliamentary debate and general endorsement. But no detailed progress on reform was made, the basic reason being that the motivation for any change lay too transparently in the Conservatives' desire to enhance the legitimacy of the Lords so as to enable it to block the sort of legislation which a majority Labour Government might introduce. Only twice in the whole inter-war period, however, did Labour take the reigns of office, but neither in 1924 nor again between 1929 and 1931 did it have a Commons majority. The legislation passed by the Commons could not therefore be of a kind to arouse strong objections from other parties or from the Lords. In 1931 one government bill was rejected at second reading by the Lords (a measure to raise the school-leaving age) but shortly afterwards the Government collapsed. Proposals for reform of the Lords continued, but governments clearly thought they had more important matters to engage their attention.

By the time Labour first came to power with a clear overall majority (of 152, no less) in 1945, memories of the bitter pre-1914 disputes had faded, replaced by immediate recollections of co-operation between leading politicians during the Second World War. Labour in office preferred to concentrate on its nationalisation measures, and the establishment of the welfare state, rather than divert attention to the Lords. For their part Conservative peers refrained from voting down government bills because they accepted guidance formulated by their leader, the fifth Marquess of Salisbury, to the effect that it was wrong for the House to reject measures which had received clear endorsement by the electorate. Even the iron and steel nationalisation bill, the introduction of which was delayed by the Government because of its more contentious character, was accepted by peers without division at second reading, though the Lords did successfully press the Government to agree to delay implementation of the bill until after the 1950 election.

Uncertain as to whether the House of Lords might become more obstructive as the prospect of an election loomed closer, the Government introduced a bill to amend the 1911 Parliament Act by reducing the power of delay from two years to one. During the passage of this bill in 1948, all-party discussions took place about the possibility of reform in the composition of the Upper House. These made some progress before breaking down over irreconcilable differences on the power the Lords should retain, though the gap between the two parties on this was ostensibly a mere three months. The Parliament Act of 1949 was therefore passed under the provisions of the 1911 Act — the first time these had been used since the First World War. In general, however, the actions of Conservative peers from 1945–51 showed clearly that they had now accepted the subordinate status of the Lords: the Upper House did not contest power with the Commons in the way it had done early in the century.

The outcome of the all-party discussions in 1948 revealed a considerable consensus. The final paragraph of the party leaders' agreed statement is worth quoting: 'The representatives of all three Parties were united in their desire to see the House of Lords continue to play its proper part in the Legislature; and in particular to exercise the valuable functions of revising Bills sent up by the Commons, and initiating discussion on public affairs. It was regarded as essential, moreover, that there should be available to the country a legislative body composed of men of mature judgement and experience gained in many spheres of public life . . . ' (Cmd 7380, 1948). The differences over powers were nevertheless held to be fundamental, preventing the carrying forward in detail of proposals for reform. The same document did indicate a number of agreed principles regarding reform of composition. These included: the view that modification of the existing House of Lords was preferable to the creation of a new body, say one based on election; that no party should have a permanent majority; that heredity alone should not confer a right of membership; that women should be included; that some remuneration should be payable to members; that peers not members of the second chamber should be eligible for membership of the Commons; and that some provision for disqualification from membership should be made for those who neglect or become unable to fulfil their duties as members.

Though no comprehensive reform could take place, it had long been obvious that some piecemeal changes were desirable. Indeed, four of the proposals quoted above made by the 1948 conference were taken up in various ways during the lifetime of Conservative governments from 1951 to 1964. The payment of expenses and the introduction of leave of absence arrangements were minor changes, though the former undoubtedly had an important impact on the work of the Lords through enabling some members who were otherwise unable to attend to do so. The admission of women and the ability for hereditary peers to remain eligible for Commons membership were further changes made in this period. Most significant though was the institution of life peerages.

Life Peerages

The principle of awarding life peerages had been considered frequently in the past. From the early nineteenth century onwards an increased proportion of new peerages went to distinguished public servants who did not possess the large estates considered necessary to support a peerage. In some cases estates were awarded by a grateful government, to Wellington and Nelson for example; in other cases substantial pensions were paid, so that at least the recipient of a peerage could live in an appropriate style. But what of the heirs of such men? Would they become landless, even penniless, peers? To guard against such distasteful possibilities, life peerages, supported perhaps by state pensions, were advocated, most commonly for victorious generals, but then especially for senior judges. And in the latter case an additional argument lay in the need adequately to staff the House of Lords for its judicial work, an activity which peers were loath to see removed. But the argument against life peerages was also strongly made, centring on the view that the independence of the Upper House could no longer be guaranteed if such peerages were conferred.

For twenty years in the middle of the last century the Lords resisted active attempts by successive governments to introduce life peers (see Bromhead, 1958, pp. 245–6). Eventually, in 1876, in the context of other judicial reforms, provision was made for two judges to be appointed as Lords of Appeal in Ordinary, with life peerages conferred upon appointment. Compromise in relation to a precisely defined group had proved possible. But further attempts to extend the life peerage principle over the next eighty years were frustrated, initially by a fear that such would weaken the independence of the Upper House, but latterly out of a reluctance to allow piecemeal rather than fundamental reform of the Lords to take place.

Because the Labour Party believed a comprehensive reform of the House ought to take place it was always ambivalent about the creation of any new peerages. In 1938 there were still only 15 Labour peers, compared with 80 Liberals and 400 Conservatives (Laski, 1938). Attlee, however, took a decidedly practical view and ennobled forty-four Labour supporters between 1945 and 1951. Labour representation in the House of Lords became adequate, but never generous. Back in opposition, Labour numbers began to decline, and Conservative prime ministers were reluctant to give hereditary awards to their opponents. In any case, with new hereditary creations running on average at almost ten per year, the House of Lords was growing in size by more than fifty per decade. Unless the flow of new creations were increased, the proportion of peers by succession would grow, a trend which had nothing to recommend it.

A simple bill to award life peerages provided a means of escape from the trap. Prior to its introduction the Government undertook some discussions with Labour leaders about possible reforms, but in the end acted on its own in bringing forward the Life Peerages Bill. During debate in both Houses Labour leaders made clear their suspicion that the Government's main intention was to enhance the prestige of the Lords, while retaining the hereditary principle. The Government for its part carefully avoided making any commitment which might constrain in any way a future prime minister's freedom to choose people as he wished. On second reading, R. A. Butler said in the Commons that life peerages would be given to distinguished people whose membership would strengthen the second chamber and ensure that it adequately and accurately reflected the life of the nation. This could well have been said of previous hereditary awards. An incidental innovation was the proposal that life peerages could be conferred on women as well as men. In the Lords at committee stage 'gentlemen's club' arguments flowed for a short while, but the men present voted by 134 to 30 in support of female eligibility to join their House — or club.

To begin with, life peers were appointed with the implication that they would be working members of the Upper House, and their names announced separately from the regular honours lists. Soon, however, the New Year and Queen's birthday honours lists included life peers, and when the Labour Party came to office in 1964, Mr Wilson announced that he would not recommend any further hereditary peerages.

The Life Peerages Act permitted the substantial reinforcement of the Labour benches in the Lords. Less foreseeable was the subsequent growth in the cross-benchers. The total number of new peerages created was much greater, and since 1958 the activity of the House of Lords has gradually and continuously increased. All these points are taken up in the following chapters. Meanwhile mention should be made of two other minor changes which took place at about the same time.

During the 1957–8 debates on the Life Peerages Bill, the Labour leader, Mr Gaitskell, emphasised the difficulty in finding Labour supporters able to spend time working without pay in the Lords. A reading of Gaitskell's diary underlines the point (Gaitskell, 1983, pp. 416, 564). The day of the penniless peer had arrived, but some of those least well-off financially were among those whose participation the Lords most required. Their presence was necessary to keep the opposition front bench from total collapse. An allowance was therefore introduced in 1957 to enable peers to claim out-of-pocket expenses incurred in attending the House of Lords. This allowance steadily increased over the following years and the definition of expenses which may legitimately be claimed widened, for example, to include secretarial costs (see Appendix A for details).

The second minor change also derived from the peculiarities of the Upper House's composition. This was the introduction of leave of absence for peers who did not wish to attend the House of which they were members. The fact that the royal writ of summons commanded the attendance of a peer at the House of Lords 'waiving all excuses' was an embarrassment to some who were near-permanent absentees. But a further and more serious embarrassment arose when peers who generally were absent suddenly appeared in quite large numbers to vote on some controversial issue. The sixty peers by succession who came to vote against the abolition of the death penalty in 1956 after four years of silent membership, gave new credence to the old cry of 'backwoodsman'. Though the Lords' rejection of abolition on this occasion did not bring it into conflict with the government of the day, it was in conflict with the House of Commons, which had approved abolition on a free vote. The reputation of the Upper House suffered because of the high turnout of peers to vote on this emotive issue. Soon afterwards a Lords' select committee was set up 'to consider the powers of the House in relation to the attendance of its members'. In agreement with its proposals (HL 60, 1957–8) standing orders were amended to enable peers to apply for leave of absence.

This arrangement does give a decent indemnity to the permanent absentee, but it is very doubtful whether it has had any other effect. The term 'backwoodsman' has no clearly defined meaning. It can be brought into use after any large turnout by those who wish to bring discredit on a particular vote or on the House of Lords itself. It popularly describes Conservative peers by succession who from deep in the shires answer a bugle call from their Chief Whip to appear for crucial divisions to swell Conservative numbers. But the very rare attenders are in fact the frail and elderly, or very busy people with heavy and genuine commitments away from Westminster. They are not predominantly hereditary peers, nor Conservatives. They include law lords and bishops and many others who owe their first allegiance to their professional duties.

The Peerage Act 1963

Proposals to allow individuals to renounce peerages which they inherit had frequently been made over the past hundred years, most recently as amendments to the Life Peerages Bill. None had succeeded. Some MPs who had become disqualified for continued membership of the Commons through inheriting a peerage had left the Lower House with considerable reluctance. In 1960 a thirty-five-year-old MP, Anthony Wedgwood-Benn, who had been elected as member for Bristol South-East in 1950, inherited a peerage. As a popular, young and very able member of the parliamentary Labour Party he had understandable ambition to remain in the Commons. When he succeeded to his peerage the Commons Committee of Privileges ruled that he was disqualified from membership of the Lower House, and a by-election for his seat was declared. Benn stood as a candidate and gained an increased majority, but then found himself unseated by an election court, which declared his Conservative opponent (who had fewer than half as many votes) elected. For the next two years the member who sat in the Commons for Bristol South-East was the man soundly defeated at this by-election!

A joint select committee of both Houses was set up to consider the matters raised by this constitutional imbroglio (HL 23, HC 38, 1962–3). Its recommendations were embodied in the 1963 Peerage Act, which permitted peers by succession to renounce their peerages for life. Mr Benn naturally took the earliest opportunity to do this, and was once more elected MP for Bristol South-East at a by-election precipitated by the immediate resignation of the Conservative member once the Peerage Act was given royal assent.

Ironically the consequences of this legislation were much more far-reaching for the Conservative party than for Labour. It enabled the Conservative succession to pass from Macmillan to Lord Home in October 1963, and brought another leading Conservative, Lord Hailsham — also a contender for the party leadership — back into the Commons as well. The Peerage Act laid down that all peers by succession could renounce their peerages; those who had already inherited, and newly succeeding peers, had twelve months to decide what to do, unless they were MPs, in which case a decision had to be given within a month. Peerages so renounced could be taken up again by the next heir upon the death of the 'disclaimer'.

Opportunity was taken in the same legislation to reduce some anomalies in regard to membership of the House of Lords. Most notable was the admission of women who had succeeded to peerages, excluded up to 1963 despite the entry of women as life peers. This represented the removal of a very minor but totally unjustified element of sex discrimination. Only eighteen ladies were involved. A second change brought into the Lords all thirty-one holders of Scottish peerages in place of the previous arrangement under which this group elected sixteen of their number for each parliament. This, it should be noted, involved the abandonment of a practice, the extension of which had been advocated frequently in the past, as a way of reducing the number of hereditary peers who had a right to sit in the House of Lords. The Labour opposition tolerated these minor extensions of the hereditary membership of the Lords because of its eagerness to establish the right to disclaim peerages.

A final effect of the 1963 Peerage Act was to regularise somewhat the position of peers of Ireland. The Union with Ireland Act in 1800 abolished the Irish House of Lords, but gave to the holders of Irish peerages the right to elect twenty-eight of their number to sit in the United Kingdom House of Lords. However, a consequence of the 1920 Government of Ireland Act had been the abolition of the machinery by which such elections took place. Despite pressure from Irish peers, no further elections were held. Existing elected peers continued to sit in the Lords, but the last of these died in 1961. Some Irish peers also held other peerages which entitled them to seats, but about seventy were not only excluded from the Lords, but were unable to vote in elections to the Commons, and though entitled to sit as MPs for any mainland constituency, not eligible to do so for a seat in Ulster. The 1963 Act relieved them of these disabilities, but failed to make it quite clear that an Irish peerage conferred no right to a seat in the Lords. In 1966 the House of Lords agreed to a report from its Committee for Privileges which rejected a petition to allow seats to holders of Irish peerages (HL 53, 1966–7).

These were relatively minor rationalisations. As far as the 1963 Peerage Act was concerned most attention focused on the provisions which allowed for renunciation. How many hereditary peers would forsake the Lords? Would there be a hundred, or even more? Was it likely that 'the shot in the arm given by the Life Peerages Act of 1958 would now be counterbalanced by the loss of good blood back to the Commons' as Crick suggested? (Crick, 1964, p. 140). Such expectations were not fulfilled. Disclaiming never caught on. Initially four of the 750 or so peers by succession renounced their peerages. Between 1964 and 1977 another eleven did so, an average of less than one a year out of fifteen to twenty-five who succeed to peerages each year. Since 1977 no disclaiming at all has taken place, and indeed two heirs have taken up the peerages renounced by their fathers and become active in the House (see Appendix B). This is not at all the outcome expected when the Peerage Act was first passed. It illustrates in a small way the changed attitude to the House of Lords over the last twenty or so years.

The 1960s: The House of Lords Re-Invigorated

From the atrophy of the 1950s the House of Lords gradually reasserted itself. Labour became a much more vigorous opposition in the early 1960s, re-invigorated by the arrival of new life peers fresh from the Commons; some bills — notably the London Government Bill — were fought with a tenacity hitherto unknown in the Upper House. Almost as many divisions took place on this one bill as had been held in the entire previous Parliament. As the 1960s progressed a marked change in the ethos of the Lords became apparent (Vincent, 1966). Instead of a large majority supporting the death penalty, as in 1956, the Lords voted in 1965 by a majority of 100 for abolition. In the late 1960s peers took a leading part in enacting the so-called permissive-society legislation on divorce, abortion and homosexuality.

But even if the character of the House of Lords had changed and Labour's strength increased, a huge party imbalance remained. With Labour back in office after 1964, the Lords inflicted numerous defeats on the Government. The Conservatives forced many more divisions than they had when last in Opposition, and these they almost invariably won. Sometimes the Government decided to compromise after defeat, but more usually it sought and obtained the deletion of Lords' amendments back in the Commons and the subsequent acquiescence of peers.

For the Conservative leadership a major concern remained the 'exercise of some control so that we don't defeat the Government too often,' as Lord St. Aldwyn, Tory Chief Whip, put the matter in a radio interview in May 1970. It was growing restiveness among Conservative peers which erupted in an ill-advised and pointless confrontation with the Government on the Southern Rhodesia Sanctions Order in June 1968. The order was defeated — the first time the House of Lords had used its veto power over a statutory instrument (see Chapter 8) — but only by a narrow margin (193 votes to 184). It was a hollow victory, the main result of which was Government anger and Opposition embarrassment (Morgan, 1975).

An immediate consequence was the breaking off by the Government of all-party talks on the reform of the Upper House which had been initiated in 1967 — for the 1960s had become a decade of institutional reform. Labour in office, with tacit support from the Conservatives under Mr Heath, sought to modernise Britain by the simple expedient of structural reform — in the civil service, in local government, in the education system, and of course, in Parliament itself, including the House of Lords. Before they were abruptly terminated, these all-party talks on the Lords had attained a considerable measure of agreement, and this became the basis of the White Paper entitled *House of Lords Reform* (Cmnd. 3799, 1968).

These proposals were a rational attempt at evolutionary reform. The Lords would have continued as recognisably the same body, but eventually all hereditary members would have been removed, and an entirely nominated Upper House emerged. Crucial to the reform was the introduction of a so-called two-writ scheme, under which some members of the House of Lords would be entitled to vote but others only to attend and speak. Non-voting members initially were to have included all existing peers by succession, but on their decease their heirs, while inheriting their peerages, would not inherit any right to membership of the Upper House. Created peers who attended less than one-third of the sittings or were over retirement age (stipulated as 72) would also be non-voting members. Those entitled to vote would therefore be the more regularly attending life peers below the age of 72, but including a reduced number of bishops and law lords. All told, the voting Lords would have been about 230 strong, with the government of the day being the largest party, though without an overall majority.

The White Paper discussed the functions of the Lords, though only briefly. The retention of some power was deemed fitting, and this was fixed at an ability to delay legislation for six months 'from the point of disagreement between the two Houses' a period not likely to be very different in practice from the twelve-month delay measured from the date of a Commons second reading established in 1949. However, in addition to the function of revising bills brought from the Commons, initiating less controversial bills and providing a forum for debate, the White Paper made particular mention of the Lords' role in considering subordinate legislation, dealing with private bills, and 'the scrutiny of the activities of the executive'. An appendix to the White Paper spoke of an enhanced role for a reformed House of Lords in such activities, and held out the prospect — enticing to some of the more active peers — of participation in a range of joint select committees of the two Houses. Reform for the second chamber was clearly being envisaged as a means to make the Upper House a more effective part of Parliament — not simply to arrest its decline (as had been done with the 1958 Life Peerages Act), but to reassert its significance.

The House of Lords voted by 251 to 56 in favour of the White Paper proposals, with the forty-three Conservatives opposing being outnumbered more than two-to-one by Conservatives in support. In the Commons a vote on the proposals also produced a majority, though a much less convincing one.

The planned reform was embodied in the Parliament (No. 2) Bill. This achieved a Commons second reading, but soon got completely bogged down in committee (taken on the floor of the House because this was a constitutional measure). Many Labour MPs objected to the continuation of the second chamber, especially one still linked to the peerage and the honours system; they feared that, thus reformed, it would prove a more formidable body than the unreformed House of Lords. Conservative MPs were fearful of the loss of independence involved in the sacrifice of the hereditary basis of membership: some would have preferred an elected element, but no consensus existed about that. Two formidable back-

benchers — Mr Foot and Mr Powell — though representing contrasting
viewpoints, joined forces in obstructing the bill. Proceedings ground to a
virtual halt and the bill was dropped. Nowhere had the proposals
generated real enthusiasm. The front benches of both parties offered
support, but only in a lukewarm manner. Those most disappointed with
the failure of the scheme were probably active members of the House of
Lords.

This debacle did affect the mood of the Lords. Peers had overwhelmingly
endorsed these proposals: they had fallen because MPs disliked them and
because the Government was unwilling to persist with them. The
unmodernised composition of the House was no longer the fault of the
peers themselves. They were embarrassed by it but helpless to remedy it.
Why then should the House take special care to avoid conflict with the
Commons? MPs had treated the Lords shabbily, so why should not peers
allow a little more awkwardness into the relationship between the Houses?
Such arguments had a partial validity. They were heard almost immediately
over the 1969 House of Commons (Redistribution of Seats) Bill, a measure
which sought to delay the revision of parliamentary constituency boundaries,
and could thus be described as having strong constitutional overtones. The
Lords showed every intention of using its legal powers to exhaustion on
this bill, but the Government side-stepped conflict with the peers by the
rather unscrupulous use of a procedural device in the Commons which
allowed it to get its way without the need for legislation at all (on all this
see Morgan, 1975).

Further conflict between the Houses was postponed as a result of the
Conservative election victory in 1970. But further evidence of the more
general reinvigoration of the House was provided by the markedly
different relationship between the Heath Government and the Lords
between 1970 and 1974 from that of previous Conservative governments.
Labour peers were three times as numerous in 1970 as they had been in the
early 1960s, and the number of crossbenchers had grown. No longer did
the Conservatives have an overall majority. On twenty-six occasions the
Government was defeated, and when this occurred, ground was usually,
though not invariably, given to the Lords. On the 1971 Immigration Bill
peers insisted (by 93 votes to 79) on an amendment providing reassurance
for existing immigrants. On the 1972 National Health Service Bill peers
voted in favour of free contraception services, and only when the
Commons asserted financial privilege (see Chapter 5) did peers give way.
The House of Lords was generally a good deal less submissive to the Heath
Government than it had been to his Conservative predecessors.

The Labour opposition flexed its new muscle in the House, exploiting
the relative absence of procedural constraints to mount an onslaught on
some of the Heath Government's more contentious bills. Notable was the

attack on the Industrial Relations Bill which took twenty-seven days for committee and report stages, and upon which 138 divisions took place — figures unsurpassed before or since on any single measure. The Government won every one of these divisions, and made few concessions (Moran, 1977). But the strenuous efforts of labour peers earned praise in quarters usually hostile to the House; Eric Heffer, spokesman for many on the Labour left, wrote of the 'magnificent fight' and the 'gallant efforts' of the Labour lords in his chronicle on this bill's enactment (Heffer, 1976, pp. 267–8). Neither Labour election manifesto of 1974 mentioned the House of Lords. But with Labour back in office again, the situation was soon drastically to change.

Labour in Conflict with the House

The period 1974–9 was exceptional within both Houses of Parliament. Two particular factors contributed to make it so. First, no longer did any special sanctions apparently attach to government defeat in the Commons. The constitutional myth that governments may have to resign if defeated on major matters had been exploded. Second, for all of this period the Government lacked a secure majority in the Commons, and for most of the time it lacked any overall majority. But whereas in the past governments with insecure majorities had refrained from bringing forward very controversial legislation, Labour showed no inhibitions about doing so from 1974 to 1976.

The Conservatives in opposition pressed divisions on large numbers of hostile amendments to government bills, defeating the Government over 350 times in the division lobby (or in over 80 per cent of all divisions which took place). Sometimes the Government found itself unable to reverse the Lords' amendments back in the Commons, for example on the Housing Finance Bill of 1975 and the Dock Work Regulation Bill of 1976; the emasculation of these measures was the result of defection by Labour MPs as much as action by the House of Lords. Where the Lords' amendments were cancelled by the Commons, peers generally gave way without more ado. But the Opposition did decide to dig in its heels and quite deliberately use the power of the Lords on three carefully chosen matters.

The first of these involved the 1975 Trade Union and Labour Relations Bill, and concerned the provision of safeguards against possible abuse of the 'closed shop' principle among journalists. The Government's leading opponent in the Upper House was the formidable crossbench peer, Lord Goodman, behind whom, through much of this controversy, the Conservatives took shelter. The bill fell at the end of the 1974–5 session, and was reintroduced in the following session, but eventually passed without the

Parliament Act procedures running their full course, mainly because the Government changed its position and the Conservative Party got in a muddle (see Beloff, 1976). The second confrontation was over the bill nationalising aerospace and shipbuilding introduced in the 1975–6 session. Again the bill fell at the end of the session because the two Houses were still in dispute over amendments to delete ship-repairing. But here a technical procedural device became available because the bill was found by parliamentary clerks to be 'hybrid' and therefore liable to an elaborate time-consuming parliamentary procedure (see Chapter 8). In the Commons the Government had the 'hybridity' rule set aside (though by only a single vote, 304–303). In the Lords no such easy way of escape from potentially lengthy select committee hearings was available, so Labour ministers reluctantly compromised and dropped ship-repairing from the bill.

The third exercise of power involved the outright rejection of a bill which would have brought Felixstowe Dock into public ownership, but because this was a private bill promoted by the British Docks and Harbour Board — albeit one with clear government support, and one which had already passed the Commons — the Government could do nothing to overcome the decision of the House (see pp. 176–9).

By 1977 the Government had lost its overall majority in the Commons, which meant that legislation which did not command support beyond Labour's own ranks could not pass through the Commons, let alone the Lords. Tension between the two Houses subsided. But by that time Labour had renewed its historic commitment to abolish the House outright, and to reform Parliament into an 'efficient single chamber legislating body'. This provoked debate elsewhere about the future of the Lords. An official Conservative Party committee recommended a scheme of reform which ultimately would have removed hereditary peers, and created a two-thirds elected and one-third appointed House, with its powers slightly enhanced. The report, though emanating from a committee chaired by Lord Home of the Hirsel, had a lukewarm reception, even within the Conservative Party (see Chapter 9).

The Thatcher Years

During the first two years of the Thatcher premiership there was, however, considerable pressure within the Conservative Party for reform of the House of Lords (see for example party conference debates in 1980 and 1981). Attempting to secure agreement with Labour would be pointless (how different from 1968), but the precedent of the 1958 Life Peerages Act — carried unilaterally by a Conservative Government — was cited.

Mrs Thatcher showed no interest in the question. Her priorities generally lay in directions other than institutional change. Talk of reform receded. In its place attention began to focus on the enhanced influence of the Lords. After the 1983 election, which gave the Government such a huge Commons majority, it was even suggested that the Lords was more effective than the Lower House in obliging the Government to change its mind on particular questions. Party leaders in the Lords talked openly of the extra responsibilities placed on the Upper House by this parliamentary situation, as they did again in 1987 (see for example HL Debs, 25 June 1987, col. 21).

On the Labour side, the very weakness of the party in Commons and country, especially at the time of the 1983 election, appeared to enhance the role of the Lords. The Labour peers were probably the most united and generally best organised section of the party in these years. The televising of the Lords emphasised how responsible and dignified they looked, perhaps confirming to some party activists the irrelevance of the House of Lords and the desirability of its abolition. But they were not irrelevant, as the party (and country) had reason to realise when the Conservative Government began to face defeat on some quite major issues, such as its strategy for abolition of the GLC. On the Conservative side Mrs Thatcher's growing ascendancy within the party throughout the early 1980s, seen clearly in the Commons after the influx of new MPs at the 1983 election, was not so readily apparent in the Lords. The sheer continuity of the Upper House ensured that the party there was less 'Thatcherite' and remained more tempered by the old paternalistic Tory tradition.

At the start of Mrs Thatcher's third term, the House of Lords looked more confident of itself and of its role in the whole business of parliamentary government than it had for many years past. In October 1987 the Leader of the House, Viscount Whitelaw, made a speech to a fringe meeting at the Conservative Party Conference in which he forecast that the Government faced the prospect of serious defeats in the Upper House during the coming session; however, rather than warning his fellow peers not to press their opposition too far, he urged MPs and ministers not to push the House of Lords too hard (*The Independent*, 9th October, 1987).

Though no fundamental reform had taken place, it is interesting to note how the House of Lords had quietly developed its activities, taking up where it could suggestions made in the 1967 White Paper. The establishment of the European Communities Committee in 1974 was a notable, but by no means isolated, example. Clearly the question of fundamental reform will inevitably return to the political agenda sooner or later, but meanwhile the activity of the House grows.

Between the House of Lords of today and its predecessor body of 600 years ago there is an unbroken institutional continuity. But along with this continuity there has also been great change. The House of Lords has become more meritocratic and rather less aristocratic. From being the senior part of parliament it has become very much a junior part. More recently, from being an ill-attended body sustained by the enthusiasm of a few amateur, part-time or retired politicians, it has become much better attended and a partly professional House. From parliament to parliament significant, if subtle, changes are continuously evident. The institution may be the same body as existed centuries ago, yet it is also completely different. It is to the analysis of the House of Lords as it is in the 1980s that the remainder of this book is largely devoted.

2

MEMBERSHIP OF THE HOUSE

At the commencement of each session of parliament the Clerk of the Parliaments prepares a roll of 'Lords Spiritual and Temporal'. This is the authoritative list of all those eligible for membership of the House of Lords; it is tabled in the House and subsequently published. In November 1986 it contained the names of 1,171 individuals, holding between them 1,205 different peerages (since some peers hold more than one peerage). Included in this list were some peers who were effectively full-time politicians, attending the House almost every sitting day and making it very much the centre of their working lives. Many others were part-time members, contributing selectively to the proceedings of the House while pursuing other careers or other activities. Some attended the House too infrequently even to be considered part-timers, while still others had nothing at all to do with the place. While it is the more active element within the House which is our major concern, it is necessary to commence our analysis by formally classifying all those who are entitled to seats. Table 2.1 does this.

Table 2.1 Composition of the House of Lords, May 1987

	Total	Of whom women	Percentage of total membership
Lords Spiritual			
Archbishops	2	– ⎫	2.2
Bishops	24	– ⎬	
Lords Temporal			
Royal dukes	5	–	0.4
Peers by succession	761	20	64.2
Hereditary created peers	26	–	2.2
Life peers created under Appellate Jurisdiction Act 1876 as amended	21	–	1.8
Life peers created under Life Peerages Act 1958	346	47	29.5
	1,185	67	
Peers without writs	89		7.5
Peers with leave of absense	133		11.2

Archbishops and Bishops

The 'Lords Spiritual' consist of twenty-six senior bishops of the Church of England. The Archbishops of Canterbury and of York sit as of right, as do the occupants of the Sees of London, Durham and Winchester. Until 1847 all other diocesan bishops also had seats in the Lords, but since that date the creation of new sees has not been accompanied by any extension of the right to seats in the House of Lords. The number of diocesan bishops with seats has therefore been fixed at twenty-one, plus the three senior diocesan bishops mentioned above. The twenty-one places are filled according to seniority as measured from the date of first appointment to a diocesan see. Apart from the Bishop of Sodor and Man (who has a seat in the House of Keys on the Isle of Man) and the Bishop of Gibraltar in Europe, an extra-territorial diocese created in 1970, all other diocesan bishops are eligible for membership of the Lords. When a bishop retires from his see (which he must now do by the age of 70) he loses his seat in the Lords, his place being taken by the most senior bishop not yet a member of the House of Lords. In recent years newly appointed diocesan bishops have had to wait between four and eight years before taking a seat in the Lords. Sometimes bishops are translated from one see to another, in which case, if already a member of the House of Lords, they are simply re-introduced in their new capacity.

The 'Lords Spiritual' are the only members of the House of Lords who do not remain for life. Several retiring archbishops have been created peers (including the most recent three), but in all other cases retirement entails departure from the Lords. Individual bishops do therefore tend to have a relatively short membership of the House of Lords: in 1986 only six of the twenty-six had been members for 10 years or more, though this was partly because no fewer than five bishops who were members retired in 1985. The bishop with longest membership in recent years was Dr Ellison, who entered the Lords in 1960 while Bishop of Chester, and retired from the See of London in 1981.

Royal Peers

The category of 'royal peers' is somewhat anomalous in that the few individuals involved could be included elsewhere in Table 2.1, but the effect of so doing would be in some degree misleading. The Duke of Edinburgh was created a Duke upon his marriage to Princess Elizabeth in 1947. He has taken his seat in the House of Lords, but has never spoken. Prince Charles was created Duke of Cornwall when Queen Elizabeth, his mother, succeeded to the Throne, but he did not enter the Lords until the age of 21. In 1986 his younger brother was created Duke of York upon marriage, and he entered the Lords in 1987. Both these royal princes were accorded full ceremonies of introduction because their peerages were regarded as new creations, though they took titles which had been held in the past by members of the Sovereign's immediate family. Prince Charles did make a maiden speech in 1974 in a debate on sport and leisure, introducing his remarks with a reference to the fact that no members of his family had spoken in the House of Lords for about 100 years. He spoke again in 1975 on voluntary community service, but has not done so since, to the time of writing.

The two other royal peers are the Duke of Gloucester and the Duke of Kent, both the second holders of peerages conferred on their fathers, the younger sons of King George V. The Duke of Kent has not spoken in the House, but the Duke of Gloucester, ten years after taking his seat, made a forthright speech on smoking and health in a debate in 1984, and spoke again in 1987 on professional liability, basing his remarks on his experience as an architect.

In the early nineteenth century royal peers spoke frequently, by no means eschewing matters of political controversy. Today members of the royal family must necessarily avoid any appearance of political partisanship. But this would not be difficult in respect of many debates which take place in the Lords. There is no reason why contributions from royal peers should not be made in a House characterised both for the breadth of subject-matter debated, and, in respect of some debates, the low or non-existent party political content.

Peers by Succession and Hereditary Created Peers

Peers by succession are all those who have inherited their peerages; hereditary created peers are the first holders of peerages which can be passed on to heirs. Taken together we may refer to these as holders of hereditary peerages. They are divided into five ranks, the most senior being dukes of whom there are twenty-four, followed in order of precedence by marquesses (28), earls and countesses (155), viscounts (103), and the barons, baronesses and ladies (445). The last non-royal dukedom to be created was in 1874; several marquesses were created in the twentieth century, but none since the Second World War, while earldoms and viscountcies have been conferred up to the present time. When hereditary peerages were regularly awarded prior to 1964, former prime ministers, if they took a peerage, became earls, and former cabinet ministers usually became viscounts. Sometimes a person awarded one peerage would later be advanced to a higher peerage in recognition of further achievements.

The distinction between various ranks of peerage is of no importance with regard to the work of the House of Lords. Peers of higher rank have higher formal precedence, but this confers no privileges over lower ranking peers in the proceedings of the Lords. However, as regards membership, the distinction between hereditary peerages and life peerages is important. It is worth noting that no new hereditary peerages were awarded after 1964, when Labour came to office, until Mrs Thatcher's second term as Prime Minister in 1983. This was a sufficiently long period under Conservative as well as Labour governments to have established an expectation that such awards would never again be made. However, in 1983 Mrs Thatcher recommended hereditary peerages at the rank of viscount for both her cabinet deputy, William Whitelaw, and for the former Speaker of the Commons (and ex-Labour Cabinet Minister) George Thomas, who became Viscount Tonypandy. This was presumably intended as a mark of special distinction for these individuals, despite the fact that by this time two other former Speakers of the Commons and two other former prime ministers had all accepted life peerages. Neither of these two had eligible heirs, so their peerages will become extinct upon their deaths, but in 1984 an earldom was conferred upon former Prime Minister Harold Macmillan, Earl of Stockton. When he died in 1987 his peerage was inherited by his grandson.

It seems unlikely that many hereditary peerages will be awarded in the future. If the motive for making such awards is to mark out individuals of exceptional achievement from the ordinary run of life peers, then it would seem more sensible to confer life peerages at a higher rank than that of baron, though this has never been done, and it is doubtful whether it could be done without further legislation.

The rules governing the succession of peerages are very complex and need not detain us here, though it is necessary briefly to explain their significance. When a hereditary peer dies he is succeeded by the nearest direct descendant of the original holder of the peerage. For the first holder of a peerage this can only be a member of his immediate family (son or grandson). For the holder of a peerage which was first conferred many generations ago, distant relatives may be eligible heirs.

An implication worth noting is that hereditary peerages most at risk of extinction are those which have been in existence for a single generation — because only direct descendants of the first holder are eligible heirs. Of the seventy-six hereditary peerages which became extinct between 1966 and 1986, forty-one had been held for a single generation only. Occasionally publicity has been given to calculations about when hereditary peerages would all become extinct (assuming no new creations took place). Such calculations by extrapolating from the overall extinction rate in recent years produce a misleading result because they do not allow for the lower extinction rate among the holders of older peerages.

All hereditary peerages awarded this century have been United Kingdom peerages, but formerly Irish peerages were awarded (with imperial peerages being of Great Britain) and prior to the Act of Union of 1707 peerages of Scotland were also awarded. As already mentioned in Chapter 1 the arrangements by which peers of Ireland and of Scotland used to elect representatives to the Lords have now ceased. All holders of Scottish peerages are members of the House of Lords, but the possession of an Irish peerage no longer qualifies a person to membership.

Many other individuals who do not themselves hold peerages use titles to indicate their blood relationship to a peer. Such titles are known as 'courtesy titles': their use is not regulated by law, though from time to time the Sovereign has issued rules to govern or at least to guide their use. Thus the eldest son of a higher-ranking peer will generally use a courtesy title deriving from a lesser peerage held by his father.

A striking feature of Table 2.1 is the small number of hereditary peerages held by women. Depending on the terms in which a peerage was originally granted, some cannot be held by a female, while others cannot be transmitted through a female line of succession. But even where either or both of these possibilities exist, any male line of succession always takes precedence over a female line. In some cases, where the first holder of a hereditary peerage has had no male heirs, the letters patent for the peerage have deliberately been framed so as to allow for succession through a female line, for example, in the case of Earl Mountbatten of Burma: he was created a peer in 1946, had no male heirs, and his peerage was inherited by his daughter upon his assassination in 1979. Viscount Whitelaw likewise has no sons: his peerage will become extinct because the letters patent do not allow for it to be passed to his eldest daughter. This is in some ways a trivial point, yet it does represent the perpetuation of sex discrimination with regard to a male-dominated institution. The reply to a parliamentary question in early 1987 indicated that the Government had no plans to remove this discrimination (HL Debs, 5.2.87, Col. 326–8).

By standing order of the Upper House no peer may take his seat until the age of 21, an age unchanged when the age of majority generally was lowered to 18. Of the eighty-nine peers shown in Table 2.1 as lacking a writ of summons, three were minors, the vast majority of the remainder being hereditary peers who would have little or no difficulty in establishing their claim to a writ, but have simply not bothered, presumably because they have no interest in attending the Lords. Quite a number of these live overseas, and in some cases their links with the UK are very slight. Peers may also have their writ of summons withdrawn if they are undischarged bankrupts.

It is peers by succession that give the House of Lords its strong aristocratic inclination. But it is worth noting that comparatively few members hold ancient peerages: less than 100 survive from before the seventeenth-century civil war, and well over half of all peers by succession hold peerages first conferred within the last 100 years.

Law Lords

As is well known, the House of Lords, as well as being the second chamber of parliament, is also the highest court of appeal in the land. Up to eleven judges may now hold office as Lords of Appeal in Ordinary. When they retire, unlike the bishops, they do not lose their seats in the Lords. Their peerages are for life, not for term only. The figure of 21 in Table 2.1 includes all serving and retired peers who were awarded peerages upon appointment as Lords of Appeal in Ordinary.

A few peers who have held high judicial office, but have not been created peers under the Appellate Jurisdiction Act, are also entitled to sit judicially. These may include: senior Scottish judges accorded life peerages; the Lord Chief Justice of Northern Ireland; and some senior English judicial figures who have been awarded peerages as well as the Lord Chancellor and all former Lord Chancellors. The term 'law lords' is usually applied to this wider group, consisting of all peers entitled to sit judicially. Their contribution to the work of the House of Lords is discussed below (pp. 48–50).

Life Peerages

The final category in Table 2.1 is life peers created under the 1958 Life Peerages Act. Not only has the great bulk of all peerages created since then been life, rather than hereditary, peerages, but the total number of peers created between 1958 and 1987 was slightly more than double the number created in the thirty years before 1958. The House of Lords has been transformed by the influx of life peers. Table 2.2 shows the varied propensities of different prime ministers to create peers. Mr Wilson has been by far the most prolific, having recommended no fewer than 217 individuals for membership of the Lords during his eight years as Prime Minister. Before analysing the background of life peers, something needs to be said about the award of peerages.

The Award of Peerages

All peerages are conferred by the Sovereign who acts on the advice of the Prime Minister. Usually the New Year's honours list and Queen's Birthday

Table 2.2   The Creation of Life Peerages, 1/1/58–1/1/88

Prime Minister	Cons	Lab	Lib/SDP	Crossbench	Total	Average per 12 months
Macmillan/Home	17	29	1	18	65	17
1958–64	(25)		(1)	(22)	(48)	
Wilson	11	78	6	46	141	25
1964–70						
Heath	23	5	3	15	46	13
1970–4						
Wilson/Callaghan	17	82	6	34	139	27
1974–9						
Thatcher	64	38	9	32	153	18
1979–87	(2)			(2)	(4)	
Total –	142	232	25	145	544	

Notes: a) Resignation honours have been attributed to outgoing prime ministers in 1964, 1970, 1974, 1979.
b) Political affiliation is that taken by a peer upon first entering the House.
c) Figures in parentheses give the number of hereditary peerages awarded (excluding advancements from one rank of peerage to a higher rank).

honours list are headed by the names of a small number of people to whom peerages are awarded. Occasionally a special honours list is announced; recent examples have been on the occasion of the Queen's Jubilee, and following success in the Falklands War.

Dissolution honours lists are always published at the time of a general election. If the election results in a change of government, then the outgoing Prime Minister customarily draws up a resignation honours list, which may replace his or her contribution to a dissolution honours list. Sometimes a dissolution honours list has been issued before an election, but more usually after. In 1983 a list containing seventeen names was issued on 21 July (following a June election), eight of whom had resigned, six had been defeated, and three had failed to be selected as candidates by their parties following constituency boundary revision. It has become customary for a resignation list to be issued whenever a prime minister leaves office, for whatever reason. Mr Heath's resignation honours list in 1974 contained nine peerages, as did Mr Wilson's in 1976; Mr Callaghan's in 1979 contained ten names.

From time to time lists of new peers quite separate from any of the above occasions have been issued, the stated intention of such lists being to increase the working strength of the House of Lords. Mrs Thatcher issued lists of so-called 'working peers' in April 1981, December 1982, April 1985 and February 1987. By no means have all the peers on such lists subsequently become active members of the Lords, though Labour nominees have tended to be more assiduous than Conservative nominees. Many of those included on such lists have been men and women of considerable public distinction: the sort of people who might quite reasonably have received awards in the regular honours lists. But some have been relatively unknown and apparently undistinguished: for example, six of the fourteen names included in a list of Labour working peers issued in August 1967 could not be found in *Who's Who* at the time their peerage was announced, though subsequently some of these became highly regarded members of the House of Lords. A life peerage is both the highest regular 'honour' awarded in our society, and the necessary qualification for membership of the second chamber, which does nowadays need to recruit a number of willing party workhorses in order to ensure that the work of the Lords is adequately completed.

In the case of dissolution or resignation honours, as well as lists of working peers, the actual choice of individuals who are not members of the Prime Minister's party is recognised as being made by the other party leaders. When a dissolution honours list or a list of new working peers is being prepared, the Prime Minister will indicate to other party leaders how many names they may put forward, and the choice of whom to suggest is left to them. In 1983 it was widely reported in the press that Mr Foot wished to recommend over twenty former Labour MPs for peerages, but Mrs Thatcher would only allow eight. It was then further reported that when the Prime Minister received Mr Foot's list of eight she sent it back to him for reconsideration because it contained the names of some relatively junior political figures, and failed to include some former Cabinet ministers. Mr Foot insisted that he would only recommend individuals who would become regular and reliable working peers. His choice of names was accepted, but in the following New Year's honours list two former Labour Cabinet ministers, omitted from Mr Foot's list, received peerages on Mrs Thatcher's recommendation. In the next dissolution honours list in 1987, six Labour nominees were put forward by Mr Kinnock, all very senior parliamentarians.

In 1985 the Social Democratic Party was invited to make a single nomination, and its leader chose a former MP who had been a Deputy Speaker in the Commons, Lord Crawshaw of Aintree. He died the following year, but in drawing up another list of working peers in February 1987 Mrs Thatcher refused to invite a nomination from either Alliance party, much to the anger of Dr Owen, the SDP leader; after the election, though, two Alliance party members were included in the dissolution honours list. The Liberal Party was disappointed by the refusal of Conservative prime ministers from 1958 to 1964 to invite nominations from the Liberal leader. The omission of Enoch Powell from the dissolution honours list in 1987 occasioned widespread and conflicting press comment.

In some cases individuals decline to accept peerages, though it is impossible to say how frequently such refusals are made. Janet Morgan lists eight who declined peerages between 1964 and 1970 (Morgan, 1975, p. 22).

Ever since the scandal associated with Lloyd-George's almost open sale of honours just after the First World War, a political honours scrutiny committee has existed. Following the considerable controversy occasioned by Mr Wilson's resignation honours in 1976, this committee was reconstituted, and it was made known that if in future it objected to any candidate, it would convey its objections not only to the Prime Minister, but, if this had no effect, to the Queen herself. The committee is responsible for ensuring that honours are not awarded in return for financial support, nor should honours be conferred on individuals about whom some public scandal is likely to arise. However, in 1983, the procedures by which the committee must satisfy itself that no honour is proposed in return for financial gifts to a political party were tightened up (*The Times,* 3 December 1983). Nevertheless, this has not silenced criticism of the fact that individuals associated with companies which have made substantial financial donations to the Conservative Party have received honours including peerages (see HC Debs 6.12.83. cols 161–5). On the other hand no single honours list has caused such notoriety as Mr Wilson's list in 1976, which included the names of several individuals whose public service was hard to recognise (see Walker, 1987, Ch. 6, and Roth, 1977, Ch. 2).

Analysis of Life Peerages

Any classification of new peers is somewhat arbitrary. Many have had varied careers with experience in several areas. For the purpose of Table 2.3 a person's major sphere of employment up to the time that the peerage was awarded has been recorded. Even in cases where a peerage has clearly been granted because of service given to a political party, and announced in a list of so-called 'working' peers, the person concerned has been classified according to whatever professional background he or she had.

The House of Commons remains the greatest single source for the recruitment of new peers. The House of Lords is undoubtedly felt by many former MPs to be a pleasant place for semi-retirement from political life. There is still the proximity to the Commons, the sense of atmosphere found at Westminster, old friends to consort with, and the possibility of doing a little useful political work from a base in the Upper House. These advantages are available without constituency work to cope with, or the pressures of parliamentary life as they are encountered in the Commons, or indeed the strain of election campaigns. 'I knew I had been right to

Table 2.3   Professional Background of Life Peers Created 1958–88

Former MPs			198
	includes	Conservative	80
		Labour	106
		Liberal	9
		Others	3
Business			71
Trade unions and Co-operative movement			26
Universities			58
Local government			32
Civil and diplomatic service			18
Military			8
Other public services			41
Doctors			9
Lawyers			24
Editors/Journalists			13
Arts			7
Ministers of religion			6
Widows			9
Miscellaneous			24

Note: 209 had at some stage been MPs, but in eleven cases their subsequent career seemed more appropriate for their categorisation.

retire from the Commons, but did not want to be completely cut off from Westminster' commented a former Labour cabinet minister in his memoirs (Stewart, 1980). Former MPs whose departure from the Commons was not of their own choosing through election defeat or even failure to be reselected, may still be relatively youthful and not without political ambition. But they may calculate that their chances of quickly getting back into active political life through finding and winning a Commons seat are relatively low, and in such circumstances be grateful for the opportunity to go to the Lords. Here they may well receive a warm welcome on their party front-bench, and even hope to gain ministerial office if their party is subsequently returned to power. Exceptionally, a minister who loses his Commons seat in an election may even continue his ministerial career without interruption through the immediate award of a peerage, as happened to Lord Gray of Contin in 1983.

About one third of the former MPs to receive peerages had attained cabinet rank within government, and most of the remainder had at some stage held ministerial office. A few former cabinet ministers never become peers: maybe because they don't want to, or maybe because their party leader declines to recommend them and the prime minister of the day is not disposed to intervene (examples since the 1960s include John Nott, Ray Gunter, Barbara Castle and Eric Varley). Only a minority of former junior ministers have been created peers after leaving the Commons. Of the thirty-four Conservative MPs who retired in 1983, eleven had received peerages by 1987. Of Labour's thirty defeated and thirty-eight retiring MPs, only eight had received peerages by 1987.

Throughout the twentieth century the House of Lords has received recruits from among the most successful men of business, including manufacturing and heavy industry, retailing and the world of finance. In some cases the individuals concerned have remained very absorbed in their business activities and have not become much involved in the work of the Lords at least until their retirement. Lord Kearton was created a peer in 1970, but did not make his maiden speech until 1982, after which he became quite active in the Upper House. Mrs Thatcher's creations included such men as Lord Weinstock (GEC) and Lord Sieff of Brimpton (Marks and Spencer), neither of whom took an active part in the House of Lords, at least initially. Typically the eminent businessman who becomes a peer while still highly committed to his business career sits on the cross-benches, and makes occasional contributions in debates on particular subjects. Some peers categorised here as businessmen were known as active supporters of a political party, for example, the February 1987 list of 'working' peers included Sir Charles Johnston, a director of various engineering companies, who had been chairman of the National Union of Conservative Associations in the 1970s and later a joint treasurer of the Party, and Sir James Goold, a former president of the CBI in Scotland, as well as chairman of the Scottish Conservative Party. Some of the businessmen ennobled on Mr Wilson's recommendation were not Labour supporters, and since his time few men of business have received peerages on the recommendation of Labour leaders. Lord Williams of Elvel, awarded a peerage in 1985, had been Chairman of the Prices Commission from 1977-9, and then for several years a senior City figure before becoming a Labour front bench spokesman in the Lords.

If the world of business has provided numerous recruits, especially to Conservative benches in the House of Lords, the trade union movement has since 1958 been a reservoir from which the Labour Party has drawn. Before the Life Peerages Act the only trade union leader to become a peer was Lord Citrine who entered the Lords in 1946 after 20 years as General Secretary of the TUC. Neither of his two successors in that post became a peer, but after 1958 a steady stream of trade union leaders entered the Lords, several on the recommendation of Conservative prime ministers. Almost all had been leaders of large unions, usually taking peerages after retirement. An exception was Lord Delacourt-Smith who continued as General Secretary of the Post Office Engineering Union after becoming a peer in 1967, and even for a time combined his union post with office in the Labour Government. Not all trade union peers become active members of the House of Lords, though all bar one have taken the Labour Whip: the exception, Lord Chapple, made a peer in 1985, chose to sit on the cross-benches. Trade-union representation in the Lords is also facilitated by peers who were formerly trade-union-sponsored MPs.

A large number of life peers have been drawn from universities which were little represented before 1958. Some of these have been former vice-chancellors or heads of colleges, whose names became household words through their chairmanship of well-known commissions or committees of inquiry, such as Lord Wolfenden, Lord Fulton, and Baroness Warnock. Other university peers have been well-known as supporters of a political party and their peerage has been awarded to enable them to voice such support in the Lords, for example Lords Balogh, Crowther-Hunt and Wedderburn of Charlton on the Labour side, and Lords Beloff, Butterworth and Bauer among Conservatives.

Almost all the life peers classified as 'local government' achieved their main distinction as elected councillors, generally in positions of leadership within their authorities. Several had also tried to win election to the House of Commons, but without success. Only two professional local authority officers were given peerages: Lord Alexander of Potterhill in 1974 after many years as secretary of the Association of Education Committees, and Baroness Faithfull, a Conservative, in 1976; she had been director of Social Services for Oxford. The original purpose of the 1958 Life Peerages Act might have implied that expertise acquired through professional work within local government would have been of potential value to the Lords, but prime ministers seemed reluctant to draw on this reservoir of talent and experience, perhaps because so many peers — both hereditary as well as life peers — had experience of local government, though as elected councillors rather than as professional employees.

The group described as 'civil and diplomatic service' changed its character after 1958, but the change seems to have had more to do with the end of Empire than with the Life Peerages Act. Before the Act was passed many hereditary peerages were conferred upon colonial governors, ambassadors, and other diplomats, but few on home civil servants. Since 1958 the disappearance of many of these great offices overseas has brought with it an attrition in peerages of this kind — and officers in the armed services have received fewer life peerages than their predecessors received hereditary peerages. On the other hand peerages for home civil servants, formerly rare, have become relatively numerous. A peerage for the retiring head of the civil service has become customary, even when (as in 1982) the person concerned — Lord Bancroft — had been prematurely retired and reckoned to be outside prime ministerial favour. On the other hand, though every recent head of the diplomatic service had received a peerage upon retirement, no such award was made to Sir Michael Palliser who retired in 1983 (a year after the Falklands conflict), which underlines the point that such awards cannot be viewed as automatic.

The category 'other public service' includes peers drawn from a variety of areas. For example: three former prime ministers of Ulster; some former chairmen of nationalised industries; and others whom it is hard to classify because of their varied experience. Sir John Hunt led the successful Everest expedition in 1953, and after many years in the army served as Director of the Duke of Edinburgh's Award Scheme for ten years before becoming a peer in 1966. Surprisingly the first former senior police officer to receive a peerage was Sir Philip Knights in 1987, an omission the more worthy of mention because the House of Lords so frequently debates law and order questions. No former prison governors have become peers.

Representation of the professions among new peerages remained irregular even after 1958. A few lawyers in addition to law lords received peerages before and after 1958, as did former presidents of the older medical royal colleges. No leading psychiatrist or veterinary surgeon received a peerage between 1958 and 1987. Two Protestant ministers, the Methodist, Donald Soper, and George MacLeod of the Church of Scotland joined the bishops and ennobled former archbishops, but no Roman Catholic priests were recruited. A small number of people prominent in the arts received life peerages, including Lords Bernstein, Britten, Olivier and Miles. Prime ministers have been only moderately imaginative in their attempts to bring in voices from other corners of the nation's life. Mr Wilson's recommendation in 1970 of a 34-year-old woman disabled in a riding accident, to assist in voicing the needs of the handicapped, deserves some credit on this score; she was Baroness Masham of Ilton, the youngest person ever to receive a life peerage. Enough women were given peerages — sixty-five all told to 1987 — to give the Upper House a female membership, among life baronesses alone, far exceeding that of the Commons. However, of these, nine were widows of prominent male politicians who, had they lived, could reasonably have expected peerages, and hence they have been classified as 'widows'. The most recent was Baroness Airey of Abingdon who received her peerage in 1979 shortly after her husband had been assassinated.

How much difference has the Life Peerages Act made to the House? Some broadening of the field of recruitment to the peerage has taken place, and undoubtedly many people — especially, but by no means exclusively, within the Labour Party — who would have refused hereditary peerages have been willing to accept life peerages. Furthermore if all life peerages had been awarded as hereditary peerages the Lords would have grown in size even more rapidly than it has, because well over 100 more heirs would have become eligible to take seats in the House of Lords over the last 30 years. But the vast majority of life peers are the same kind of people as might have been offered hereditary peerages in the past. Some are elder statesmen, others are eminent men and women because of their achievements in various walks of life. Some are party nominees appointed in expectation of their regular and reliable support for their party in the Lords.

The House of Lords in 1987

In the House of Lords as a whole the 750 or so peers by succession still dominate, even if in terms of the active House they are more or less balanced by the 340 or so life peers. Though taxation may have destroyed the opulence of earlier generations, peers by succession remain predominantly men of substance. Over half can be described as landowners, many of whom own vast estates. About a quarter of all those who own fine stately homes and large landholdings are members of the Lords (A. Roth, 1986). There are very few tenant-farmers. There are more heads of Oxbridge colleges than comprehensive school teachers — or head-teachers for that matter. Some three dozen life peers have had experience as manual workers, but most of these are separated by at least two decades from their last direct experience of factory or mine. Five times as many work in banking and finance as in engineering. When the Lords debated the Lloyds Bill in 1982, over half the peers who took part in the second reading declared an interest as Lloyds underwriters. A survey of peers' directorships in 1985 indicated that 355 peers held *in toto* 1,755 directorships; 201 of these were Conservative, 89 non-party, 33 Alliance parties, and 31 Labour. (By way of comparison, 180 MPs held cumulatively 435 directorships.) All kinds of companies were represented, but with a particular concentration in banking, insurance and finance; 136 peers were found to be directors of 'Square Mile' companies or partners in stockbrokers and jobbers (*Labour Research,* December 1985, Vol. 74 No. 12; see also *Labour Research,* April 1986, Vol. 75 No. 4). The same emphasis can be noted from Andrew Roth's figures for 1972. His book, *Lord on the Board* gave information on the financial interests of all peers, and at the end of his work he listed peers with interests in various areas. This showed, for example, 678 peers with interests in property, 171 with interests in insurance, 139 with interests in investment trusts and stockbroking, and 131 with interests in banking. In 1987 Andrew Roth was working on a new study, giving similar information for all peers. Unlike MPs, peers have no register of interests, and information has to be gained from a variety of published sources, supplemented by direct inquiry from peers themselves.

Table 2.4 summarises the occupational background of peers. It is based

Table 2.4 Occupational Background of all Peers

Occupation	Number of hereditary peers	Number of life peers	Total as % of House
Landowner/farmer	463	60	44
Public service/administrator	109	238	30
Industrialist/service/ manufacturing/retail	155	109	23
Military (regular)	156	25	15
Political work	23	143	14
Banking/insurance	89	32	10
Judge/barrister/solicitor	45	75	10
Civil service/diplomatic	48	66	10
Journalist/author/publisher/printer	70	44	10
Teacher (university, school)	27	77	9
Arts/entertainment	39	36	4
Church	3	31	3
Advertising/public relations	20	6	2
Accountant/economist	15	10	2
Engineer	12	13	2
Other	178	91	22

Sources: This Table is adapted from one published in the *News of the World*, 15 March 1987, which in turn had been taken from N. Baldwin, PhD Thesis, Exeter University.

Note: Occupations have been used as the basis of analysis in this Table. Since some peers have more than one occupation, totals exceed the membership of the House of Lords.

on the careful researches of Nicholas Baldwin, and relates the position as he found it in 1981. Again, the difficulties in categorising peers must be emphasised, but the overall balance in membership presented here is indicative of the character of the House of Lords. In terms of occupational class background, Baldwin summarised the position in 1981 as 86 per cent drawn from business or professional classes, 2 per cent from the working classes, and 13 per cent miscellaneous or not known.

Even more striking are figures regarding peers' education. In 1981 no less than 431 peers were old Etonians — over a third of the total membership of the House of Lords. Overwhelmingly these were peers by succession (over half of all peers by succession went to Eton), but as many as 10 per cent of life peers had also been to Eton, a slightly higher figure than the proportion of old Etonians in the Commons. Over 86 per cent of peers by succession and as many as 45 per cent of life peers have been educated at public schools — the latter being almost exactly the same proportion as for all MPs — though only five per cent of the total population attended such schools.

The House of Lords remains disproportionately composed of men, public-school-educated and financially well-to-do. This fact must be emphasised because it is sometimes claimed, half jokingly, that peers by succession being in the House of Lords through the accident of birth (and death) are a cross-section of society. Any such claim is nonsense. However, it is also true that the device of succession does provide by chance a representation different from, and in some respects wider than, that which would be provided by nomination or election. The House of Lords in the course of its business hears little or nothing from people straight up from factory shop-floor or lorry-driving, or small-scale tenant farming. But unexpected and unlikely contributions do occur, and are heard with gratitude. Debate on transport questions can be assisted by contributions from a London bus driver or a lorry driver; a debate on prisons must surely be enriched by someone who has recently served a jail sentence. Peers by succession are more likely than MPs in the contemporary world to include men with such experience, and these are in fact actual examples.

On one point at least the succession system does produce welcome variety. Through the chance of birth and death the House of Lords' membership includes a few dozen people in their twenties and early thirties who have time to contribute to its business, and very few of these possess those special ambitions without which it is impossible to gain election to the Commons at an early age. In 1982 some seventy peers by succession were under 40 years old and over half were under 60; but only thirty-nine life peers were under 60, and at that stage none were under 40 years old. The average age of all peers was 63, but the average age of life peers alone was 70 years old. An entirely appointed House of Lords would almost certainly be a very elderly House indeed.

The Active House of Lords

In some senses the House of Lords defies definition. It consists of peers who belong to it, but some belong so loosely that they are scarcely members in any real sense. The Lords resembles many clubs or other organisations — even trade union branches — in that it has a nucleus and a bigger membership. In 1984–5 three peers attended all 151 sittings and sixty-one others attended 140 times or more; but at the other extreme fifty-seven attended only once and over 350 not at all. At any single sitting most of those present are likely to be people who attend most of the sittings, but there will also be a few who have for some reason selected that sitting for a rare appearance.

Technically it may be correct to say that the House of Lords consists of all peers eligible to receive a writ of summons. But at any one time one should obviously subtract those not in receipt of the writ, and also those on leave of absence. Perhaps one should go further and deduct all who fail to attend in any given session, even if they have writs and are not on leave of absence (though non-attenders must positively ask not to be placed on leave of absence, otherwise they are automatically given leave). Peers who attend just once or twice cannot be excluded from an analysis, but they are members to a lesser degree than peers who attend over a hundred times a year.

Attendance is one yardstick for assessing the active House of Lords. But some members attend frequently without apparently contributing much to the work of the Lords; in the 1984–5 session fifteen peers who attended over two-thirds of the sittings said nothing (four of these were life peers). On the other hand some peers attend seldom, but when they do come they make weighty speeches. For example, in the 1984–5 session Lord Grenfell, a hereditary peer who worked for the UN in New York, attended only once to make his maiden speech on third-world starvation; Lord Marshall of Goring, chairman of the Central Electricity Generating Board, attended once to be introduced to the House (as a new peer) and a second time to make his maiden speech on electricity generation; Lord Lane, Lord Chief Justice, attended only once, to speak in a debate on drug-trafficking.

In the following analysis we examine both attendance and interventions in debate as recorded by the Hansard Sessional Index. The total number of peers eligible to attend the House of Lords at the close of the 1984–5 session was 1,174. Of this total ninety-five were without writs of summons and 142 were on leave of absence. If we exclude these we are left with a total of 937, of whom over 80 per cent attended once or more during the

Table 2.5   Peers' Attendance and Interventions in Debates, 1984–5*

	Eligible for attendance	Attended once or more	Intervened in debates once or more
Hereditary created	29	22	15
Life peers (1958 Act)	341	320	248
All created peers (including bishops and law lords)	415	384	293
Peers by succession	759	435	215
Total	1,174	819	508

Sources: Calculated from Hansard Index and information supplied by House of Lords Journal and Information Office.

Note: * Peers eligible for membership at end of session, i.e. excluding peers who died during the session, but including those who became eligible during the session.

previous session, leaving 118 peers who did not attend, even though they were not on leave of absence. In the same session 508 peers spoke in debates, leaving 311 who attended at least once, but never spoke on the floor of the House during that year.

The most striking feature of Table 2.5 is the contrast between created peers and peers by succession in terms of their relative likelihood to attend or to speak. Prior to the 1958 Life Peerages Act most of the regular attenders had inherited their peerages and most were Conservative. By the late 1960s this was no longer true, and by the 1980s Conservative and hereditary dominance within the working House had been further eroded. It was the arrival in considerable numbers of relatively active life peers which brought about this change. Over 90 per cent of created peers attended, and over two-thirds spoke in debates in the House of Lords. By contrast less than 60 per cent of peers by succession attended, and less than 30 per cent spoke.

Table 2.6 gives a more detailed analysis of attendance in the same 1984–5 session. The 1968 White Paper defined regular attenders as those who were present on more than one-third of the sitting days and also gave figures for those attending up to one in twenty sittings. Table 2.6 uses both these criteria, but also incorporates the more demanding criterion of

Table 2.6 Attendance Frequency of Peers, 1984–5 Session*

			Number of attendances				
		Nil	*Up to 5% (1–7)*	*Over 5% (8–49)*	*Over 1/3 (50–99)*	*Over 2/3 (100–151)*	*Total*
Conservative	C	8	9	34	24	38	113
	S	32	68	97	42	64	303
Labour	C	1	7	21	29	54	112
	S	2	–	3	3	5	13
Lib/SDP	C	2	5	7	9	23	46
	S	8	4	9	8	11	40
Cross-bench	C	17	14	36	16	16	99
	S	282	52	37	10	22	403
Bishops		1	7	17	1	0	26
Law lords		2	4	10	2	1	19
Life peers		21	32	90	72	126	341
All created	(C)	31	46	125	81	132	415
All succeeded	(S)	324	124	146	63	102	759
Total		355	170	271	144	234	1,174

Source: Author's calculations, based on information supplied by Party Whips and by House of Lords Information Office.

Note: C = created; S = succeeded.

* Excludes peers who died during the session.

attendance at over two-thirds of the sittings. The relative assiduity of life peers and the predominance of created peers among regular attenders is clear. The table also shows that while the Conservative Party was the largest group in the House of Lords, at every attendance frequency level Conservative peers were outnumbered by the other groups combined. Noticeable too is the high proportion of Labour peers who attended regularly compared with peers in other parties. Almost half of all Labour peers attended over two-thirds of the sittings, and almost three-quarters at least one-third, while for the Conservative Party the corresponding figures were one-quarter and two-fifths.

Intervention in debates by peers is analysed in Table 2.7. No less than 80 per cent of all Labour peers who attended the Lords also spoke, whereas less than 60 per cent of Conservative or non-party peers who attended spoke in the chamber. Though peers by succession formed the majority of those who attended the Lords, they were outnumbered by created peers when contributions to debate are considered, and among the most regular contributors — who intervened over fifty times in the session — created peers outnumbered peers by succession by two to one. In this group of the most frequent speakers, a majority were front-bench spokesmen, whose role is further considered in the following chapter.

Table 2.7   Intervention by Peers in Debates, 1984–5*

		Number of interventions			
		1–10	*11–50*	*Over 51*	*Total*
Conservative	C	39	30	14	83
	S	88	32	15	135
Labour	C	31	34	22	87
	S	3	7	1	11
Lib/SDP	C	12	19	7	38
	S	10	7	4	21
Cross-bench	C	43	10	1	54
	S	32	14	2	48
Bishops		20	–	–	20
Law lords		9	–	1	10
Life peers		114	91	43	248
All created	(C)	154	94	45	293
All succeeded	(S)	133	60	22	215
Total		287	154	67	508

Source: Number of interventions calculated from Hansard Index; interventions made on the same day on the same motion, question, or stage of a bill have been counted as a single intervention.

Note: C = created; S = succeeded.
   * Excludes peers who died during the session.

In examining the activity of the House of Lords, it is helpful to conclude by considering specifically the work of particular groups of peers. Two easily recognisable groups are the bishops and the law lords, both already referred to in our analysis of membership. These deserve particular attention because a second chamber designed on corporate lines would consist of groups essentially similar to bishops and law lords.

Bishops

The activity of the bishops in the House of Lords has changed a good deal during this century. Before the First World War they took an active part, not least in matters of sharp political controversy; but in the inter-war period the activity of bishops in the Lords declined until, by the Second World War, most bishops had become rare visitors, though there were a few individual exceptions (Bromhead, 1958, pp. 56–8). A sense of caution about voting on political issues was accentuated during the 1940s and 1950s, but reversed in the more lively atmosphere in the House following the introduction of life peers in 1958. In 1953 only one bishop voted against the Government on the Central African Federation and in 1956 two voted when the Government's Suez policy was debated. But in 1968 no fewer than eighteen bishops voted (all with the Labour Government) in a sharply contested division on sanctions against Rhodesia. Throughout the 1970s and 1980s bishops have from time to time taken a significant part in the business of the Lords, including politically controversial matters.

Bishops have been prominent when so-called issues of conscience have come before the Lords, notably in the late 1960s. The Divorce Reform Bill of 1969, which introduced the concept of breakdown of marriage as a ground for divorce, followed a considerable debate in which the Church had taken a leading part. When legislation to reform the law on homosexuality was introduced, Lord Dilhorne, a former Lord Chancellor, could not remember any bill on which the bishops had taken so much part. On abortion, in 1968, the bishops were divided, with the Archbishop of Canterbury, Dr Ramsey, supporting an amendment to remove the so-called social grounds for abortion from the bill, but some of his brother prelates helping eventually to defeat this amendment. On the death penalty question bishops were divided in 1948 (when only two voted) and again in 1956, but by 1965 all were abolitionists, and in 1969 no fewer than twenty bishops voted when the death penalty was finally abolished (following a four-year trial period of abolition). This was the largest voting turn-out of bishops since twenty-four bishops had voted in 1927 on the prayer book controversy.

Legislation on these issues of conscience has usually been introduced by private members, and passed on free votes. A good deal of government legislation also deals with matters where ethical, moral or social questions are raised, and the bishops have not infrequently taken a vigorous part on such bills too. Immigration is one such subject. In 1968 six bishops voted against the Labour Government on the Commonwealth Immigrants Bill; in 1970 five voted against the Conservatives on the Immigration Bill (though one bishop, Dr Allison of Winchester, voted in support of the Government on this bill); in 1981 eight bishops voted against the Conservative Government on the British Nationality Bill. At committee stage on this latter bill several amendments were put down to retain the principle that any child born in the UK would be entitled to British citizenship, including one amendment in the name of the Archbishop of Canterbury and three other bishops. The opposition parties deliberately did not move their amendments so as to allow debate to be focused on this episcopal proposal, which was nevertheless lost by 134 votes to 92.

On some government bills the bishops have effectively acted as spokesmen for the particular interest they represent, though this should not be thought of as simply a narrow Church of England interest. For example, in 1976 the Labour Government's Community Land Bill gave rise to great concern on the part of land-owning charities, the largest of many affected being the Church of England. In the Lords the Bishop of London (Dr Ellison) led the attack, eventually pressing his amendments which were carried by large majorities against the Government on divisions in which bishops acted as 'tellers'. When the changes made were altered by the Commons, the bishop wanted the Lords to insist on its amendments, but the Conservative Opposition decided to concentrate its attack against the Government on another bill, and the bishops had to accept defeat. In 1985 during a debate on the Local Government Bill which abolished the Greater London Council, the Bishop of London, Dr Leonard, speaking as Chairman of the Church of England Board of Education, moved an amendment which was approved on division, giving the newly formed ILEA greater stability (see p. 141).

When, in 1985, the Conservative Government introduced a bill to remove restrictions on Sunday trading, its action provoked widespread opposition from the churches. This bill was first introduced in the Lords where the bishops led the attack, and though the Government got the bill through virtually unscathed, an unusually intense campaign had been unleashed in the country, which led to the bill being defeated outright at second reading in the Commons. In the Lords, bishops had forced a division at second reading (lost by 141 votes to 85), and in committee up to nineteen bishops voted at one time, but in the only Government defeat on this bill (which concerned continued protection for shop-workers under employment law), no bishop voted.

In almost any area of legislation an episcopal contribution may be forthcoming. Sometimes this will be a second reading speech drawing attention to the social or moral questions which underlie much legislation. The Bishop of Durham, Dr Jenkins, gained some headlines for his claim made during the debate on the 1985 Transport Bill that the doctrine behind this measure looked dangerously like idolatry. He took no part in the later stages on that bill. In 1984 the Bishop of Rochester, Dr Say, spoke at the second reading of the Local Government (Interim Provisions) Bill, explaining that it was only with reluctance that the bishops joined debate on such a highly charged party political matter, but that they did so because the churches in London were united in their opposition to the abolition of the GLC. Subsequently three bishops voted against the Government on this bill in a division which entailed the Thatcher Government's most serious defeat in the Lords (see Chapter 6).

Bishops do not appear to show any inhibition in voting against the government, even helping to bring about a government defeat. During a debate in 1971 on disestablishment of the Church, a peer suggested that bishops take care not to use their voting strength against the government of the day, but he was immediately contradicted by the Archbishop of Canterbury and other bishops (HL Debs 20 Jan 1971, Vol 520). In the 1980s tension between the Church of England and Mrs Thatcher's Conservative Government became very obvious, and bishops in the Lords found themselves voting against the Government much more frequently than in its support. But it must also be said that bishops were not on the whole either regular attenders or regular voters. In 1984–5 not a single bishop voted in 92 of the 130 divisions for which the Government placed a whip.

Bishops also take part in the non-legislative work of the House of Lords. The Archbishop of Canterbury has three times in the last ten years initiated a full day's debate, most recently on the fortieth anniversary of the United Nations in 1985. Other bishops, too, occasionally put down motions, or ask questions, the latter sometimes dealing with matters relating especially to their dioceses. But participation by bishops in debates on motions is, on the whole, rather low. In 1984–5 bishops spoke only in fourteen out of forty debates on motions for papers (the formula on which general debates are held), and only in two out of forty-five debates on unstarred questions. Among subjects debated without an episcopal contribution were mentally ill prisoners, overseas aid policy, the problems of the disabled, and the problems of rural areas. The motion which drew most bishops as speakers concerned the effect of the Government's social and economic policies; three bishops spoke in this debate, contributed to by no less than forty other peers. The reason for such enthusiasm undoubtedly lay in the fact that this was the first full debate televised live from the Lords!

Bishops are busy people and attendance at the House of Lords has to be fitted in around a very full schedule. The business of the Lords is not generally arranged with long enough notice to facilitate the presence of a bishop, let alone the most suitable bishop, for all the occasions where a speech from the bishops' benches might be considered appropriate. The occasional high turnout of bishops may arise for quite fortuitous reasons. A meeting of bishops in London took place on the day that eighteen voted on Rhodesian Sanctions in 1968, and when nineteen bishops voted in February 1986 on an amendment to the Shops Bill, none spoke in the preceding debate because they arrived *en bloc* directly from a Synod meeting, just in time to vote (HL Deb, 6 February 1986, Col 1314). A rota ensures that a bishop is present for prayers, which means that at least one bishop is present for the first part of the day's proceedings. Drewry and Brock found a high correlation between bishops' interventions in debate and their reading of prayers (Drewry and Brock, 1971). Given the large cross-bench element and the independent-mindedness of peers generally, individual speeches can sway votes in the Lords, and the contributions made by bishops undoubtedly have an impact quite disproportionate to their numerical strength.

Some bishops give much more attention to the Lords than others but very few in recent years have attended more than one-third of the sitting days. The Bishop of Norwich, Dr Wood, a member from 1975–85, was for several years the most frequent speaker, making up to two dozen speeches annually on a wide range of subjects. When he retired in 1985 several peers hoped he would return as a life peer but this was not to be (Whale, 1985). The Bishop of Rochester, Dr Say, the senior bishop in 1987, having been a member of the Lords since 1969, was also a regular attender and quite frequent contributor to debates. Other bishops took very little part, though in recent sessions very seldom has any bishop been totally silent.

Should the bishops take their responsibilities in the Lords more seriously? It is certainly reasonable to argue that, given the fact of their membership (in some strength), more effort should be made to ensure that bishops are present and do contribute on a wider range of topics than at present. Even on the Sunday Trading Bill, to which the Church took strong exception, no bishop spoke or voted on several crucial amendments, and not infrequently peers express their regret at the absence of the bishops during debates on social questions. The Bishop of Rochester acknowledged their erratic attendance on Sunday trading, explaining that this had been due to 'our commitments to our parishes and people (which) must always have our first loyalties' (HL Debs, 25 February 1986, Col 949). One view would be that where the Church as a body is openly and publicly critical of the government, its bishops ought to be prepared to use the forum of the House of Lords to join debate with government ministers, not in a spasmodic way, but in a regular, detailed and hence more responsible way.

Law Lords

Legal expertise may be regarded as an essential requirement in any legislature. About one-sixth of the members of the House of Commons are lawyers (far fewer than in many other legislatures, notably the US Congress), but only one-tenth of peers (see Table 2.4). The law officers of the Crown have usually been members of the Commons, though since 1976 one of the Scottish law officers has been a member of the Lords. Legal learning in the Upper House is chiefly represented by the Lord Chancellor, and his predecessors still living, together with the law lords. Serving law lords are not forbidden from taking part in any business before the Lords, though there is a predisposition against their participation in matters of political controversy. Their judicial duties also inevitably impose restriction on the amount of time they can give to the work of the House. Once retired they may have more time to participate, and need no longer feel that the independence of their role as judges is threatened by their entry into matters of political controversy. But advancing years may well limit the activities of some, and others may feel that discretion and a sense of decorum ought still to inhibit participation in political matters.

Some serving law lords hardly ever speak in the House (Blom Cooper and Drewry, 1972, Ch. 10). Those who are active concentrate their contributions on bills which involve the judicial system, the administration of justice, or law reform. On such matters law lords may play a substantial part, even occasionally dominating the proceedings. Some law reform measures are technical and complex and political discussion never really emerges, but in other cases matters which do excite party controversy in the Commons may well be debated in the Lords simply from a technical or expert point of view. Law lords are by no means always united, and it is recognised that when they speak, they are simply offering their own views. They may sound out opinion within their profession, or even be subject to a little discreet lobbying from fellow judges, but only in exceptional circumstances do they claim to speak on behalf of their colleagues. An example of the latter occurred in 1976 when Lord Wheatley, a Scottish judge, explained in a debate on the proposed devolution legislation that his speech expressed the unanimous views of all the High Court Judges in Scotland, whom he had specifically consulted, and whose views were unlikely to be placed on public record by any other means (HL Debs, 27 January 1976 col 836). In his speech he expressed serious misgivings about the proposals, but took no part in the subsequent devolution debate. On the question of the death penalty, all law lords who took part in the

1948 debates supported retention; in 1956 seven voted for retention, two for abolition. By 1965 judges were painfully aware of the imperfections of the 1957 Homicide Act (which had categorised murder into capital and non-capital). Lord Chief Justice Parker argued strongly for abolition, undoubtedly exerting an important influence over a number of peers. He was supported by four other law lords, but his predecessor, Lord Goddard, and the Master of the Rolls, Lord Denning, both supported retention.

The most obvious conflict between serving law lords and the government in the post-war period arose over the War Damage Bill of 1965. It was the retrospective character of this measure — introduced to remove a liability to damages which the courts had found against the government — which angered the judiciary. The Lord Chief Justice, Lord Parker of Waddington, attacked it at second reading, and along with another law lord and several retired law lords, voted for a wrecking amendment carried by a substantial majority at committee stage. When the Commons returned the bill with the Lords' amendment deleted, Lord Parker again spoke and voted against the Government, but no other law lord supported him in the lobby, and the Government comfortably won. This was a Labour Government bill, but the Conservative Party which had left office the previous year had clearly been preparing a similar measure. Two former Conservative Lord Chancellors supported the bill along with most opposition frontbenchers.

Where serving law lords have been asked by the government to chair commissions or committees of inquiry their subsequent participation in Lords' debates on these subjects is to be expected. Lord Donovan took an active part at all stages in the passage of the Industrial Relations Bill in 1971 following his chairmanship of the Royal Commission on Trade Unions in the later 1960s. Following inner city unrest, Lord Scarman was asked to conduct an inquiry in 1981, but several of his recommendations were not accepted by the Government. During the passage of the Police and Criminal Evidence Bill in 1984 he sought a number of changes, one of which was carried on division against the Government; this made racial discriminatory behaviour by the police a specific disciplinary offence, an alteration reluctantly accepted by the Government. In 1987 he gave an ironic welcome to a government statement which he claimed marked the acceptance of a recommendation made in his report as 'recently as 1981'. For a serving law lord he was unusually active in the House, prior to his retirement in 1986.

Serving law lords also take some part in the non-legislative work of the House of Lords. Lord Chief Justice Lane made his maiden speech in a debate on crime in 1983, and has contributed to other debates on this frequently debated subject. When the Lords debated the report of the committee on Fraud Trials, chaired by Lord Roskill, a serving law lord, nine of the eighteen speeches were made by serving or retired law lords

(10 February 1986). A serving law lord always chairs the Law and Institutions Sub-Committee of the European Communities Committee, and the expertise of law lords is also made available through their membership of some other select committees.

Contrasting approaches to the House of Lords are illustrated by Lords Devlin and Denning. Lord Devlin retired in 1964 after only three years as a serving law lord; during that time he rarely ättended the House of Lords and never spoke. He was only 59 at retirement, and despite his public activities — for example as Chairman of the Press Council for five years — and his authorship of interesting and controversial books such as *Trial by Jury* and *The Enforcement of Morals,* he remained a silent and virtually non-attending member of the Lords to the time of writing. By contrast Lord Denning — who became a Lord of Appeal in Ordinary in 1957 — has been a prolific contributor to debates since his retirement in 1982.

The law lords do play a significant role in the House of Lords. In part this is a matter of being 'resident technical consultants to the legislature on legal points arising out of proposed legislation' (Blom-Cooper and Drewry, 1972, p. 203); in part it is their capacity to contribute generally to debates on crime and the penal system, though their contribution here is fairly irregular: in part it is their readiness to act as guardians over the whole machinery of justice when they see this being affected by some change they consider foolish. Among the law lords of each generation there also appear to be one or two who choose to become House of Lords men, drawing on their legal expertise, but applying this in an unabashed way in debate on a wide range of topics.

Other Groups of Peers

It is possible to identify many different groups of peers, distinctive because of their professional background or by reason of such characteristics as disablement or membership of other bodies such as the European Parliament. A brief comment about the activities of some such groups is helpful in developing an understanding of the House of Lords.

Though the few civil servants who received peerages prior to 1964 had taken little part in the activities of the House of Lords, some of their successors, for example Baroness Sharp, a former Permanent Secretary, and Lord Helsby, formerly Head of the Civil Service, did not regard their examples as precedents to be followed when they entered the Lords in the late 1960s. Both took active parts in proceedings on some bills, including occasions on which the government was defeated, especially on matters where their specialised knowledge based on their professional experience in the civil service could be deployed. This has also been the pattern for activity within the House of Lords by Lord Allen of Abbeydale who became a peer in 1976, four years after retiring from his post as Permanent Secretary at the Home Office. Some of the subjects on which he has spoken persistently have been Home Office matters; his courteous yet razor-sharp interventions have occasionally left government spokesmen reeling with discomfiture. Another former civil servant who has taken part in the Lords has been Lord Bancroft, making occasional speeches indicating his disquiet with government attitudes, for example over the summary banning of trade unions at GCHQ (8 February 1984). Others have taken no part whatsoever in the proceedings, notably the former Head of the Civil Service, Lord Armstrong of Sanderstead, who never made a speech while a member of the House of Lords from 1974 to 1980.

Several peers from the Foreign Service and Diplomatic Corps have been active in the Lords. Lord Strang, former Head of the Foreign Office, entered in 1954, and became the first co-ordinator of the cross-bench peers, a group to which his successors, including Lords Caccia, Garner, Gore-Booth, and Greenhill of Harrow, all belonged. Lord Brimelow, who served for two years as Permanent Secretary at the Foreign Office before his entry to the Lords in 1975, departed from convention by joining the Labour peers instead of remaining on the cross-benches. He has chosen to take little part on the floor of the House, but has actively engaged himself in the work of the European Communities Committee. Lord Gladwyn, whose last diplomatic appointment was as Ambassador to France, entered the Lords in 1960, and has been an active Liberal spokesman ever since.

Several former military leaders have taken a regular part in debates on defence and related matters, as well as acting as spokesmen for such interests as the Officers' Pensions Society. The annual debate on the Defence White Paper customarily draws half a dozen or so speeches from such peers. Some ask questions and take a regular part in the business within their particular interests. Such peers invariably sit on the cross-benches, though they may informally link up with peers in whichever party has their sympathy. Many hereditary peers have also had experience as regular officers, and some of these, together with politicians who have had responsibilities for defence, formed the House of Lords all-party defence study group in 1976, an unofficial group which sought to act as a forum within the Lords to develop a better understanding of defence issues.

Several elected members of the European Parliament have been peers (four in 1979, three in 1984); these have naturally used their membership of the Lords to bring European Community concerns to the notice of government and public. Lord Bethell and Baroness Elles, both MEPs, tabled amendments to the 1985 Representation of the People Bill designed to enfranchise all British officials working in EC institutions. Their amendment was carried with the support of Labour peers, but the Labour front-bench in the Commons opposed the change, and the Government was unwilling to break a concordat reached across the floor of the Commons, so the changes were eventually reversed.

From the early 1970s onwards a group of disabled peers have taken an active part in the Lords, seeking to improve public awareness of the needs of the disabled, and urging government to take action to alleviate the problems faced by disabled people. Legislation on employment, social security and housing, as well as bills dealing specifically with the sick and disabled, have been amended at the instigation of disabled peers. The presence of several peers in wheelchairs — sometimes four at a time — adds a certain immediacy to debates on the problems faced by the disabled. Individuals who suffer such handicaps are not likely to become sufficiently active as politicians to win election to the Commons, so their presence in the Lords has added significance.

Finally, mention must be made of women peers. Though heavily outnumbered by men, those women who have been peers have tended to be disproportionately active, as was shown by Drewry and Brock (1983). Baroness Young was Leader of the House from 1981 to 1983; Baroness Hylton-Foster has been Convenor of the Cross-bench Peers and Baroness Seear Leader of the Liberal Peers. Baroness Llewelyn-Davies of Hastoe was Labour Chief Whip from 1973 to 1982, and then followed Baroness White as salaried Chairman of the European Communities Committee before being herself succeeded in the latter role by Baroness Serota in 1986. Proportionately the female element on the front-benches in the Lords has been considerably higher than in the Commons. Of the 134 life peers shown in Table 2.7 as speaking more than eleven times in the 1984–5 Session, twenty-seven were women. Female peers have initiated debates, asked questions and put down amendments to bills on subjects of obvious interest to women, such as Baroness Seear on equal pay, Baroness Ewart-Biggs on female prisoners, Baroness MacLeod of Borve on widows, and so on. When Baroness Lockwood — Chairman of the Equal Opportunities Commission — initiated a debate on the position of women in public life in May 1985, six of the twelve speeches were made by women. But Drewry and Brock's study found that women's contributions in the Lords taken overall did not differ substantially from those of their male colleagues in terms of subject matter.

Conclusion

The working House of Lords is hard to describe. A nucleus of peers can be thought of as professional politicians. For some this has been their whole career, for others it is an interlude. Around this nucleus a very large number of peers are part-time members of the Lords, some regular and systematic part-timers, others very infrequent and probably casual attenders. In part, the House has become a meritocratic chamber where leading figures in various walks of life mingle with politicians. In part, the House is a representative chamber, not according to any elective principle, but simply through the accidental membership, as it were, of doctors, practising dentists, bee-keepers, opticians, accountants, lecturers, social workers, journalists, retailers and so on. In part, the House remains an aristocratic chamber, some of its most active members being there because of peerages awarded to their forebears, and a high proportion having grown up in families marked by privilege or conspicuous success.

It is a surprising blend. It could be a highly fragmented institution. Certainly, if all peers were like bishops or law lords, eminent and successful, but owing their presence in the House of Lords to offices they hold outside it, fragmentation would be likely. Nor do the other groupings we have briefly considered here really bring coherence to the Lords as a working institution. It is the parties which are the great organising force within the chamber, bringing co-ordination to its activities and drawing peers together from all the diverse elements which constitute the House of Lords. It is to the parties, and their rôle in the Lords, that we turn next.

3

THE ROLE OF POLITICAL PARTIES
IN THE HOUSE

The party system has been aptly described as the single most dominating feature of the British constitution. An idealised model of British politics sees one party monopolising government, and another party, Her Majesty's loyal Opposition, just as organised and cohesive, taking its place as the alternative government. In practice, third parties may intrude to a greater or lesser degree, but at the parliamentary level it is the two-party model which has predominated.

In modern conditions it is control of the Commons which is crucial in deciding which party becomes the government. The Commons is directly elected and is therefore the centre-piece of the party political struggle. The House of Lords by contrast has no rôle in the making or unmaking of governments, nor do any of its members owe their place to election. Nevertheless although governments do not depend for their existence on the Lords, they are answerable there and they must get their legislation through both Lords and Commons. All governments must therefore appoint a team of ministers in the House of Lords. For each item of business the government spokesman has his place with his supporters beside and behind him. The Opposition spokesman for that business faces him across the table, similarly supported by his colleagues.

Government and Opposition parties keep lists of their supporters, to whom a party whip is issued in relation to most of the business which comes before the Lords. This indicates whether votes are expected, and if so, the importance attached to specific items by the party leadership. This is done, as in the Commons, by underlining either one, two or three times, the latter being the strongest summons. The salience of party is heightened in the Lords by the expectations of the many peers who come to the Upper House after a lifetime's experience of the party-dominated Lower House.

Despite these factors, the general environment within which parties operate is very different in the Upper House from the lower. Fundamental to this is the fact that peers do not owe their position to election, and no election can remove them from the House of Lords. They may be loyal party members, but they were not elected on the basis of any party manifesto, so their obligation to support such is not the same as that of

MPs. They have no constituents to bother about, no local parties to humour, no reselection anxieties to trouble them. Nor do peers receive a parliamentary salary which might generate some obligation to attend regularly. If they disagree with their party, they need not openly rebel because they can just quietly stay away from the Lords, or at least stay out of the division lobby. The party whips can encourage and try to persuade their colleagues, but they cannot in any sense command, coerce or bully them. A rebellious MP may ultimately face expulsion from his party and the likely loss of his seat at the next election. If a rebellious peer is expelled from his party, he simply moves to some other quarter of the House, where he may become an even greater nuisance or embarrassment to his former colleagues.

The presence of a large number of non-party or cross-bench peers has also been significant in mitigating the impact of party politics upon the House of Lords. Many cross-bench peers have been active, even in committee on contentious bills, seeking to promote changes which have lain outside the party battle-lines. A description given by a prominent cross-bench peer in 1975 still accurately describes the role of crossbenchers: 'Some are genuinely non-party; some are retired public servants who have served governments of both parties. Some have definite party sympathies, but because they hold some public office prefer for the time being to lay aside their active party allegiance. Some are not in full sympathy with their parties. Some just do not like to be at the receiving end of a whip. In our opinions we range widely from right to left' (Lord Strang, HL Debs, 3 July 1975, Col 382). The presence of a sizeable body of this kind is a highly unusual if not unique feature of any legislature. It helps to muffle party politics.

The considerable imbalance between the two major parties has been a final factor restraining the development of competitive party politics in the House of Lords. There is a sense in which the Labour Party (because it is so markedly smaller than the Conservatives) whether in or out of office is always in opposition in the Lords, usually losing divisions, just occasionally winning. Competition can never be so keen if teams are so unevenly matched. Yet though the Conservatives retain a marked majority over Labour, the total picture of party strength in the Lords has changed a good deal in recent years, changes which merit closer attention.

The Changing Party Balance in the House

Figures about relative party strength in the Lords need to be interpreted with some caution since peers who take a party whip may attend the House so seldom (or even never come at all) that their inclusion in party totals is misleading. For many years the parties were reserved about publishing any lists of their supporters, and the information given in reference books was certainly incomplete as well as sometimes unreliable. Not until the 1968 White Paper on reform were authoritative figures about party support published.

Table 3.1 gives the picture for three selected sessions over the last twenty years, differentiating between 'regular' attenders, who come on over one-third of sitting days, and mere attenders, but excluding altogether peers who did not attend at all in the sessions indicated. Total Labour strength rose steadily, peaking at 161 in 1979, but then declining to 119 in early 1987. There were two reasons for this. The first was the loss of Labour peers to the newly formed Social Democratic Party. By 1985 twenty-three peers had migrated direct from the Labour to the SDP benches. For several years prior to this, a trickle of Labour peers had made their way to the cross-benches (some of whom moved on to the SDP in 1981). The second was the reduced flow of new Labour peerages following Mrs Thatcher's arrival in Downing Street. As Labour peers became old and frail or died, replacements were slow to follow. Successive Labour leaders urged the Prime Minister to replenish the Labour benches. When she did so, she ensured that the supply of new Conservative peers outnumbered Labour, Liberal and Social Democrats combined (see Table 2.2, p. 31).

Table 3.1   Party Strength in the House of Lords

		Cons	Lab	Lib (and SDP)	Independent incl. Cross-benchers, bishops and law lords
1967–8	Attenders	314	113	37	215
	Regulars	125	95	19	52
1975–6	Attenders	292	149	30	281
	Regulars	141	104	24	60
1984–5	Attenders	376	122	76	245
	Regulars	168	91	51	68

Sources: 1967–8 figures from Cmnd 3799, *House of Lords Reform.*
1975–6 and 1984–5: Author's calculation based on information provided by House of Lords Information Office and by party whips.
See also HL 9 (1987–8) Annex B, Tables 1 and 2.

Notes: 'Attenders': Those who actually attended once or more during the session, excluding any who died during the session (or bishops who resigned before the end of the session).
'Regulars': Those attending who were present on one-third or more of sittings during the session, i.e. 'regulars' also included in 'attenders'.
Figures for total party strength for November 1986 issued by the House of Lords Information Office were: Conservative 412, Labour 118, Liberal 43, SDP 43, Crossbench (excluding bishops and Lords of Appeal) 236.

The larger number of Conservatives created life peers in the 1980s was one reason for the growth in Conservative strength. Another was Conservative recruitment from new peers by succession (some of whom first sat on the cross-benches). From the Conservative point of view, the crucial question was the margin the party held over the combined opposition parties. Labour's loss to the Social Democrats was no gain to the Conservatives. The increased difficulty faced in the Lords by the Thatcher Government in the mid-1980s, no doubt reinforced caution on the Prime Minister's part about her new nominations.

Later in this chapter we examine further the nature of party cohesion in the House of Lords, discussing party organisation and the character of whipping. Before that however, we examine more closely the front benches in the Lords.

Conservative and Labour Front Benches

There are some striking contrasts between the two major parties' front-benchers in the Lords (see Tables 3.2 and 3.3). Labour's has become dominated by life peers; of the twenty-seven peers who held office when Labour was in government from 1974–79, all but three were life peers, and in 1987 only a single hereditary peer remained in an expanded front-bench team of thirty-one spokesmen. By contrast less than 30 per cent of the Conservative front-bench team since 1979 have been life peers, and in the early 1970s the proportion was considerably lower.

Because it consists overwhelmingly of life peers, the Labour front-bench tends to have a higher average age and also contains peers with a shorter experience of the House of Lords than the Conservative front-bench. In 1986 the average age of the latter was 51, while the average age of the Labour front-bench was 67; four Conservative spokesmen were under 40 but only six of Labour's thirty-one spokesmen were under 60, and as many as thirteen were over 70 years old. While Conservative front-benchers were younger than their Labour opponents, they had on average spent twice as many years in the Lords as their opposite numbers. However, if Commons experience is taken into account the position is altered because half of Labour's list of spokesmen had experience as MPs, but this was true of only two Conservative front-benchers.

The Conservative front-bench is mainly made up of peers by succession who have chosen, at least for a time, to follow a political career. The choice may be made quite suddenly. In 1973 the Earl of Limerick was appointed parliamentary under-secretary at the Department of Trade on the day following reports that he had joined the Conservative Party. He had previously sat on the cross-benches, and after the Conservatives lost office

Table 3.2 (a) Government Ministers, House of Lords, October 1987

Peer	Office (Departments also covered)	Peerage	No. of yrs as member of the House	Age (attained by 1987)
Whitelaw	Lord President of the Council Leader of the House	H 1st V[a]	3	68
Mackay of Clashfern	Lord Chancellor	LP	8	60
Young of Graffham	Secretary of State, Trade and Industry (Treasury, Employment)	LP	2	54
Cameron of Lochbroom	Lord Advocate	LP	2	55
Belstead	MS, Environment Deputy Leader of the House (Arts, Civil Service)	H 2nd B	28	54
Trefgarne	MS, Defence Procurement (FCO, Employment, Wales)	H 2nd B	24[b]	45
Glenarthur	MS, Foreign and Commonwealth Office (Defence)	H 4th B	10	42
Caithness	MS, Home Office	H 20th E	17	38
Lyell	US, Northern Ireland	H 3rd B	26[b]	47
Trumpington	US, Min. of Agriculture (Home Office)	LP	6	64
Skelmersdale	US, Department Health and Social Security	H 7th B	13	41
Brabazon of Tara	US, Transport (Treasury)	H 3rd B	12	40
Hooper	US, Department of Education and Science (Foreign and Commonwealth Affairs)	LP	1	47
Sanderson of Bowden	MS, Scottish Office	LP	2	44

Notes: [a] Former Member of the House of Commons.
[b] Became eligible to sit at age 21.

Abbreviations: MS: Minister of State   H 2nd: second holder
US: Parliamentary Under   of peerage
Secretary of State   LP: Life Peer
H: Hereditary Peerage   B: Baron
E: Earl   V: Viscount

in 1974 he quickly returned to his City business interests. For those who happen to inherit peerages the House of Lords does provide an inside track for rapid advancement in a political career. Lords Beaverbrook and Hesketh in 1986 both joined the government in their thirties without having had any significant political experience. In 1971, the Earl of Gowrie

Table 3.2 (b)   Government Whips, House of Lords, October 1987

Peer	Office	Peerage	No. of yrs as member of the House	Age (attained by 1987)
Denham	Captain, Gentleman at Arms Chief Whip	H 2nd B	38[b]	59
Davidson	Captain, Yeoman of the Guard, Deputy Chief Whip (Energy, Transport)	H 2nd V	16	58
Long	Lord-in-Waiting (Defence, N. Ireland, Foreign and Commonwealth Affairs)	H 4th V	19	57
Beaverbrook	Lord-in-Waiting (Treasury, Employment, Trade and Industry)	H 3rd B	1	35
Hesketh	Lord-in-Waiting (Agriculture, Arts, Environment)	H 3rd B	15[b]	36
Dundee	Lord-in-Waiting (Scotland, Energy)	H 12th E	3	37
Arran	Lord-in-Waiting (Health and Social Security, Education, Home Office)	H 9th E	4	49

Notes: [b] Became eligible to sit at age 21.
Abbreviations: H: Hereditary Peerage   H 2nd: second holder
                 V: Viscount   of peerage
                 E: Earl   B: Baron

forsook the teaching of poetry to join the Conservative Government. His ability was quickly recognised, but his general political outlook would not have commended him for political advancement under Mrs Thatcher. Nevertheless he received rapid promotion and became a cabinet minister in 1984 — though he resigned the next year because he had come to feel the pay was inadequate, a point taken up later in this chapter.

The Labour front-bench, in addition to former MPs who had taken peerages prior to their final retirement from political life, consisted mainly of middle-aged or elderly party activists, mostly with experience in local government. Among the few exceptions were: Lord Williams of Elvel, a prominent City figure who continued as a stockbroker after entering the Lords in 1985; Lord Wedderburn of Charlton, a professor of law; and Baroness Ewart-Biggs, who had been the wife of a diplomat assassinated in 1980. The sole hereditary peer in 1987, Lord Ponsonby of Shulbrede, had been general secretary of the Fabian society and a local councillor. From 1974–9 Lord Melchett was a Labour minister; he had succeeded to a

Table 3.3 (a)   Labour Front Bench (Principal Spokesmen), House of Lords, October 1987

Peer	Principal Spokesman	Peerage	No. of yrs as member of the House	Age (attained by 1987)
Cledwyn of Penrhos	Leader of the Opposition Civil Service, Foreign Affairs, Welsh Affairs	LP[a]	7	70
Underhill	Deputy Leader Transport, Electoral Affairs	LP	7	72
Ponsonby of Shulbrede	Chief Whip	H 3rd B	10	56
David	Deputy Chief Whip Environment	LP	8	75
John-Mackie	Agriculture, Food, Forestries, Fisheries	LP[a]	5	77
Birk	Arts, Libraries, Heritage Cable, Broadcasting	LP	19	N.K.
Irving of Dartford	Defence	LP[a]	7	68
McIntosh of Harringay	Education and Science	LP	3	53
McCarthy	Employment	LP	10	61
Stoddart of Swindon	Energy	LP[a]	3	60
Ennals	Health	LP[a]	3	64
Mishcon	Home Office	LP	8	71
Elwyn-Jones	Legal Affairs	LP[a]	12	77
Prys-Davies	N. Ireland	LP	4	63
Ross of Marnock	Scotland	LP[a]	7	75
Jeger	Social Security	LP[a]	7	71
Williams of Elvel	Trade and Industry	LP	1	53
Bruce of Donington	Treasury	LP[a]	11	74

Note: [a] Former Member of the House of Commons.
Abbreviations: H: Hereditary Peerage
                          LP: Life Peer

peerage in 1973 at the age of 25, but soon after Labour lost office in 1979 he left the front-bench in order to earn his living elsewhere, though he remained quite active in the House of Lords on behalf of countryside interests. His career pattern was unique on the Labour side, but would have been quite typical on the Conservative side.

Table 3.3 (b)   Labour Front Bench (Assistant Spokesmen), House of Lords, October 1987

Peer	Assistant Spokesman	Peerage	No. of yrs as member of the House	Age (attained by 1987)
Oram	Peers' representative on the Parliamentary Committee. Overseas Development	LP[a]	10	73
Dean of Beswick	Whip Environment	LP[a]	3	63
Gallacher	Whip Agriculture	LP	3	66
Graham of Edmonton	Whip Defence, Sport, N. Ireland	LP[a]	3	61
Nicol	Whip Green Issues, Trade and Industry	LP	3	63
Jenkins of Putney	Arts	LP[a]	5	78
Wedderburn of Charlton	Employment	LP	9	59
Ewart-Biggs	Home Office	LP	5	57
Silkin of Dulwich	Legal Affairs	LP[a]	1	68
Carmichael of Kelvingrove	Scotland, Transport	LP[a]	7	75
Morton of Shuna	Scotland (Legal Affairs)	LP	1	55
Turner of Camden	Social Security	LP	1	63
Stallard	Planning	LP[a]	3	65

Note: [a] Former Member of the House of Commons.
Abbreviations: LP: Life Peer

Representation of the Government in the House

As Table 3.2 shows government is represented in the Lords by some twenty peers who hold salaried offices as ministers or whips. Between them these peers act as spokesmen for all departments. Almost half the time of the Lords is spent on government legislation, and for most other items of business peers expect a contribution from the government front-bench, even if this is only to declare strict government neutrality in the matter under debate, as is sometimes the case with private members' bills or motions. Generally peers give very close attention to the contribution made by the government spokesmen. The number and relative seniority of ministers in the House of Lords are matters of importance to the Lords as a whole.

At the beginning of this century the prime minister and up to half the Cabinet were in the House of Lords. Today very few senior ministers sit in the Lords. Furthermore, as the total number of government ministers has increased, following the greatly expanded scope of government activity, the number of ministers in the Lords has remained fairly steady. The result is that the proportion of ministers in the Upper House is a good deal lower today than it was generally in the nineteenth century (see Table 3.4).

Table 3.4 Government Ministers (Including Whips[a]) in the House of Lords

Administration	Total size of Government	Number of peers in Government	Number of peers in the Cabinet
1945–51 (Attlee)	84–95	16–20	2–4
1951–7 (Churchill/Eden)	83–84	18–19	3–7
1957–64 (Macmillan/Home)	82–89	15–21	3–4
1964–70 (Wilson)	100–109	15–19	2
1970–4 (Heath)	84–95	16–20	3
1974–9 (Wilson/Callaghan)	98–111	14–17	2
1979–87 (Thatcher)	103–108	19–21	3–4

Source: Derived from *Hansard* list of ministers; first volume for each session.
Note: [a] Includes unsalaried government whips in office 1945.
           Excludes non-political appointments to Royal Household.

One obvious reason for this change was the confirmation of the political ascendancy of the Commons provided by the 1911 Parliament Act. Lord Curzon's failure to become prime minister in 1923, though not wholly due to his being a peer, was taken as having established a convention requiring the prime minister to sit in the Commons. In 1951–2 Churchill had seven peers in his cabinet, but since then Conservative cabinets have never had more than four peers, and Labour never more than two. By 1960 it was a matter of some surprise and opposition protest when a peer was appointed Foreign Secretary, and though this post was filled again by a peer in 1979, it had long been obvious that the great bulk of senior ministers must be members of the Commons. That is the elected House, and it is only there that the elected representatives of the people can directly question ministers about the discharge of their responsibilities.

The decline in the proportion of ministers in the Lords also results from a more general change in the nature of political life. At the turn of the century politics was still an activity dominated by the non-professional politician. In that respect Lords and Commons were alike; the members of neither House received salaries, and the great majority followed other occupations. In 1911, pay for MPs was introduced and throughout this century politics has increasingly become a sphere dominated by professional or near-professional politicians. For such ministerial office is the natural climax to their career. There is therefore immense demand for ministerial posts from MPs. Furthermore the work-load for all ministers has become extremely onerous. The House of Lords is not generally composed of professional politicians (indeed, if we exclude those who go there towards the end of their political careers, virtually none of its members could be so described). In contrast to the clamour for posts in the Commons, there is some evidence that ministerial posts have been difficult to fill in the Lords. For the non-professional part-time politician, the work involved may be very demanding, the salary offered relatively poor and, perhaps most seriously, the interruption of another career too serious to contemplate.

Four different catagories of government office-holders may be distinguished in the Lords, namely cabinet ministers, ministers of state, junior ministers and whips. The House of Lords always contains at least two cabinet ministers: the Lord Chancellor, and the Leader of the House. The Lord Chancellor acts as front-bench spokesman primarily on legal aspects of government legislation, but he speaks for the government on other matters too. Some holders of this office have been much involved with major policy, others less so. The Leader of the House, who has overall responsibility for the passage of government legislation, always holds a senior non-departmental post. Viscount Whitelaw, who was appointed Leader at the commencement of Mrs Thatcher's second administration, was Lord President of the Council. He was frequently also described as deputy prime minister. (The work within the House of these ministers is described in the following chapter.)

Sometimes Leaders of the Lords have been assigned specific ministerial duties, frequently responsibility for the Civil Service. Lord Whitelaw had no departmental responsibilities, but as senior cabinet minister chaired a number of important cabinet committees. According to Harold Wilson (1971) Lord Longford felt that leading the House was a part-time job and pressed for a departmental post in 1964–5; he was rewarded by becoming Secretary of State for the colonies in late 1965. Lord Longford himself argued (1974) that a Labour Leader of the House who lacks a departmental portfolio is at a disadvantage compared with a Conservative Leader, because leading the Lords is regarded as a junior job in a Labour Cabinet.

In addition to the offices of Lord Chancellor and Leader of the House, peers have since 1979 held a variety of departmental cabinet posts including Foreign Secretary, Secretary of State for Trade and Industry and Secretary of State for Employment. Lord Gowrie was Chancellor of the Duchy of Lancaster from 1984 to 1985, and had responsibility for the Civil Service and the Arts. From 1970 to 1974 Lord Carrington was Secretary of State for Defence, then briefly head of the newly created Department of Energy until the fall of the Heath Government. Where departmental Cabinet posts have been held by peers, it has been usual to have a second Cabinet minister who is an MP attached to the same department and directly answerable to the Commons. Thus, when Lord Carrington was Foreign Secretary, first Sir Ian Gilmour, then Mr Humphrey Atkins were appointed Lord Privy Seal and dealt with Foreign Office matters in the Commons. When Lord Young became Employment Secretary, Mr Kenneth Clarke became Paymaster General and was also described as Minister for Employment. The Labour Opposition were critical of the fact that the senior minister in the department dealing with the politically-sensitive and highly-important subject of unemployment was in the Lords, but the fact that the department concerned thereby had two cabinet ministers told against their criticism somewhat.

Below cabinet level are ministers of state and parliamentary under-secretaries all of whom are full ministers, though the former are more senior with higher salaries and wider responsibilities. Promotion from one rank to the other usually, but by no means always, involves a move to a different department. In 1987 there were five ministers at each of these two levels in the Lords; when Mrs Thatcher first came to office in 1979 she appointed eight peers at minister-of-state level and three at under-secretary level. The actual balance of numbers between the two ranks depends on a variety of factors, among them the need to recognise seniority and perhaps the need to ensure adequate financial reward to peers who might otherwise decline to serve in the government. A Lords' departmental minister will usually answer in the House for all the business of his department (as well as helping as spokesman for at least one other department). He will also be assigned a particular area of responsibility as a minister within the department concerned, and within that area civil servants will seek policy direction from him. In 1987 Lord Caithness had particular responsibility for prisons within the Home Office (and was quite frequently referred to as the minister for prisons), and Lord Brabazon of Tara had special responsibility for shipping while parliamentary under-secretary at the Department of Transport.

The whips' offices are political appointments to the Royal Household. The Chief Whip is styled the Captain of the Gentlemen at Arms (the title was unchanged when a woman, Baroness Llewelyn-Davies of Hastoe, was appointed to this office in 1974); the Deputy Chief Whip is the Captain of the Yeomen of the Guard. Assistant Whips, three or four in number until 1974, but five since then, hold offices as Lords in Waiting: they are to be distinguished from the non-political Lords in Waiting, whose functions are in the Royal Household, and whose appointments are not affected by changes of government.

Apart from the Chief Whip, all other whips unlike their Commons counterparts, act as official government spokesmen, supplementing the departmental ministers. Most Chief Whips only intervene in debates on business-of-the-House matters (though exceptionally the Chief Whip and his Labour opposite number made speeches in a debate on 9 April 1987 on the unity of the nation).

Lords in Waiting usually could expect to act as spokesmen for at least three departments, mostly of course in a supplementary capacity (see Table 3.2 (b)). But this could give them a great deal to do, for example, at committee stage on bills, or generally in answering questions or replying to debates, especially if the departments they spoke for were ones with a lot of parliamentary business. Though not ministers, Lords in Waiting since the mid-1970s were regularly but not invariably provided with offices in one of the departments for which they spoke. The whole House knew that as Lords in Waiting they were spokesmen and not in any sense originators of policy. When they spoke in the House of Lords it was necessary for them to stick closely to the brief provided by the department concerned, and probably make generous use of the civil servants waiting in the box in the corner of the chamber ready to brief government spokesmen. Being a Lord in Waiting may be viewed as an apprenticeship to ministerial office. It represents an opportunity to get to know the Lords well, and learn how it is best handled; it also gives an insight into the workings of government. Some peers enjoyed the challenge of this office precisely because of the range of topics dealt with and the opportunity for contact with a number of departments. Others found it frustrating and were relieved when a 'proper' ministerial post came their way. But once it did they were likely to find the Lords a little less forbearing. Certainly ministers of state, and even more Cabinet ministers, could expect the Lords to press them much harder in debate because of their senior ministerial status.

The Government front-bench was organised in such a way that each department had at least two peers who spoke for it. If no minister was in a department, the main spokesman may have been a minister elsewhere, or a Lord in Waiting. Baroness Young dealt with Education while Minister of State at the Foreign Office after 1983; however, she had previously been an education minister, though when at that department she also dealt with health and social security legislation. Energy was dealt with by two whips in 1987 but no minister. For major bills the usual spokesmen may need to be supplemented by others drawn in so as to help spread the burden of work. This raises the important question of the adequacy of government representation.

Government Appointments in the House

At no time in recent years have all departments had at least one minister in the Lords. Mrs Thatcher's second administration began with Education, Trade, Transport, the Treasury and the Welsh Office without ministers. Sometimes the situation has been much more unsatisfactory. When the Labour Government of March 1974 took office, only fourteen peers (including whips) were appointed, giving direct representation in the Lords to only seven departments. Among departments then lacking any ministers in the Lords, with the numbers of ministers in the Commons in parentheses, were: Environment (nine); Education and Science (four); Employment and Productivity (four); and Health and Social Security (five). In June 1974 Lord Windlesham, speaking from the Conservative front-bench, expressed disquiet at the representation of the Labour Government in the Lords, and argued that the reputation of the House depended to a very considerable degree on the number and seniority of ministers appointed from among peers. In reply the Leader of the House drew attention to the way in which the representation of the government tended to improve during the lifetime of each administration (HL Debs, 25 June 1974, Cols 1322–5).

The implication of these remarks appeared to be that an incoming prime minister first sought to satisfy the aspirations for government office among MPs before looking to the Lords. In time, however, the need for stronger representation in the Lords became obvious, and this resulted in some strengthening of the government in the Upper House. The Conservative Government started in 1970 with sixteen peers, but this later rose to twenty. Labour in March 1974 had only fourteen office holders in the Lords, but by 1975 there were seventeen. When Mrs Thatcher came to office in 1979 the number immediately rose to twenty-one, but this total was not exceeded during either of her first two administrations. Richard Crossman recorded in his diary the resentment expressed by Labour MPs when Baroness Serota was appointed Minister of State at the Department of Health and Social Security in 1969 because a 'good job has gone to a peeress', though he added that London MPs who knew how good she was from her work as Labour Chief Whip on the Greater London Council 'congratulated me' (Crossman, 1976, p. 380).

The House of Lords, generally, is well pleased when it can deal with senior ministers. If a Secretary-of-State post is conferred on a peer, the expressions of pleasure in the Lords may well be in sharp contrast to the attitudes expressed in the Commons at such appointments. Peers were delighted when Lord Home became Foreign Secretary back in 1960, but in the Commons Labour MPs secured immediate debate for a hostile motion. Likewise in 1970 the appointment of Lord Carrington as Defence Secretary pleased peers, but in April 1971 a Labour back-bench MP introduced a ten-minute rule bill seeking to debar the appointment of peers as senior ministers heading departments, on the grounds that they should be 'subject to the scrutiny and if necessary the ribaldry and hostility of the House of Commons' (HC Debs, 7 April 1971, Col 465–70). Lord Carrington's inability personally to speak in the Commons' debate following the Falklands invasion in 1982 probably increased his determination to resign immediately in face of the strong criticism vented in the Lower House. Undoubtedly, peers who are senior ministers need to tread cautiously when dealing with MPs. A good junior minister and parliamentary private secretary in the Commons can be helpful. The attitude of the Lords' minister himself is important. One ex-minister peer spoke in an interview of his particular care over letters to MPs, which he frequently found he had to modify because they had been drafted by civil servants in a tone suitable for a Commons' minister, but, in his view, unsuitable for a Lords' minister.

A prime minister who wants to give ministerial office to a person who has no seat in either House of Parliament may do this by bringing that person straight into the Lords. In 1979, Mrs Thatcher decided to include in the Department of Environment ministerial team the Leader of Leeds City Council, who was thereupon created a peer, Lord Bellwin. In 1984 she decided to bring a businessman who had been an adviser to the Government and then for two years chairman of the Manpower Services Commission into her Cabinet: he too became a peer, Lord Young of Graffham, and subsequently Secretary of State for Employment. Sometimes individuals have been brought into the Lords on the nomination of the Leader of the Opposition shortly before an election, with the expectation that if the election brings a change of government, they are likely to be given office. In 1978, Mrs Thatcher, as Leader of the Opposition, nominated for peerages Sir Christopher Soames, a former Conservative Cabinet Minister turned diplomat, and Sir Arthur Cockfield, a businessman. Both received office when the Conservatives came to power a year later. In 1964 and again in 1974 Mr Wilson brought a small number of non-parliamentarians directly into his Government.

It may be an advantage for the holders of some offices to be peers. When, in 1964, Mr Wilson wanted to have a government minister rather than an official as British representative at the UN in New York, it was understandable that the post should go to a peer, the more so in view of the Government's very slender Commons majority. In 1974 Lord Goronwy-

Roberts became a junior Foreign Office minister, the only minister in that department not an MP. Because of the parlous state of the Government in the Commons, he was the only one who could go on lengthy overseas trips! Back in 1956 a former Permanent Secretary at the Foreign Office pointed out the advantage it would be if the Foreign Secretary sat in the Lords, though he added that 'in modern conditions this is perhaps asking the impossible' (Strang, 1956, p. 300). But in this judgement he was wrong because in 1960 a peer became Foreign Secretary, as happened again in 1979.

Work on the Front-Bench

While peers who are ministers are relieved of some of the tasks which fall upon their Commons' counterparts, such as constituency duties and the need to be present in the Commons a great deal, at least if the government of the day lacks a secure majority, in other respects ministers in the Lords may have to work harder. A Commons minister can expect to speak in his House only on matters for which he has a very direct departmental responsibility. He will only answer questions on set days, usually once every three or four weeks, or less frequently. But as we have noted Lords' ministers may have to speak on behalf of several departments (they can have a 'long waterfront', Theakston, 1987, p. 137), and may also find themselves answering oral questions very frequently (see p. 167). Baroness Young had responsibility for nine bills in less than two years while Minister of State for Education 1979–81. Lord Trefgarne was on his feet answering oral questions in the Lords on 70 of the 147 sitting days in the 1981–2 session while he was a junior minister at the Department of Trade, but also helping with Foreign Office questions.

In 1983 the Top Salaries Review Body commissioned management consultants to investigate and report on relative pay levels for ministers; among those whose jobs were analysed were two peers. The report concluded that because ministers in the House of Lords had to range over a wider area than their Commons counterparts, they needed wider knowledge, and this meant 'perhaps more work (rather than necessarily a more important job)' (Cmnd. 881–I–II). The Review Body had in earlier reports recommended that ministerial salaries be the same in both Houses, but because ministers in the Commons were entitled to draw part of their parliamentary salaries too, this in effect meant lower pay for the Lords' ministers. In 1981, against the advice of the Review Body, the Cabinet decided to pay a higher ministerial salary to Lords' ministers, a decision in effect endorsed by the management consultants' report two years later. The Government had no doubt discovered that low pay was a problem in recruiting Lords' ministers. Up until 1980 Lords in Waiting were paid substantially less than back-bench MPs. One former minister in interview told of the amazement of his business associates when in 1979 he felt duty bound to take ministerial office at a salary so very much lower than he had been receiving for his work outside politics. In 1985 Lord Gowrie, who had been promoted to the Cabinet the previous year, at the age of 45, and was widely thought of as a future Leader of the House, resigned altogether from government, publicly stating that his reason for doing so was the low level of pay; he received £33,000 per year, some £8,000 less than Cabinet ministers in the Commons.

The resignation of Lord Elton, Minister of State for the Environment, in September 1986, deprived the Lords of another experienced minister, and at the same time Lord Swinton, Deputy Chief Whip, departed. In the resulting reshuffle the two peers who newly joined the Government were Lord Beaverbrook and Lord Hesketh, both of whom had made their maiden speeches as recently as that summer. At the same time Lord Caithness, who had first joined the Government as Lord in Waiting as recently as 1984, was promoted to Minister of State at the Home Office; in October 1987 the difficulties he had in coping with the Criminal Justice Bill caused government embarrassment (and according to newspaper reports hastened the departure of the sick Lord Havers from the woolsack). A good deal of muttering was being heard in the Lords about the overall adequacy of government representation. The business of the House of Lords had become more onerous, and its importance had increased. Was the House being accorded sufficient ministers of the standing and experience it merited?

In a very few cases the general abilities of government spokesmen may be called into question, but most of the time peers have nothing but praise for the individuals involved. But there is a recognition in the Lords that because too few peers hold government office, those that do simply have too many subjects to deal with. Furthermore, if they are spokesmen only, or relatively junior ministers, they do not have the authority to deal with a subject in a way that seems fitting to many members of the Lords. Participants in debates may include peers of considerable expertise and experience in certain areas, for example, former Permanent Secretaries or Cabinet Ministers, or those with immense experience of a relevant kind elsewhere. A Lord in Waiting or junior minister answering debate may have received instructions not to give way, and not even to promise another look at a particular clause in a bill. Sometimes the mood of the Lords alters quite quickly in such circumstances, opposition hardens and a division begins to look likely with possible government defeat and consequent awkwardness. The Chief Whip and Leader of the House may have to be hurriedly summoned, and sometimes a sudden change of tack

by the government spokeman at the Despatch Box can be observed. But
equally there can simply be frustration on the part of peers at the
difficulties they face in ensuring that their views are being taken seriously
enough by government. Lord Houghton of Sowerby, a senior back-bench
Labour peer and vastly experienced parliamentarian, who was formerly
Chairman of the PLP as an MP, expressed such frustration during a debate
on a government bill in 1985. His remarks are worth quoting:

> I think we are moving into a different regime in this House. We have become
> more important and more publicised, and there is a desire to become more
> powerful and to take a more definite place in the combined activities of the two
> Houses of Parliament . . . the Government Front Bench in this House . . . do
> not have the authority to do what a Minister in . . . (the Commons) . . . would
> very frequently feel bound to do, or at least feel that it was desirable to do . . . I
> think that greater authority, more flexibility and more room for manoeuvre
> should be in somebody's hands in this House.
>
> (HL Debs, 4 July 1985, col. 1390)

But the generally unsatisfactory nature of government representation in
the Lords is a function of the unsatisfactory situation in which the House
now finds itself. A full minister in each department would be a minimum
desirable improvement. But beyond that, it seems unfortunate that senior
ministers are not empowered to speak in either House, while retaining full
membership of only one House. In most European countries with
bicameral legislatures ministers are entitled to speak in both Houses
(though in some cases they are members of neither). It may be objected
that this would increase demands upon ministers, but this need not be the
case, for example, where answerability in the Commons replaced full
membership of that House.

The Opposition Front-Bench

Given the legislative role of the House of Lords and the answerability of
the Government in the upper chamber, it is incumbent upon the major
Opposition Party to make arrangements to ensure that its point of view is
officially stated in the debates which take place. When Labour was in
opposition before 1964, the number of active Labour peers was too few to
permit anything other than informal, flexible arrangements for the
organisation of their front-bench. Since 1964 when either Conservative or
Labour have been in opposition, a front-bench team at least as large as the
government team has been maintained. Indeed in recent years the major
parties when in opposition have named more peers to their front-bench
than when in office. Labour had a list of eighteen principal spokesmen and

thirteen other spokesmen in 1987 (Table 3.3); the Conservatives in early 1979 had a list of twenty-six front-bench spokesmen. The absence of any pay or extra allowances for Opposition front-benchers (other than the Leader and Chief Whip) necessitates using some peers who have careers elsewhere to which they must devote at least some of their time. If this has been one reason for expanding the list of spokesmen when in opposition, another has been the straightforward desire to make use of whatever expertise is available.

Whenever the Conservative Party has been in opposition, the Leader and Deputy-Leader in the Lords were appointed by the overall party leader. These two peers always served as members of the Leader's Consultative Committee, or 'Shadow Cabinet'. Lord Carrington was Leader of the Opposition from 1964–70 and again from 1974–9. In addition there has always been at least one further peer appointed to the Conservative 'Shadow Cabinet': between 1974 and 1979 Lord Hailsham was a member, described as being 'without specific duties', though not surprisingly he did act as party spokesman in the Lords on legal matters. The chairmanship of the party has frequently been held by a peer, as it was from 1975 to 1981 by Lord Thorneycroft, and he, too, spoke from time to time from the opposition front-bench, though he had no specific sphere of responsibility.

In the Labour Party the offices of Leader of the Labour peers, Deputy Leader and Chief Whip were all open to election when the party was in opposition. The Leader and Chief Whip, together with an elected representative of back-bench peers, were ex-officio members of the party 'Shadow Cabinet', where according to Punnett (1973, p. 430) 'their contributions are certainly not restricted to House of Lords matters'. Until 1973 no elections had been necessary because there had never been more than one nomination for each post. But in that year, when Lord Beswick resigned, three nominations were received for his former post of Chief Whip. The victor was Baroness Llewelyn-Davies of Hastoe, who comfortably defeated her two rivals, Lord Davies of Leek and Lord Peddie.

Lord Peart, who had entered the House of Lords and became Leader in 1976, remained as Labour Leader after 1979 as well. But Labour peers became restless with his lack of drive and ineffectiveness. Despite hints and private appeals to step aside he refused to do so. In 1982 Lord Cledwyn of Penrhos stood against him, and defeated him by sixty votes to thirty-seven. At the same time Lord Ponsonby of Shulbrede emerged triumphant after a contested vote for Baroness Llewelyn-Davies' post as Chief Whip. The leadership of the opposition therefore underwent a considerable change that year, and a reinvigoration followed. Lord Cledwyn improved the organisation of the Opposition front-bench and generally rekindled enthusiasm among Labour peers.

In both the major parties, when in opposition, it is the party leader in the

Lords who selects the team of front-bench spokesmen and allocates duties between them. There does not seem to be much difficulty about this. A Labour left-wing peer who thought he had been appointed to the Lords to speak from the front-bench on a particular subject found himself quickly shifted to the back-benches because of his general rumbustiousness. This was unusual. More often it is a matter of persuading peers to take a rôle rather than removing them from the front-bench. The work involved for an opposition spokesman can be quite onerous, especially when dealing with major and complex legislation. The only opposition front-benchers to receive salaries are the Leader and Chief Whip. The absence of salaries is no doubt one reason why some peers, especially younger peers, leave their front-bench when their party is in opposition.

Back-Bench Party Organisation

The parties and the cross-bench peers each hold weekly meetings every Thursday at 2.15 p.m. The main concern at these gatherings is to outline future business, and to sound opinion about the most desirable way of handling such business. A document is prepared each Thursday while the House is sitting and sent to peers indicating the timetable for the forthcoming week. For this the party whips are responsible, and the document — or whip — includes mention of expected divisions with appropriate underlining. Cross-bench peers, if they so wish, may receive an 'unlined whip' prepared by the Chief Whip, which indicates the expected timetable and may include other helpful notices (such as when dinner will be available).

On the Conservative side a body known as the Association of Conservative Peers (ACP) is the equivalent of the 1922 Committee in the Commons. All Conservative peers belong, and they elect a chairman and a committee of about ten others, all backbenchers who retire in rotation. Since 1980 the Chairman has been Lord Boyd-Carpenter, a former MP and sometime Chief Secretary to the Treasury. He left the Commons in 1972 upon appointment as Chairman of the Civil Aviation Authority, a post he held until 1977. His predecessors as Chairman of the Conservative peers had been Lord Drumalbyn (1975–80), and Lord Brooke of Cumnor (1970–75), both also former MPs and ministers; in their time the Conservative peer's organisation had been called the Independent Unionist Peers. Its change of name in the early 1980s was at Lord Boyd-Carpenter's suggestion.

The executive committee of the ACP holds a meeting immediately prior to the general Thursday meeting. At this earlier meeting the committee decide what proposals to make to their colleagues, for example, as to the motions to be debated in the time allocated on the floor of the House to the party. Front-benchers do not on the whole attend the 2.15 meeting (they have their own meeting at 2.00 instead), but the Chief Whip attends the ACP meeting, and he can relay opinion to ministers as necessary, as no doubt can the Chairman. The Chairman of the 1922 Committee from the Commons was said to attend quite frequently, though Lord Boyd-Carpenter never attended the 1922 Committee, not because of any feeling of unease about doing so, but simply because he hadn't the time. In the mid-1980s the ACP held special meetings about six times a year, usually with senior ministers giving talks and with the Prime Minister coming once a year.

On the Labour side a Labour peers' co-ordinating committee exists. While the party was in opposition in the 1980s this consisted of five elected back-bench peers and the five office-holders within the party in the Lords, namely the Leader, Deputy Leader, Chief Whip, Deputy Chief Whip and the peers' representative on the 'Shadow Cabinet'. This last post was held by Lord Oram from 1983 onwards; his predecessor had been Lord Lee of Newton, who had also sat as representative of the Labour peers on the Liaison Committee, a body representing ministers and back-bench members of both Houses when the party was in office. The co-ordinating committee of ten peers was chaired by a backbencher by deliberate choice. It met fortnightly and among other tasks considered how to use time allocated to the party for debate in the House of Lords.

On Thursdays prior to the 2.15 party meeting, the party whips met at 1.00 p.m., and at 1.30 p.m. all principal opposition spokesmen met. These meetings prepared the ground for the main party meeting, at which in addition to front-bench peers reporting briefly on matters within their area of responsibility, reports were given from the Chairman of the co-ordinating committee and the peers' elected representative on the Shadow Cabinet. Usually about fifty Labour peers attended this meeting. When Labour was in office in the 1970s front-benchers attended the Thursday 2.15 p.m. meeting quite regularly, which contrasts with Conservative peers' practice, but in fact both parties parallel their Commons counterparts in this respect.

Labour peers also hold occasional meetings on an *ad hoc* basis addressed by leading party members. On most Wednesday mornings the Parliamentary Labour Party (PLP) in the Commons holds meetings to discuss policy issues which are open to interested Labour peers, and quite a few attend. Lord Cledwyn also encouraged suitable Labour peers to participate in PLP subject groups, but it would seem that very few do this; even those who do were excluded from voting in elections for PLP group officers. Prior to 1983 the PLP in the Commons held a single regular meeting for discussion of policy questions and business matters. Curiously all Labour peers were entitled to attend these PLP meetings and indeed to vote on policy matters. Richard Crossman in his diary recorded disquiet about this (Crossman, 1976, p. 376). Lord Kennet in a letter to *The Times* (14 April 1972) claimed that the Labour Government in the 1960s had sometimes put pressure on Labour peers to attend and vote at PLP meetings 'in order to uphold government policy against the objections of Labour backbenchers in the Commons'. By dividing the Commons PLP meeting in the 1980s into a business meeting (at which votes were taken) and a separate meeting for discussion of policy, it became natural to exclude peers from the former.

Liberals and Social Democrats

Liberal peers elect their Leader, who then appoints other party office holders and party spokesmen. From 1967 until his death in 1984 Lord Byers, a former Liberal MP, was Party Leader in the Lords. Baroness Seear, who had retired from her post as reader in personnel management at the London School of Economics, was elected Leader in 1984, comfortably defeating two rivals, Lord Banks and Lord Mackie of Benshie. The Deputy Leader, Lord Gladwyn has had a remarkably long and active retirement since leaving the Diplomatic Service in 1960. Lord Tordoff, Chief Whip since 1984, was Chairman of the Liberal Party before becoming a peer (see Table 3.5).

Table 3.5 (a)   Liberal Party Office Holders, January 1988

Peers	Office	Peerage	Years in House	Age attained by 1987
Seear	Leader	LP	16	73
Gladwyn	Deputy Leader	H 1st B	27	86
Tordoff	Whip	LP	6	58
McNair	Deputy Whip	H 2nd B	12	71

Table 3.5 (b)   Social Democratic Party Office Holders, January 1988

Peers	Office	Peerage	Years in House	Age attained by 1987
Diamond	Chairman	LP[a]	17	79
Kilmarnock	Deputy Chairman	H 7th B	12	59
Stedman	Chief Whip	LP	13	70

Note: [a] Former Member of the House of Commons.
Abbreviations: H: Hereditary Peerage
                 LP: Life Peer

In addition to the Leader, Deputy Leader and two whips, no fewer than twenty-five peers were named as party spokesmen in 1987. Only a few of these would normally speak from the front-bench, though all when speaking would be expected faithfully to represent their party line, unless they specifically disclaimed to be doing so. The line between front- and back-bench in the Liberal Party was therefore somewhat fuzzy. This arrangement meant that not only was every subject covered, but on most more than one peer was designated a party spokesman, so that hopefully the presence of a party spokesman could be more readily assured.

The Social Democratic peers elected a chairman rather than a leader. They reached agreement about other office holders, and like the Liberals published a list of party spokesmen which included most party members in the Lords. Their first Chairman was Lord Aylestone, but in 1983 he gave way to Lord Diamond, a member of the Lords since 1970, and a former Cabinet minister in the Labour Government of the 1960s. Lord Kilmarnock was the Party Whip, but when he became deputy chairman Baroness Stedman, formerly a junior Lords' minister in the Labour Government of the 1970s, took his place as Whip.

To begin with SDP peers sat on the rear opposition bench behind Labour peers, but after a short while the Liberals invited them to share their benches, which at least facilitated communication between the parties. Liaison between the parties became close. In early 1987 in addition to short separate meetings on Thursday afternoons, they also held frequent joint meetings for all peers in both parties. The leaders and whips of both parties always met after the party meetings on Thursday afternoons. Though separate whips were issued, the level of whipping was always the same. When first founded the Social Democrats had resisted the idea of whipping their members altogether, but the necessity for this was soon recognised. In 1987 their weekly whip was a much more chatty document than the more formal, traditional whips issued by all the other parties, including the Liberals. The Alliance parties together employ a part-time research assistant in the Lords, in addition to the highly-competent 'whips' assistant' employed by the Liberals and a secretary employed by the Social Democrats.

Relative to their numbers in the Commons, Liberals (and since 1981 Social Democrats) have enjoyed a considerable strength in the Lords. When the Lib-Lab pact was formed in 1977 David Steel announced a 'Shadow Cabinet' which included seven peers along with fourteen MPs. Some Liberal peers remained as leading party spokesmen until 1983, when all such posts were reassumed by MPs. But in January 1987 when a joint Alliance team of parliamentary spokesmen was announced, two peers were included, Baroness Seear on Social Services and Baroness Stedman on environmental protection.

Three or four Liberal peers usually attended the meeting of Liberal MPs, though no MP regularly attended the meeting of peers. The arrangements for this remained somewhat fluid, depending on the party offices held by individual peers. David Steel came to the Liberal peers' meeting two or three times a year. The Leader and Chief Whip of the SDP peers usually attended the SDP MPs' meeting, and the Commons SDP Whip usually came to the peers' meeting. While such arrangements were helpful, the most important liaison between Liberal peers and MPs took place through the policy panels set up within the party organisation.

Cross-Bench Peers

There have always been non-party peers in the Lords. In the post-war period their number grew steadily, and in the mid-1960s some of the more active non-party peers began to meet regularly, with Lord Strang (formerly of the Foreign Office) emerging as their co-ordinator. When he retired in 1974, Baroness Hylton-Foster, widow of a former Speaker of the Commons, was elected in his place. She has been re-elected unopposed every year since. She took the title Convenor of the Cross-bench Peers.

Every Thursday at 2.15 p.m., when the parties have their meetings, crossbenchers meet as well. Usually some twenty to thirty attend. They decide on the subject-matter for debate in time allocated to them, and may discuss any concerns they have about the House. Sometimes they meet earlier in order to hear from a guest speaker they have decided to invite, for example, the chairman of a nationalised industry or a prominent trade unionist. In some respects cross-bench peers may look like another party in the House of Lords, but this is misleading. Their opinions range widely and their organisation is minimal. They have no leader, and could not have one in the usual sense of the term because they neither seek to formulate common views on issues coming before the Lords, nor could they. But having a regular meeting, a recognised spokesman, and an unlined whip are all useful devices for keeping non-party peers in close touch with the work of the Lords. For example, their convenor sits on the various select committees which deal with domestic House of Lords' matters, such as procedure, leave of absence and expenses, privileges and the Committee of Selection. She can report back on matters covered by these committees, and sound out the opinions of cross-bench peers, and feed these in as necessary.

As Tables 2.4 and 2.5 show, quite a number of cross-bench peers are active on the floor of the House. It is worth particularly noting their role on subject select committees, where a cross-bench figure has frequently been sought for the post of chairman. In recent years most of the chairmen of the six European Communities' sub-committees have been crossbenchers.

This suggests non-party status can be seen as a definite advantage for some aspects of the work of the Lords. The voting habits of cross-bench peers are of particular interest.

A few are habitual or at least fairly regular supporters of one or other party, but most vary their voting pattern. Not having the guidance of a party whip, crossbenchers are slightly more inclined to abstention than are party members. A few when in doubt say that they support the government of the day — whatever party is in office. More look to other cross-bench peers, taking a lead from those whose opinion on a particular subject they respect. Whips are even known to calculate that an intervention for or against the government by x on subject y will be worth, say ten votes. Sometimes gentle overtures are made by party front-benchers to individual crossbenchers whose contributions they have reason to believe may be of particular assistance to them on a certain matter.

Analysis of 222 divisions for which the Government had a whip in the 1983–4 session shows that the balance of cross-bench votes went against the Government 48 times and in support of the Government 174 times. All told, cross-bench peers cast more than twice as many votes with the Government as against it (2,548 to 1,293). However, if the twenty Government defeats alone are examined, in fifteen of these the balance of cross-bench votes went against the Government, and in six of these fifteen that balance was crucial to the outcome of the division. Analysis of divisions in the 1975–6 session showed crossbenchers voting heavily against the Labour Government. (Research conducted by the author.)

Such statistical analysis shows that cross-bench votes are of greater assistance to the Conservatives than to the Labour Party in the Lords. Baldwin analysed cross-bench peers in terms of their education, career and peerage, and found that on a comparative statistical basis they were 'overwhelmingly similar' to Conservative peers (Baldwin, 1985, p. 136).

Whipping in the Lords

There may possibly be some validity in talking about the 'black arts of whipping' in the Commons, but such a phrase would be utterly inappropriate in the Lords. Commons whips have a variety of sticks and carrots which they may use to encourage party loyalty. Aspiration to front-bench office or to membership of certain select committees or to positions on delegations to exotic foreign parts, or even hopes of recognition in future honours lists: all these and more may be factors which a Commons' whip can trade against. But such inducements are not part of the currency with which a Lords' whip deals. For most peers the high-point of their career is over; ambitions have either been fulfilled or have subsided. Appeals to party loyalties developed over a lifetime may be an effective approach to whipping, but possibly more effective still are reasoned arguments, carefully framed, possibly put privately by a minister to doubters, rather than publicly on the floor of the House. The whips may be active in identifying waverers, exploring their views, communicating these to party spokesmen and facilitating intra-party discussions.

The arrangements for whipping in the Lords therefore remain low key. In addition to a Chief Whip, the Conservative and Labour Parties both have Deputy Chief Whips, and several assistant whips. But these all act as party spokesmen on specific subjects. No regional whips exist, as in the Commons, though subjects may at times be allocated as the special responsibility of individual whips. Such arrangements, if made, are flexible, low profile and short-lived. Labour for a time in the 1970s tried dividing up the entire party among the various whips on an alphabetic basis, but the arrangement was not sustained.

For many years past Chief Whips have sub-divided their party lists according to the relative availability of different peers and their regularity in attendance. Such categories as 'do not attend', 'age and health make attendance unlikely', 'distance and commitment make attendance unreliable' and 'regular and reliable' have been identified. More recently, during the 1983 parliament, Labour has made use of a 'telephone whip', with a list of supporters who may be telephoned and urged to attend for particular divisions. Occasionally the Conservative Chief Whip has written a letter to the more likely attenders within his party's ranks, urging more regular attendance for divisions on particular bills, and possibly including some statistics about attendances and voting figures. In 1983 a pro forma was sent to all Conservative peers asking for commitments to attend at particular times, but the response to this was so disappointing that the exercise was not repeated.

Occasionally a party Chief Whip has decided that the voting record or general conduct of a particular peer is such that a talk with that peer is necessary. A Conservative peer who was frequently drunk had the whip withdrawn in the 1960s. The next Conservative to lose the party whip was Lord Alport in December 1984. His offence was to launch what the press described as a stinging attack on Mrs Thatcher during a debate on a Labour motion on unemployment, and to follow this by voting against the Government at the end of the debate. Nor was this an isolated act of rebellion on his part: twice during the 1983-4 session the Government ran a three-line whip, and on both occasions Lord Alport voted in the Opposition lobby. According to the *Financial Times* (19 December, 1984) the situation was further exacerbated by the fact that 'Lord Alport was unable to make himself available to discuss the position' with his Chief Whip following his rebellion. But the withdrawal of the party whip simply meant that he became an 'independent Conservative', remaining outside the Lords a member of the party he had earlier served as an MP and Commons minister.

The Labour Party in the Lords frequently uses a three-line whip, but sometimes there has been surprise and disappointment at the relatively modest turnout of Labour peers though it is important to remember the high average age of Labour peers. Only twice in the 1983 Parliament did more than 100 Labour peers vote — both occasions being on the Local Government (Interim Provisions) Bill. On the substantive abolition bill, only twice did over ninety Labour peers vote and for several crucial divisions at report stage fewer than eighty did so, a turn-out which compared unfavourably with that of Alliance peers, some of whom believed the problem lay in Labour's rather indiscriminating use of the three-line whip. A further problem may have been that on these measures Labour allowed some of the initiative on whipping to be taken by those compaigning outside the House of Lords, notably those assisting the GLC campaign (see Livingstone, 1987, Chapter 8) and peers may have responded less well to this approach. Labour turn-out however was in general much better than it had been in the 1970s. The Liberals used three line whips somewhat more frequently in the 1983 Parliament than previously, but still much less often than Labour.

When the Conservative Party used a three-line whip a turn-out of over 200 Conservatives could be expected; on the second reading of the Local Government (Interim Provisions) Bill 212 Conservatives voted with the Government, and on the second reading of the Local Government Bill, the next year, 221 voted. However Lord Denham, Government Chief Whip, was very reluctant to use a three-line whip other than in exceptional circumstances. He argued that heavier regular whipping would in the long term prove counterproductive. In the 1980s, he remembered well the intense pressure put on Conservative peers to prevent any amendments being made to the European Communities Bill in 1972. This he felt had a devastating effect on the morale of peers, and he determined to avoid the repetition of such pressure. One cannot put excessive pressure on volunteers, or else they may cease to be volunteers.

An analysis of all 222 divisions in the 1983–4 session in which the Government placed a whip, shows that some Conservative cross-voting took place in 104 of these, or almost half. In 88 of these 104 divisions the Government won; the number of Conservative rebels averaged between two and three. In fifteen cases the Government was defeated in divisions where the Labour Opposition also had a whip on; the average number of Conservative rebels in these divisions was eight. In one case the Government was defeated outright by its own backbenchers rebelling. This was a division on the Trade Union Bill, which some Conservative peers thought should insist on secret ballots for office holders (it was even suggested in some quarters that they received a nod and a wink from Downing Street); forty-nine Conservative peers voted against the Government, forty-three in its support. Conservative defeat from the political right had become comparatively infrequent; there was only one other example during the 1983 Parliament — on the 1986 Education Bill (see Chapter 6).

Labour peers cross-voted in only 22 of the 180 divisions in which both Labour and Government had placed a whip. In only two cases did more than one peer cross-vote, and in thirteen of the remaining twenty, the cross-voting was by the same peer — Lord Plant — who voted against his party whip repeatedly on the Police and Criminal Evidence Bill. Lord Plant, a former trade unionist, had been a member of the Police Pay and Conditions Review Board before becoming a peer in 1978. He was retained as spokesman by the Police Federation, and obviously found himself quite out of sympathy with his party and its attitude to this major piece of legislation. One other peer cross-voted four times; this was Lord Northfield, formerly Donald Chapman, a Labour MP; he voted against his party twice on the Housing and Building Control Bill, and on two other different bills. Two other peers cross-voted twice, and the remainder were isolated instances of disobedience to the whip. Abstention is a much easier course of action than actually voting against party colleagues.

Abstention

Unlike the Commons the House of Lords has no arrangement for 'pairing' absentees, a fact which reflects the more irregular pattern of attendance and voting in the Upper House. It is difficult to do other than provide a rough estimate of the extent of calculated abstention by peers. Sometimes peers indicate in speeches their opposition to, or misgivings about, their party line on a particular issue, and then fail to vote in the division immediately following. For example, four Conservatives criticised the Government in speeches during the second reading debate on the Rates Bill in April 1984, then failed to support it in the division lobby, despite a three-line whip. The total turnout of peers for particular divisions can also be considered. Some references have already been given to this, for instance, to the very low turnout of Labour peers for divisions on some legislation in the mid-1970s; on the bill nationalising aerospace and shipbuilding, the average turnout of Labour peers was only forty. In 1976 the *Sunday Times* published the results of a survey into the voting records of the ninety-nine Labour peers created between 1964–76, based on the fifty-three most important divisions over the previous two years. This found that only thirty-five of them voted in as many as half of the divisions for which they were eligible as members of the House (*Sunday Times,* 30 May, 1976). Baldwin found that in one month the Labour Government lost forty-six divisions in the Lords, half of which it would have won if half of its peers had turned up and supported it in the division lobby (Baldwin, 1985, p. 258).

It is possible for any particular day to consult the *Journals of the House of Lords* to see which peers actually attended, but failed to vote in a particular division. For example, the *Journals* record the names of twenty-eight Conservative peers present on 13 March 1980, none of whom voted in the crucial division on school transport charges held that day. Some were almost certainly deliberate abstentions, but it is impossible to say how many. Peers come and go throughout the day, as a study of successive divisions at the same sitting indicates. Three major divisions took place on the afternoon of July 22 1980, at report stage of the Housing Bill. The *Journals* list 358 peers as attending that day. The first division took place at 3.44 p.m., and 228 peers voted; the second at 6.55 p.m. with 199 peers voting and the third at 9.52 with 136 peers voting. Of the total attending the Lords, 72 voted in none of the three well-spaced divisions, and only 163 or well under half, voted in more than one division. These were keenly contested divisions, the middle one of which the Government lost. On private members' legislation, with the whips not operating, there may be even less regularity about voting. Hindell and Simms (1971) found that in two divisions held at 5.12 and 6.47 p.m. on the same afternoon during the committee stage of the Abortion Bill in 1968, of 140 peers who took part in the two divisions, only 57 voted in both.

In the early 1980s the Opposition Whips usually managed to arrange matters so that crucial votes occurred relatively early in the day, at least before the evening dinner period, the Government Chief Whip acquiescing in this provided that Opposition accepted a timetable ensuring the completion of successive stages on major bills at appointed times. In 1984–5 only twenty-nine divisions took place after 8.00 p.m., but eight of these were on items of business for which the Government had no whip (mainly private members' bills). In the remaining twenty-one late divisions, the average turnout of peers, expressed as a percentage of the total recorded as attending the House on the days concerned, was 30 per cent. Only on two occasions did over half the peers who attended vote in divisions held after 8.00 p.m. At the other extreme, only in seven divisions did over 80 per cent of attenders vote, and in all the whipped divisions the average voting turn-out was just over half the total of peers attending the House of Lords on the days concerned.

Because of the way the House of Lords is composed the parties cannot organise support in anything like the way they do in the Commons. Most peers subscribe to a party whip, and when they turnout to vote they are almost invariably loyal to their party. But comparatively few feel an obligation to attend and vote in the Lords in a truly regular manner. It is the relatively casual or spasmodic nature of the participation of peers which limits the hold of the major parties, and the fact that even among active peers only a minority could be described as professional politicians.

4

THE ORGANISATION AND
PROCEDURE OF THE HOUSE

The previous two chapters have indicated both the similarities and the contrasts between the House of Lords and the House of Commons. An examination of the procedure and organisation of the House of Lords must once again embrace this theme. Many of the basic rules of debate are very similar in both Houses, as are the stages of the legislative process. But the style of debate and the detailed use made of procedures are very different. For example, the House of Lords, like the House of Commons, has a speaker, the Lord Chancellor, but his rôle contrasts sharply with that of the Commons' Speaker. In both Houses a prominent part of each day's proceedings is the asking of oral questions, but the procedures and practices of the two Houses have developed in quite different ways.

A second general theme to any discussion of procedure and organisation in the House of Lords must be the increase in the pressure of business which has taken place over recent decades, yet alongside this there is the relative lack of procedural restriction. Despite higher attendances and increased professionalism among peers, very few formal restrictions on their freedom have been introduced. Some consequences of increased activity in terms of changed behaviour and minor adaptation of procedure have been evident. But broadly speaking peers still remain as free as MPs were in the mid-nineteenth century. This matter will also be explored in this chapter. However, we begin with a brief look at the physical arrangements of the House of Lords.

The Lords' Chamber: Peers' Facilities and Allowances

Unlike the nearby Commons chamber, that of the Lords was not destroyed during the Second World War. The present chamber dates from 1847, and therefore retains the lavish decoration associated with the names of Barry and Pugin. With the Sovereign's throne as its centre-piece rather than the Speaker's chair, and with the rich deep red upholstery rather than the mellow green of the Commons, the Lords' Chamber is a good deal more spectacular than that of the Commons. In 1980 the ceiling was found to be in need of repair (part of it fell down one day while the House was sitting), and over £2 million was spent in restoration work. Although the chamber is much more ornate than the Commons, it is no less functional. In its centre is the Clerk's Table, furnished with two despatch boxes, from which Government and main Opposition party front-bench spokesmen speak. In the corners television cameras may now regularly be observed, recording proceedings for edited daily and weekly transmission, again a contrast with the Commons where, in 1987, TV still had not been admitted.

The seating within the chamber is arranged in three blocks on each side of the Table, unlike the Commons' two blocks (see Figure 4.1). The front benches of Government and main Opposition party are in the middle block. The side of the House to the right of the Throne is known as the Spiritual side, that on the left, the Temporal side. Nowadays the bishops occupy the front two benches in the first block on the Spiritual side, and the Government of the day and its supporters the remaining benches on that side of the House. Nearest the Throne on the Temporal side are the benches of the Alliance parties. Facing the Throne and below the Table are the cross-benches, occupied by peers who adhere to no party: in recent years as their numbers have increased, cross-bench peers have spilled over into some of the benches facing the centre of the House below the Table.

The benches on the floor of the House provide seats for some 250 peers, a number which is small in relation to the total membership of the House of Lords, but until recent years adequate for the active membership. However, with average daily attendance of over 300 by the mid-1980s, for some proceedings there was often the same shortage of seating as for members of the Commons. Peers listening to debates may sit on the steps of the Throne, or stand nearby, but these areas are technically outside the House, and may also be occupied by various categories of non-members, such as the eldest sons of peers, privy councillors (senior ministers from the Commons may also sit on the steps of the Throne), peers of Ireland and retired bishops who had had seats in the Lords. On the floor of the House there are no prescribed places for individual peers, though those who attend regularly usually sit in the same spot. In front of the Throne is the Woolsack upon which the Lord Chancellor sits as Speaker of the House. This is also technically outside the House, which means that the Lord Chancellor steps two paces into the House when he wishes to make a speech himself.

Immediately behind the debating chamber is the Princes Chamber, a relatively small area used as a sort of gossip room by peers. Leading off this is the Royal Gallery, a large and splendid room, sometimes used for a visiting head of state to address parliamentarians, sometimes as the debating chamber when, for emergency reasons, the main chamber has

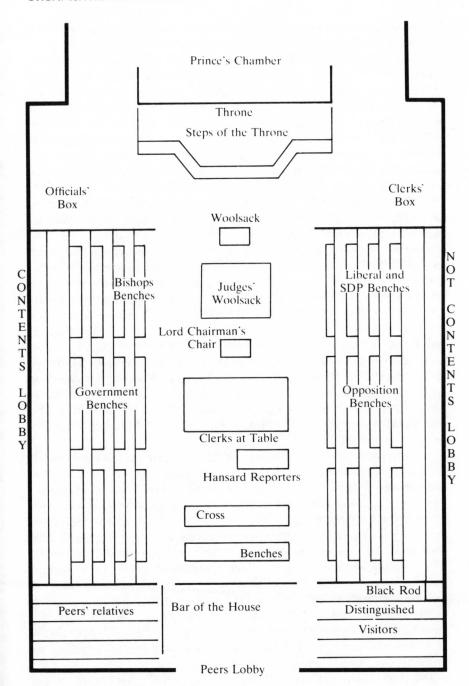

Figure 4.1 The House of Lords' Chamber

had to be vacated. It is now modestly furnished, so as to enable peers to take guests there for conversation. Through the Royal Gallery the Queen processes when she opens Parliament, on her way from the Royal Robing Room to the Throne. Its walls are covered with 'a vast picture of the battle of Waterloo on the one side and the battle of Trafalgar on the other' (the description is Crossman's, and for his somewhat irreverent description of the State Opening of Parliament in 1968, see his Diary, Vol. II, pp. 543–4).

The accommodation available to peers away from the chamber itself is far from generous. There is no equivalent to the Common's smoking room, and though being without constituents, peers' needs for offices or for rooms in which to hold small *ad hoc* meetings are less than MPs', nevertheless, they find the paucity of such facilities something of a handicap. The Opposition Party's major spokesmen, for example, must all share a room, as must all six chairmen of the European Communities sub-committees. Certain parts of the Palace of Westminster remain within the control of the Lord Great Chamberlain (acting on the Sovereign's behalf), but responsibility for most of the Palace passed in 1965 to the respective officers of the two Houses, Black Rod in the Lords and the Serjeant-at-Arms in the Commons. The House of Lords Offices Committee looks after the accommodation and services used by the Lords. In 1987 this operated mainly through seven sub-committees, the titles of which adequately indicate their activities: Administration; Computers; Finance; Library; Refreshment Department; Staff of the House; and Works of Art. Work of considerable practical importance to the running of the House of Lords was carried on through these sub-committees, which tended to be dominated by about a dozen senior peers, mostly office holders within the party groups in the Lords.

In 1987 peers remained without salaries for their parliamentary work (unless of course they were ministers or held one of the very few remunerated offices in the House of Lords). The expense allowance introduced in 1957 had enabled peers to claim out-of-pocket expenses within specified daily maxima ever since, and certainly by the mid-1980s the allowances payable had become relatively generous compared with what they had been in the 1960s and 1970s (see Appendix A for details). But the whole allowance system, while adequate for peers whose work in the Lords is very much a part-time affair, is manifestly inadequate to provide a reasonable recompense for the more or less full-time working peers — on Opposition Party front-benches or on the back-benches anywhere in the House. (It is, of course, also open to abuse if a peer simply looks in for a short time on most sitting days without actually contributing to the work of the House in any way.)

The Top Salaries Review Board was obviously well aware of the anomalies when it made its 1987 Report (Cm. 131), but, nevertheless, felt unable to endorse a recommendation made by its management consultants, namely that parties within the House of Lords should be allowed to nominate a limited number of active back-benchers for a higher level of allowance. The opposition parties in Parliament have since 1975 received a financial grant to defray expenses; this is — perhaps aptly — known as 'short' money (after Mr Edward Short, later Lord Glenamara) who introduced this provision when Leader of the Commons. The parliamentary parties are themselves responsible for the distribution of this money, very little of which has ever been channelled towards peers. The paucity of services available to opposition front-benchers had, by 1987, resulted in the Leader of the House of Lords entering into discussions with the other parties about the possible introduction of a new allowance or system of support for opposition parties in the Lords.

Arrangements Regarding Peers' Attendance

Certain formalities must be attended to before a new peer becomes a member of the House of Lords. In the case of a peer by succession the claim to a writ must be established, and this can be a lengthy process. Lord Avebury, who succeeded his cousin in 1971, was surprised by the care with which his claim to a peerage was examined. The *Daily Telegraph* of 5 August 1971 quoted him as saying that the process of establishing his claim to the peerage was 'complicated, lengthy and expensive' and that the need to produce 'a mass of supporting evidence including birth, death and marriage certificates of various members of the family' had delayed him taking his seat. For straight succession to an elder son, the process is speedy. In cases where claims are uncertain for some reason, the Committee for Privileges may investigate; this sometimes involves detailed and complex argument being deployed by petitioners through counsel. When such cases are being heard, at least three Lords of Appeal must be present, and the fact that several days may be taken up delving into arcane matters (such as the precise nature of Scottish peerage law before the Act of Union) inevitably at considerable public expense, has drawn criticism. But, hitherto, the House of Lords has not been disposed to recommend any fundamental change: in truth the time spent on such cases per decade is not large (see HL Debs, 27 June 1977, cols. 897–918).

Peers by succession have no ceremony of introduction. When they take their seats for the first time they simply take the oath of allegiance, or they affirm, and are recorded in Hansard, as having 'sat first in parliament'. Newly created peers must be ceremonially introduced before taking their seats in the House of Lords. The custom is that two peers of the same rank act as sponsors: all appear in their full robes, and the ceremony takes about ten minutes. Usually not more than two introductions take place on any one day, which means that it would take a very long time to introduce the 1,000 peers Mr Benn suggested a Labour Government may create in order to abolish the House (though Mr Benn has argued that mass creations could be effected by an appropriate Commons' motion). In 1975 a motion calling for a Select Committee to examine the ceremony was moved by a peer who argued it was absurd, time consuming and open to ridicule, but the Lords decisively rejected his motion by 106 votes to 31.

Peers who have taken their seats may subsequently apply for leave of absence. The reasoning behind the introduction of this facility has been explained in Chapter 1. Under the relevant standing order peers may apply for leave for a parliament but they are warned not to do so if there is any likelihood that they may wish to attend, however infrequently. A peer who fails to attend in one session receives a letter pointing this out and inviting him to apply for leave of absence. If he fails to respond to this letter, he is now automatically granted leave. In all cases leave may be cancelled at 28 days' notice. Very occasionally a peer on leave has attended, even tried to vote, in which case the party whips will seek to dissuade him, though it is not clear — given the wording of the relevant standing order — that they have any power to prevent him.

The leave of absence arrangements do allow a peer formally to sign off, as it were, from the House of Lords for a period. The party whips presumably fall silent to a peer on leave. But the arrangements do seem somewhat pointless. They certainly do nothing to discourage infrequent attendances by so-called backwoodsmen. In recent sessions up to 100 peers have not attended at all, but also failed to take leave of absence. It would be sensible — and save both time and money — to scrap the leave of absence arrangements altogether.

Peers, like MPs, enjoy certain privileges, notably freedom of speech within the House of Lords, and freedom to attend, involving some protection from arrest or detention. This latter point had to be considered by the Committee of Privileges in 1983 when a peer detained under Mental Health legislation asserted parliamentary privilege to secure his release. In a special report the Committee for Privileges recommended that future legislation should make clear that peers could be detained notwithstanding their parliamentary privilege (HL 254, 1983–4).

The Rules and Practice of Debate

Peers do not address the Lord Chancellor or other peer presiding when they speak (as MPs do the Speaker), but make their speech to the rest of the Lords in general. Except in committee, no peer may speak more than once in the same debate, except the mover of a motion who has the right of reply. Brief interventions to ask questions, or to clarify earlier points, are usually permitted. As in the Commons, peers refer to each other in the third person during debate, for example, the noble viscount, Lord so-and-so. Not all military members are 'gallant' as in the Commons, but only Admirals of the Fleet, Field-Marshals or Marshals of the Royal Air Force; similarly not all barristers are 'learned', but only the holders, or former holders, of high judicial office. Members of the same party refer to one another as 'my noble friend . . .', relatives as 'my noble kinsman. . . .'

Elaborate courtesy remains the norm in Lords' debates. The lack of any disciplinary powers vested in a presiding officer is illustrated by the adoption in 1626 of SO30, 'all personal, sharp or taxing speeches be forborn' and SO31 of 1641 which enjoins any peer who feels he has been affronted to appeal to his fellow peers generally for reparation. Personal attacks of any kind on fellow peers are rare: a peer who is rude to another peer may find his rudeness simply ignored (as Lord George Brown did on 10 November 1983 when he attacked Baroness Birk). Lord Hailsham for many years displayed a habit of providing his own running commentary on proceedings from the Woolsack, and occasionally his *sotto voce* remarks were not *sotto voce* enough. However when protests about his behaviour were made on the floor of the House, he was quick to apologise (see, e.g. HL Debs, 25 November 1970, col. 129–30; also *The Times, 26 November 1970*).

Peers tend not to interrupt each other and to listen to speeches in near silence. Former MPs may find this a greater ordeal than the noisy hostility they learned to cope with in the Commons, as apparently did the first Earl of Avon (R. Rhodes-James, 1987, p. 610). Peers making maiden speeches are expected to avoid controversy. This supposedly allows the next speaker always to congratulate them, and indeed most maiden speeches draw congratulations from almost every following speaker throughout a debate, frequently laced with personal reminiscences about previous dealings with the peer or, in the case of a hereditary peer, his father or even grandfather! The House of Lords is a great place for nostalgia, with peers enjoyably recounting each other's exploits when given the opportunity.

The House of Commons is always called 'another place'. Peers may quote ministers, but may only paraphrase speeches made in the same session by other MPs to which they may wish to refer. Peers are not meant to read their speeches, such a practice being described in the *Companion to the Standing Orders* as 'alien to the custom of the House and an obstacle to good debate'. However 'extended notes' are allowed, and as any visitor to the public gallery can see such 'extended notes' often amount to a full text, which peers not infrequently then hand in to the editor of *Hansard,* presumably in corroboration of what the shorthand writers recorded. As in the Commons peers may make minor corrections themselves to the *Hansard* proofs of their speeches, and then to the daily parts before the bound volumes are printed, but not to such an extent as to alter the sense of what they said.

Peers wishing to speak in a debate do not have 'to catch the Speaker's eye' as MPs must in the Commons. Instead they may hand in their names before the debate and, under the general guidance of the Leader of the House, his office prepares a list of peers in the order in which they will speak after consultation with the party whips and the mover of the motion concerned. This list of speakers is then supplied like a programme along with the day's order paper to all who attend the debate. This practice has certain advantages; it promotes decorum in debate, and it enables the overall length of a debate to be calculated reasonably accurately. It also ensures that no peer need leave the debate having had no opportunity to deliver his carefully prepared remarks. But it does tend to produce a series of disjointed, if eloquent, speeches, unrelated to each other, even if well-informed. The order is not rigid, and may be varied by mutual agreement and peers sometimes remove their names, especially if there is a very long list. A peer who has not put his name down can usually speak immediately prior to the closing front-bench speeches, though in some debates this would not be possible.

Peers have no official register of interests as MPs have had since 1975. By custom, however, peers begin speeches by declaring any interest they may have in the matter under discussion. This is clearly desirable, to safeguard the integrity of peers' debates, but it has an additional purpose in that it enables a peer to explain his credentials for taking part. Where a peer is a member of a public board he is not debarred from speaking in debates which concern that board, but the Addison rules (so called after the Leader of the House in 1951), urge restraint upon him, emphasising that it is ministers and not board members who are responsible to parliament for the board's activities. The Chairman of the Central Electricity Generating Board, Lord Marshall of Goring, sat through a four-hour debate on the Layfield Report on 2nd March 1987 without speaking. This was a particularly sensitive subject at that time, with the Government about to announce its decision on the building of a nuclear power station at Sizewell. Peers who hold offices on public boards do sometimes take part in debates dealing with the work of that body, explaining why they have felt it right to do so (e.g. HL Deb, 26 November 1970, col 1294). The interpretation of the Addison rules must ultimately be a matter for an individual's judgement.

Servants of the Crown, both civil servants and military officers, who are members of the House of Lords are required to observe restrictions on their participation in the proceedings of the Lords, in the same way as their participation in any political activity is likely to be restricted. The extent of this limitation therefore depends on their seniority and the precise duties they undertake. When a peer who was also a former Cabinet Minister was appointed a European Community Commissioner, he — Lord Cockfield — was obliged by EC rules to take leave of absence from the Lords, but no other public office requires such detachment from the House.

Peers who speak in debates are expected to attend the greater part of that debate, at least so the Companion to the Standing Orders declares. Frequently this proves difficult: no fewer than four of the first seven peers to speak in a debate on the NHS on 1 April 1987 expressed regret that they had to leave the House during the debate. While general rules relating to the length of speeches have been eschewed, clocks were introduced in 1972 to provide clear indication of the length of each speech as it progresses. In the same year an experiment with limited time debates was introduced. Subsequently, these have become a permanent feature of Lords' procedures, and effectively such debates do involve strict and sometimes very short time limits for speeches (see below, pp. 102, 105).

For divisions peers walk through two lobbies, 'content' and 'not content', and are counted by two tellers, whose votes are also included (unlike the tellers' votes in the Commons). If less than thirty peers vote during proceedings on legislation, the question is not decided, which in modern conditions very seldom happens except on private members' bills. The peer on the Woolsack or (in Committee) at the Table, may vote in a division, which means there is no scope for a casting vote. If there is an equality of votes on legislation, the rule is that the bill proceeds in the form in which it was before the House, while motions are resolved in the negative unless a majority of peers vote in their favour. The quorum for ordinary business is three.

Normal sitting days are traditionally Tuesdays, Wednesdays and Thursdays, though in recent years Monday has become a normal sitting day as well (from approximately one in two Mondays in the late 1950s to nine out of ten Mondays in the mid-1980s). Friday sittings were once very rare, but have become unremarkable. The customary sitting time is 2.30 p.m. (and 3.00 p.m. on Thursdays), but if a Friday sitting takes place it commences at 11.00 a.m. as do the final sittings before a recess. Occasionally these times are varied, for example, when an unusually long debate is anticipated: on two of the three days in July 1971 when the House of Lords held its longest ever debate — 110 peers spoke on entry into the Common Market — the Lords met at 2.00 p.m. The House merely adjourns when everyone who wishes to speak in a debate has finished. There has, however, been a noticeable tendency to sit later in recent years, with the House sitting after 10.00 p.m. on over half the sitting days in 1985–6, an hour regarded as quite exceptional in the 1950s. All-night sittings remain unusual, but over particularly hard-fought bills, they do sometimes occur. The longest ever sitting in the Lords was on June 3rd 1986, and lasted 19 hours and 38 minutes, the main business being the Gas Bill, then in its committee stage.

The Select Committee on Procedure, consisting of about two dozen quite senior peers, keeps under constant review the procedures of the House of Lords. It issues regular reports, usually quite brief, sometimes suggesting slight modifications in procedure, but as often re-emphasising existing rules and conventions of the Lords. Under the authority of this Committee the *Companion to the Standing Orders* is published, which gives peers detailed guidance about the interpretation of standing orders, as well as other information concerning the practices of the House.

Broadcasting in the House

It is paradoxical that the unelected House should have become the first part of Parliament to be televised regularly. The concern of peers not to offend the sensitivities of MPs on this matter was eventually overcome by the eager media and by peers' growing self-confidence. In 1966 the House of Lords debated and approved a motion, moved by Lord Egremont, in which a welcome was extended to television as an additional means of demonstrating the usefulness of the House of Lords. In the various subsequent debates on this subject the confidence of most peers that television would enhance the public reputation of their House has been noticeable. (See Appendix C for a list of debates and select committee reports.)

As a result of Lord Egremont's motion an experiment with closed circuit television took place over a three-day period in February 1968. Five large cameras, two actually within the chamber itself, were necessary, a degree of intrusiveness which caused some misgivings. None the less in 1969 the Lords endorsed a report from the select committee it had set up on the subject which called for a proper public experiment to take place. But this did not happen. Broadcasters were clearly not very interested in televising the House of Lords without the House of Commons, and few peers thought this appropriate either.

In 1978 both Houses agreed to the commencement of regular sound broadcasting. This probably enhanced the relative public reputation of the House of Lords compared with the Commons; extracts from Lords' debates generally sound better on the radio because the House is quieter and debate more courteous and generally decorous. Sound broadcasting may have contributed a little to the general growth in the self-confidence of the Lords, which certainly had several causes in the early 1980s. After the 1983 election, Lord Soames, formerly Leader of the House, moved a motion calling for a public experiment in televising the House of Lords.

The Government made clear that public funds would not be available, but the attitude of the new Leader of the House, Viscount Whitelaw, was definitely favourable, and the Lords voted heavily for an experiment.

In January 1985 regular television broadcasts commenced. The first debate to be carried live was an Opposition motion on economic and social policies. A very large number of peers wished to speak, among them the Lords' most distinguished new recruit, the 90-year-old Earl of Stockton, formerly Harold Macmillan. On this and several subsequent occasions over four million people watched at least part of the debate (compared with a daily attendance in the public gallery of between 200 and 900). Varied use was made by BBC and ITV of edited extracts from debates: BBC II used material frequently on Newsnight; and Channel 4 produced summaries on the Local Government Bill which were watched on average by almost 300,000 people, despite the fact that they were not broadcast till midnight. A quarter of a million viewers watched a late-night Channel 4 documentary programme on the Lords' Select Committee on Overseas Trade.

In July 1985 the Lords agreed on division to extend the experiment. Expectations were high that the Commons would agree to be televised too, but in November MPs voted narrowly (275 to 263) against this. Almost immediately the broadcasting authorities, manifestly displeased with the Commons' decision, cut back on the amount of television coverage of the Lords. But by this time the experiment had run for almost a year, and viewing figures remained very respectable. In April the Lords' select committee on televising the House made a full report on the experiment. This was cautious but nevertheless firm in its recommendations that the experiment be made permanent, and in May 1986 the Lords endorsed this view. Over the following year regular edited programmes were televised showing the Lords at work. Concern about the effect of television on the behaviour of peers soon subsided; the television cameras used were relatively unobtrusive and the lighting necessary was not troublesome. Difficulties over achieving party balance in edited summaries were encountered, but the nature of party strength in the Lords, with cross-benchers and bishops to consider, as well as the four political parties, meant no precise balance could ever be defined, let alone achieved. This in a sense obviated the problem: it was more a balance in arguments made on a particular subject for which broadcasters had to strive rather than an exact balance in the political allegiance of individuals televised (see Franklin, 1986).

Officers and Officials of the House

Several peers have roles of particular significance within the House of

Lords, as do some non-members who serve the House in various ways. Of first importance is the Lord Chancellor who is ex officio Speaker of the House. But his rôle is quite different to that of the Commons' Speaker. With regard to the latter a large body of conventions has grown up designed to ensure that he will be absolutely and irrevocably separated from party politics, but there is no suggestion of the requirement of political impartiality with the Lord Chancellor. As a senior member of the Government he speaks and votes in the House, defending the Government's policies and replying to Opposition attacks. When the House goes into Committee, he removes his wig and sits on the Government front-bench. Indeed his duties as Speaker are confined to putting the question on motions submitted to the Lords. As far as maintaining order is concerned the 'Speaker has no more authority than any other lord, except in so far as his own personal weight and the dignity of his office may give effect to his opinions and secure the concurrence of the House' (*Erskine May*, 1983, p. 484). In fact it is the Leader of the House who customarily offers guidance when points of order or procedural difficulties arise.

All the most sacrosanct rules regarding the separation of powers are broken by the Lord Chancellor's office. In addition to being an active member of the legislature — and recent Lord Chancellors have been assiduous in attendance at the House of Lords — he is an important member of the Cabinet, with a considerable part in planning legislation. But the most significant anomaly arises from his headship of the third arm of state power, the judiciary. Most recent Lord Chancellors have not sat judicially other than on rare occasions, but Lord Hailsham in 1970 determined to depart from this practice, and in order to do so arranged to spend less time than his predecessors on the Woolsack and with Prime Minister Heath's agreement, largely avoided service on Cabinet committees (Hailsham, 1976, ch. 36). Apart from sitting judicially, the Lord Chancellor has many important responsibilities in relation to the courts and the administration of the judicial system.

In most legislative assemblies, the presiding officer is chosen by the members themselves, almost invariably from among the more long-serving of their own number. But most recent Lord Chancellors have not had significant experience of the House of Lords prior to their appointment: of the last fourteen no fewer than nine received their peerages upon taking office. Nor do peers have any say in the appointment. If there is any body of people whom the Prime Minister must consider in making his choice, it is the lawyers, because the Lord Chancellor must be a man of the highest eminence in the legal profession. Usually the Lord Chancellor is a barrister who has spent some years in the House of Commons, and been prominent enough in his party to hold ministerial office, probably as a law officer. Of the last fourteen Lord Chancellors, eight had previously been law officers in the Commons, while three more had, as peers, held other government offices, including Lord Mackay of Clashfern who, as Lord Advocate, had dealt with Scottish law from 1979 until his appointment as Lord Chancellor in October 1987. Two of the remaining three were law lords prior to their appointment, while the third was Lord Gardiner who had been a prominent member of the bar, prior to his appointment in 1964. Lord Hailsham, Lord Chancellor from 1970–4 and again from 1979–87, has occupied the Woolsack for longer than any other peer this century. Lord Mackay is the first Lord Chancellor not formally qualified in English law.

When disputes or difficulties arise over the interpretation of the rules and procedures of the House of Lords, it is to the Leader of the House that peers look for guidance. For example, during oral question time it is the Leader who tries to move proceedings on if they become protracted, and he will usually do so by suggesting when the Lords should move to the next business. If there is a dispute about the arrangement of business, again the Lords will expect to hear from the Leader. But the advice he offers is not binding. If necessary disputes can be resolved by votes on the floor of the House, and the Leader, in offering his advice, has to bear in mind that in a formal sense he has no more authority than any other peer.

The Leader is the senior member of the Government front-bench, and has responsibility for seeing that the Government gets its business through the House of Lords. The Leader has usually been appointed from among peers who know the Lords well from years of personal experience, but two recent leaders were senior Commons politicians created peers simultaneously with their appointment to this office, namely Lord Peart in 1976 and Viscount Whitelaw in 1983. However, both of these men had been leaders of the Commons. Another minister in the Lords is usually appointed as Deputy Leader and in the Leader's absence he assumes the role of guiding the Lords on procedural matters.

Opinion among peers has consistently been against appointing a Commons style Speaker, who would, for example, rule on points of order (HL 227, 1970–1, para. 6; HL 9, 1987–8, paras 12–16). If a peer insists on speaking when it appears his fellow peers generally think he should give way to another peer, cries of 'order, order' reverberate through the chamber. The Leader or acting Leader may then intervene, and if his advice is still not accepted, it is possible for the motion 'That the noble Lord be no longer heard' to be put. This is a very rare occurrence, having taken place only seven times in the last century (most recently on 29 January 1985, when a prolix Labour peer was silenced at question time).

A third key office held by a member of the House of Lords is that of Lord Chairman of Committees. This is a salaried appointment, made by the House itself, the holder of which withdraws entirely from party politics. The Lord Chairman is ex officio Chairman of all committees of the House of Lords, unless the House directs otherwise. When the House of Lords goes into committee on legislation, it is the Lord Chairman who takes the Chair (or one of his deputies).

In 1974 a new post of Principal Deputy Chairman of Committees was created. This was partly in recognition of the increased workload of the Chairman of Committees, but mainly to enable a salaried Chairman to be available for the European Communities Committee, the Principal Deputy Chairman becoming Chairman of that committee, the work of which particularly involved the scrutiny of draft legislation from the EC Commission. Counsel are appointed to assist both the Lord Chairman and the Principal Deputy Chairman.

The appointments to the office of Chairman of Committees and Principal Deputy Chairman are always for the current session only, but in practice, like the Speaker of the Commons, the holders remain in office until they choose to resign. The work of the Chairman of Committees, especially that on private bills, is very complex (see below, Chapter 8). There are obvious advantages in avoiding frequent change in this post; the average tenure of the office of Chairman of Committees since 1800 has been 16 years.

When the office becomes vacant informal consultations take place with a view to fixing on a suitable candidate. The peer selected is then appointed by the Lords on a motion moved by the Leader of the House. During debate on this it may be made clear why the peer appointed has been chosen, in preference to another peer who has also been considered. The qualifications most desired appear to be a long experience of the House of Lords combined with comparative youth and the likelihood of occupying the office for a number of years. Not surprisingly, in view of this combination of qualities, appointees have always been peers by succession. Lord Aberdare was appointed Chairman of Committees in 1976, and remained in office in 1987: he had previously been a deputy leader of the Conservative peers. Baroness Serota was appointed Principal Deputy Chairman in 1986, after Baroness Llewelyn-Davies of Hastoe had held the post for four years.

There are in addition several deputy Chairmen of Committees, who really correspond to the members of the Chairman's panel in the House of Commons. They are not expected to renounce partisan activity and these offices have frequently been held by prominent back-bench peers. As the pressure of business in the House of Lords has increased, so has the number of deputy chairmen: in 1966 there were eight; by 1987 there were twenty.

The actual arrangement of business is carried out by the party whips, who, when this aspect of their work is under consideration, are referred to as 'the usual channels'. The need to take elaborate care in making arrangements for the conduct of business is accentuated by the remarkable degree of freedom individual peers possess both to speak and to initiate debates. What the whips do is simply get together and hammer out an arrangement about the time-tabling of the business which is as near as possible to a mutual agreement. The danger is that the whips of the two major parties, in their desire to meet one another's demands, may be neglectful of the wishes of others. Occasionally there are protests on the floor of the House about the arrangements made, and in such cases hasty re-arrangements may sometimes take place. For example, in early July 1986 the Alliance parties were angered by the fact that business was altered at less than a week's notice without their spokesman for the item concerned being consulted. In exchanges on the floor of the House the SDP whip asked for an assurance that he would be consulted when business was altered in this way in the future, but the Leader of the House in reply could only promise consultation 'when possible' (HLD, 8 July 1986, col. 179).

Some peers have expressed unhappiness with the degree of control exercised by the 'usual channels'. Lord Alport suggested that a committee with back-bench representation as well as party whips, perhaps under the chairmanship of the Chairman of Committees, should be set up for this task. But no widespread support for such a change has been evident. In fact the party whips appear to constitute a body well-suited to the difficult and delicate task of arranging business. They certainly cannot afford to ignore the wishes of backbenchers. They want to keep party morale high and to secure good turn-outs in divisions, so they are predisposed to meet the wishes of backbenchers whenever they can.

Certain officials have an important role as the professional servants of the House. The permanent staff is under the Clerk of the Parliaments, who is the Lords' equivalent to the Clerk of the Commons. All told the number of clerks working in the Lords is approximately one third of the number who work in the Commons. Like their Commons counterparts they service select committees, take responsibility for the formal records of parliamentary proceedings published in the Journals of the House, prepare the order papers for each day's business and generally advise peers on matters of procedure.

Of particular importance to the smooth running of the House of Lords is the clerk seconded to be private secretary to the Leader of the House and to the Chief Whip. He is the official who services the 'usual channels'. Party whips are constantly in touch with him about the timing of business, and individual peers anxious for advice about when or how to raise a matter in the Lords may go to him. In his office details about the organisation of business both large and small are settled. Here in the mid 1980s a good-sized board was kept with the future time-table of business throughout a session provisionally marked out (together with information about hazards which may reduce attendance, such as Ascot Gold Cup Day!). There is constant liaison between this official and civil servants in departments with legislation before the House of Lords. This is chiefly a question of pinpointing matters likely to cause delay to bills, and seeking to make arrangements which balance the needs of the Lords with those of departments. This is a job which demands a thorough knowledge of the procedures of the Upper House, together with real sensitivity to changes in the political mood of the Lords, as well as copious discretion and a capacity to command and retain the confidence of various groups of peers.

The Organisation of Business

Despite the increased activity of the House of Lords, compared with the Commons (and most other legislative assemblies) it remains relatively free of procedural rules. There is provision for a closure, but the *Companion to the Standing Orders* emphasises that this is a most exceptional procedure; it was in fact last used in 1927! There is no provision for allocation of time orders, nor is there any formal restriction on the right of any peer to initiate a debate on any subject on any sitting day. Yet it must be emphasised that alongside this formal freedom, powerful constraints can be applied within the House of Lords, through the demands made by governments (which need to get their business passed), buttressed by the strong tradition of collective self-discipline which still pervades. *Erskine May* takes twenty-one pages to deal with the order of business and the conduct of debate in the Lords, and 144 pages to do the same task for the Commons, a difference indicative of the contrast between the two Houses. In this section we consider first the daily order of business and then discuss some of the procedures a little more fully, before returning to the question of the pressures imposed on the House of Lords by increased business.

Usually oral questions immediately follow prayers, though certain items of business may intervene such as messages from the Crown, personal statements by peers (for example correcting erroneous remarks or making apologies) or obituary tributes (confined in practice to the exceptionally distinguished, the exceptionally old or those who have died suddenly while office holders). There is no fixed length for question time as in the Commons; instead the number of oral questions is limited. Since 1959 the limit has been four per day, and while SO32 provides that 'no debate may take place on such questions and supplementary questions must be confined to the subject of the original question', exchanges on questions are frequently quite lengthy — at least compared with the Commons —

and it usually takes at least 25 minutes to get through four questions. Periodically the Select Committee on Procedure has expressed concern at 'the growing disorderliness of question time' (to quote a 1971 report, HL 37, 1971–2), but until 1987 no new or more rigid rules had been introduced to limit the practices the committee deprecated, which included the reading of supplementary questions, and the giving of lengthy replies by ministers (which provoke lengthy rejoinders and hence precipitate a kind of mini-debate). Oral questions are starred as in the Commons, and in theory are asked for information only. Oral questions may be set down up to one month in advance for any sitting day. On most days in recent sessions the maximum of four per day have been asked, and not infrequently the order paper shows all available spaces for such questions already taken. Suggestions for a further increase in the number, or the introduction of a regular slot for short-notice 'topical' questions have not been taken up. As in the Commons attendance is usually high for questions, and the proceedings relatively more lively than those which follow.

At a typical sitting the Lords will move rapidly from oral questions to the main business of the day. But it is possible for several types of business to intervene. Immediately after starred questions, private notice questions are taken. These deal with matters of urgency, and must be submitted in writing to the Leader of the House by twelve noon of the day concerned. The Leader decides whether the matter is one of genuine urgency, but his judgement may be challenged on the floor of the House. A similar procedure is available to MPs, and the practice in the mid-1980s was to repeat answers given to such questions in the Commons as ministerial statements in the Lords (rather than create artificial private-notice questions in the Lords whenever such a question was accepted in the Commons, as has been the practice prior to 1983). As a result only one or two such questions have been asked in the Lords in each recent session.

Ministerial statements are made immediately after questions in the Commons, and repeated in the Lords, but because it is considered important to synchronise the time at which statements are made in the two Houses, in the Lords they usually interrupt the main business of the day, maybe coming after the first or second speeches in a debate, or, as it is euphemistically described by the Government Whip, 'at a convenient moment after 3.30 p.m.'. Statements are frequent, with two sometimes being made on the same day. Front-bench responses follow a statement, and back-bench questions may be asked for information, but SO33 stipulates that statements 'should not be made the occasion for immediate debate, unless the House so order'. None the less, exchanges can be quite lengthy, as indeed can statements themselves, and the interruption they cause can be disruptive to the flow of debate. In the early 1970s the practice developed of not repeating all statements; instead, if agreement was reached through the 'usual channels' a statement was simply printed in *Hansard*. For a while about one-third of statements were dealt with in this way, but in recent sessions the number has declined (in 1985–6 only 7 out of 112 were not given orally). Opposition spokesmen generally wish to have statements repeated in the Lords. If the senior minister concerned is a member of the Lords, the statement is made by him immediately after questions, and repeated later in the Commons. If one House is not sitting statements may be made in the other alone, and sometimes this means important statements are only made in the Lords because the Commons is in recess. Where a statement is repeated in the Lords, the television cameras are not allowed to show Lords' proceedings, so as not to hurt the sensitivities of the still untelevised Commons.

Messages from the Commons may then be read out by the Clerk of the Parliaments from his position at the Table in the Centre of the House, and business of the House motions may be taken, for example, altering business already set down on the order paper, or suspending SO44, which disallows more than one stage of a bill to be taken on any one day. The Chairman of Committees may also bring forward business, for example, concerning private bills; this is usually dealt with quickly, sometimes not so, as when, for example, a private bill receives a full debate at second reading. Motions to appoint select committees or to approve the report of a select committee may be taken. Again these are usually quite brief, occasionally not so.

Essentially there are two types of business which follow: proceedings on bills and general debates. On Wednesdays proceedings on motions have precedence, but on all other days Standing Orders give precedence to legislation. This does not mean that days other than Wednesdays are 'Government days'; private members' bills as well as Government bills may be taken, and the precedence given to legislation does not inevitably squeeze out all other debate. Wednesdays are, however, generally reserved for debates on motions.

Finally on the order paper are unstarred questions. These are questions on which speeches may be made; they may be put down on any sitting day, and they always come last in the day's business. Unlike Commons adjournment debates, no time limit exists for debate on unstarred questions, which may range from half an hour or less to three hours or even more. Questions for written answers receive replies printed in *Hansard* at the end of the record of each day's proceedings.

How the House Spends its Time

Table 4.1 indicates, for the 1985–6 session, how the total time of the House of Lords was allocated as between various categories of business. Though it is not possible from these figures to state precisely what proportion of time was spent on business initiated by the Government, or by frontbenchers generally as opposed to backbenchers, the table does show that over half the time was spent on Government bills, a proportion somewhat higher than in other recent sessions (instead of almost 54 per cent, it was around 45 per cent in the previous two sessions), while the time spent on private members' bills was slightly lower. Most motions are moved by back-bench peers, and almost all questions come from backbenchers. Thus well over a quarter of the time of the House was spent on motions, questions or bills initiated by back-bench or cross-bench peers, and in other recent sessions this proportion has probably been nearer to a third.

Table 4.1 Allocation of Time to Various Categories of Business (1985–6)

Category of business		Percentage of total time
Prayers and introduction		1.3
Legislation		
Public bills		57.9
Government bills	53.9	
Private members' bills	4.0	
Lords' bills	18.6	
Commons' bills	39.3	
Private bills		0.5
Statutory instruments and measures		3.7
Motions and Questions		
Starred questions		5.7
Motions for general debates		15.9
Debates on Select Committee reports		2.9
Unstarred questions		5.1
Statements		3.9
Other (including formal business and adjournments during pleasure)		3.1

Source: Adapted from figures provided by House of Lords Information Office.

Public bills may be introduced into either House, by Government ministers or by private members. Private members' bills which are successful in the Commons are brought to the Lords, but peers may also introduce their own private members' bills. On the more important public bills about half the time is spent in committee, the remainder on the other stages (see Chapter 5).

Private bills (not to be confused with private members' bills) are largely dealt with off the floor of the House in select committees, though all must be accorded a second and third reading by the Lords; and sometimes extended debate takes place. Most debates on Statutory Instruments are brief, occasionally not so. Instruments must be approved by the Lords. Sometimes the House debates a motion of regret at the content of an instrument, while at the same time formally approving the instrument (see Chapter 8). 'Measures' are the form in which Church of England business comes before the House of Lords: this relates to those few areas where Church matters are still subject to parliamentary control. They are introduced by bishops, but only one-tenth of one per cent of the time of the House was taken up with Measures in 1985–6, a proportion typical for recent years.

Motions in the Lords may be of four kinds. First is a motion for address, the form used for debate on the Queen's Speech, and for certain items of formal business. The Queen's Speech debate typically extends over three days, usually with a concentration on foreign affairs and defence one day, home affairs and social policy another, and the economy and industry on the third. Second are motions to 'take note', the formula usually used by government when it wishes the Lords to debate a situation or a document without coming to a positive decision. Select Committee reports, almost invariably, are debated on 'take note' motions. Third are motions calling for a definite decision of the Lords, which, if not withdrawn or agreed without a division, result in a vote taking place. Fourth, and most frequent, are motions for papers. These call attention to a particular subject, but are not usually worded in a contentious manner. The motion ends with the somewhat cryptic formula 'and to move for papers', the addition of this phrase ensuring that the mover of the motion has the right to reply to the debate, at which point the motion is withdrawn. Thus a motion for papers enables a debate to be held without the Lords formally expressing any opinion, or as the *Companion to Standing Orders* states, 'The opinion of the House is expressed in the speeches made by its members rather than on division' (page 78).

On most Wednesdays only one motion is debated as the day's main business. But in 1972 a procedure was introduced whereby one Wednesday a month, up until the Whitsun recess, was set aside for two limited time (2½ hours maximum) debates on motions chosen by ballot. Back-bench and cross-bench peers only are entitled to enter the ballot, which they do simply by placing their motion on the Order Paper. The ballot is conducted by the Clerk of the Parliaments, but not at the Table: instead it takes place in the office of the Chief Whip, in the presence of the 'usual channels', a minor example of the relatively relaxed procedures in the Lords. For limited-time debates peers indicate their wish to speak as they do for other business and at the commencement of the debate the Chief Whip announces how much time is available for each speaker. In 1984 the Lords agreed to extend the principle of limited-time debates to allow for some five-hour debates. It is argued that the advantages of time limits are: they encourage short, and hence perhaps more pithy, speeches; they make it more reasonable for peers to attend throughout a debate; and in the case of motions for resolution they ensure a definite time at which any division can be anticipated. However time limits tend to make peers very unwilling to give way to allow other peers to put questions or interject, and this, in turn, can inhibit peers from expressing controversial views. Those who value the cut and thrust of debate more highly than the eloquence and charm of set-piece speeches have been lukewarm about time limits.

Those Wednesdays not set aside for balloted debates are allocated to various party groups in the House of Lords. A formula has been established which gives eight days to Labour, five to government back-benchers, three to the Alliance parties and three to crossbenchers. In the 1970s when Labour was in office the formula used gave half the time to the Conservative Opposition, a quarter to government backbenchers and a quarter to crossbenchers and Liberals together. The changes since then reflect changes in the political complexion of the Lords, although the Alliance presses for a still larger share. A party may decide to use one of its Wednesdays for two 'short' debates rather than one longer debate.

Increased demands on the time of the Lords, both from the Government with more legislation to consider, and from a more active body of peers, have made it less easy for individual members to obtain opportunities to initiate debate and to secure the discussion of private members' bills. Whilst any peer can put down a motion or introduce a bill, it is only with the co-operation of the 'usual channels' (or possibly by the luck of the ballot for a motion) that this will be taken as early business on a particular day. If this is not forthcoming the peer concerned will find that his only opportunity to raise the subject will occur very late in the evening.

Motions and unstarred questions usually make their first appearance on the order paper under the heading 'No day named'. A peer may approach the secretary to the Leader of the House and Chief Whip directly to explore possible times for an unstarred question and he may seek the support of his own party whip. But there can be no guarantee that time at a reasonable hour will be made available. SO41 lays down that no motion or question may be put on the order paper for a date more than one month of sitting time ahead. Informally, however, debates on motions are frequently arranged at longer notice, especially when it is considered desirable to secure the participation of peers with very heavy commitments away from the House of Lords.

There is no weekly announcement of forthcoming business as in the Commons, but a provisional future business paper is prepared by noon on Thursday each week in the Chief Whip's office. This contains a detailed statement of business for the forthcoming week, as well as provisional information for later weeks. It has been drawn up by the 'usual channels' and is the basis both for discussion at the parties' Thursday afternoon meetings, and for the party whips issued by the parties to their members at the end of each week.

The House of Lords is often said to have more time than the House of Commons, and therefore to be well-placed to revise legislation hurriedly considered — maybe under a 'guillotine' — by the Lower House, as well as to debate issues which MPs overlook or ignore. But these are only partial truths. Commons financial privilege is one clear factor which limits the time spent in the Lords on some bills compared with the Commons. But almost all legislation is debated a great deal more expeditiously in the Upper House than in the Lower (see Tables 5.2 and 5.3). This is because peers conceive of their work as being the revision of bills, and therefore give most bills much less scrutiny than does the Commons. Furthermore, the House of Lords is not engaged in contesting the will of the Government as the Opposition in the Commons seeks to do. Much less time is spent in the Upper House on the repartee of party politics. The peers' whole style of speaking tends to be much more concise. In moving amendments to bills, peers more usually go straight to the point of the amendment wihtout accompanying political banter. They are less inclined to repeat points made by earlier speakers.

On second reading debates and debates on motions the same sort of points apply. In the Commons party whips know a debate must be kept going until 10.00 p.m., and not infrequently Opposition whips, since 1979, have had to cajole backbenchers into speaking, so as to fill up the time available. But this kind of thing simply isn't necessary in the Lords (even if occasionally party leaders are embarrassed at the small number of speeches from their members in a particular debate).

Of course all this is generalisation, the description of a tendency. Sometimes debate in the Lords is protracted, repetitive and generously laced with party rhetoric. On other occasions it is brief, not because peers are well-informed, but because on some subjects the spokesmen concerned appear so very ill-informed that they have little or nothing to say.

A Busier House

Indisputably though, the Lords' timetable has become much fuller in recent years. Sessions vary a good deal according to a government's legislation programme, but an unmistakable trend towards a busier House is clear both throughout this century, and in particular over the last thirty years. A more active membership is one cause for this increased activity.

Table 4.2 Increased Activity of the House of Lords, 1959–86

Session (at approximately 4-yearly intervals)	Total number of peers on roll	Total number who attended	Total number who spoke	Average daily attendance	Number of days House sat	Total number of hours House sat	Average length of sittings in House (hrs)	Number of sittings after 10pm
1959–60	907	542	283	136	113	450	4	1
1963–4	1,012	525	289	151	110	534	4¾	3
1967–8	1,061	679	424	225	139	803	5¾	31
1971–2	1,073	698	419	250	141	813	5¾	28
1975–6	1,139	752	486	275	155	969	6¼	39
1981–2	1,174	790	503	284	147	930	6⅓	41
1985–6	1,171	798	529	317	165	1,213	7⅓	93

Sources: Calculated from information supplied by House of Lords Information Office and from the sessional index to *Hansard*.

Another is the heavier legislative programme imposed on Parliament by Conservative, as well as Labour governments. Table 4.2 summarises some of the changes of the last 30 years consequent upon both the altered membership of the House of Lords and the increased burden of Government legislation.

In this table figures have been given for sessions of normal length at roughly four-yearly intervals. Of course no session is absolutely typical: certainly both 1975–6 and 1985–6 were unusually heavily congested. But a clear overall long-term trend is evident. More peers attend the House of Lords; more speak; the House sits on more days and until later in the evening than used to be the case. It is true that the House of Lords sits fewer hours than the Commons: in 1985–6 the Commons sat 1,552 hours, excluding time spent in standing committees. But the Lords still sits for longer than any other European legislative assembly. It is not the relatively short hours of the Lords, but the immensely long hours of the Commons which is unusual in an international perspective.

The most serious timetable problems faced by the House of Lords result from the uneven flow of legislative business, a matter discussed further in the next chapter. Here we may simply take note of the fact that even when the House of Lords has been manifestly, if not hopelessly overburdened with work, the 'usual channels' have never broken down, nor indeed has there been any serious threat of this happening. The House of Lords has retained its flexible procedures and in a formal sense individual peers have retained their unusual freedoms. This has been possible because, collectively, there has been the acceptance of a remarkable degree of collective self-discipline. A group of peers, appointed in December 1986 to examine the working of the Lords and suggest alterations, conducted a survey of opinion among all members of the House of Lords. Its report published in Summer 1987 strongly endorsed the existing system of self-regulation and made only minor recommendations for changes in procedure. The case for a Speaker with controlling powers received virtually no support whatsoever (HL 9, 1987–8). When this report was debated in the House, the pride peers take in their lack of procedural restriction was very evident, and peers who were former MPs seemed especially inclined to contrast favourably the procedures of the Upper House with those of the Commons (HL Debs, 4 November 1987, cols 988–1053).

5

THE LEGISLATIVE WORK OF THE HOUSE

The legislative work of the House of Lords is generally regarded as its most important task. Bryce emphasised this in 1918, as did the White Paper on Lords Reform in 1968. Surveys of peers' opinions suggest this is the view of active members of the Lords (Baldwin, 1985; Bromhead and Shell, 1967). Since almost all major legislation is introduced first into the Commons, it is the revision of bills brought from the Lower House which must be regarded as having first importance. But some bills are introduced into the Lords, and the work of the House on these is by no means insignificant. Private members' bills can of course be introduced in either House.

The Upper House is often spoken of as a revising chamber. But in an important sense both Houses are revising chambers because, in the modern legislative process, bills are shaped and drafted in government departments and the work of both Commons and Lords is chiefly one of revision. Nevertheless the Lords is clearly the junior chamber, and its rôle in relation to legislation is formally circumscribed, a point which is best discussed before the legislative procedures and the use made of them is examined.

Limitations on Power

The formal powers of the House of Lords are limited, first by the financial privilege of the House of Commons, and second by the Parliament Acts. These two limitations need to be considered separately, though the terms of the Parliament Acts differentiate, for special treatment, a category of bill known as 'Money Bills'.

Financial privilege arises from 'the ancient rights and privileges' of the Commons: these require that all proposals dealing with 'aids and supplies' must originate from the Commons, and that once approved by the Commons, they cannot be altered by the Lords. These principles were embodied in the seventeenth century resolutions passed by the Commons, (see Chapter 1, p. 7) and have never been disputed. In modern times 'aids and supplies' are brought together in Finance Bills which deal with taxation and Consolidated Fund Bills which authorise expenditure. Together these are known as Supply Bills.

Though the power of the House of Lords in relation to such bills is strictly limited, they must, nevertheless, be passed by the House. The current House of Lords never even debates Consolidated Fund Bills (though a peer attempted to speak on such a bill in 1981 (see HL Debs, 22 December 1981, cols. 395–400; HL 86 (1981–2)).

As regards the annual Finance Bill, embodying budget proposals and authorising taxation, debate at second reading is usual, generally, on the overall economic situation, though sometimes particular aspects of the Finance Bill may be attacked, as, for example in 1978, when Conservative peers were critical of the allegedly retrospective character of clauses on tax avoidance. After second reading, remaining stages are taken formally.

The seventeenth-century resolutions, however, were incomplete in two respects. First, though the Lords could neither initiate nor amend any bill of aid or supply, the House could still reject such a bill in its entirety. This is what happened to the 1909 Finance Bill, and that episode resulted in the Parliament Act which introduced a quite distinct limitation on the power of the Lords, considered below.

Second, the resolutions left room for debate over definition. Complaints were soon heard that some bills of aids and supplies included clauses dealing with extraneous matters, which the Lords was prevented from amending because they were 'tacked' on to bills protected by Commons' privileges. So in 1702 the Lords adopted a standing order which condemned 'tacking', defined as 'the annexing of any clause . . . to a bill of aid or supply the matter of which is foreign to and different from the said bill'. In modern times the question of 'tacking' has rarely been raised, though it was in 1976 when a peer argued that the power conferred in that year's Finance Bill (to allow inland revenue staff to seek a court order empowering them to break into private premises to take away papers) altered the law on trespass, and *prima facie* appeared to breach the House of Lords SO No 50 (quoted above). His view was not accepted by the Lords as a whole, though his assiduity in raising the matter was widely welcomed (see HL Deb, 7 July 1976, col. 1225–9, 15 May 1978, col. 6–44). In effect the House of Lords Standing Order on 'tacking' is the Upper House's way of safeguarding *its* privilege, which otherwise could be eroded by a creeping extension of Commons' financial privilege.

Other bills, besides Supply Bills, frequently contain some provisions which deal with taxation or public expenditure (technically, 'charges', either imposed on the people or on public funds), and, where this is so, Commons' financial privilege is involved. However, it may often be difficult to disentangle in such bills provisions dealing with 'charges' from other provisions concerned with policy and administration. Some relaxation of Commons' financial privilege is therefore desirable, otherwise the legislative rôle of the Lords could be unduly inhibited. In practice, the Commons is less emphatic in asserting its privilege in relation to such bills. If, for example, the House of Lords introduces amendments which impinge Commons' financial privilege, the Commons may accept such changes, and even if it disagrees with them, the Lower House does not necessarily assert privilege in order to get its way. However, if the Commons does reject a Lords' amendment on grounds of financial privilege, the Upper House will not press the matter, though peers may sometimes try to find another form of amendment which circumvents financial privilege. For example, in 1985, the House of Lords carried on division (by 77 votes to 62) an amendment (opposed by the Government) to the Films Bill. This would have enabled financial assistance to be given to film production from funds derived by levies on films shown on TV, levies on video cassettes of films and blank video tape. The Commons rejected this amendment, advancing financial privilege as its reason for doing so. Back in the Lords a further amendment was proposed to remove the proposed levy on blank video tape (a form of tax), but retain the other two proposed levies; this alteration, it was argued, would mean the amendment no longer infringed Commons' privilege. The Government, however, secured a better turn-out in the division lobby, and the compromise amendment was rejected by 100 votes to 83.

Bills which deal with 'charges' are quite often introduced into the Lords, before being dealt with by the Commons. When the House deals with a bill which involves any kind of financial provision a 'privilege amendment' is moved at third reading specifically disclaiming that the bill affects 'charges'. When the bill arrives in the Commons this amendment is removed. Such procedural nicety illustrates further the care taken to avoid even a technical infringement of financial privilege.

The second major limitation on the power of the House of Lords arises from the Parliament Act of 1911 (amended in 1949). This introduced a wholly new category of legislation, Money Bills, over which the power of the Lords was limited to a single month's delay. Somewhat simplified, a Money Bill is one which deals exclusively with 'charges'. This means that Finance Bills embodying budget changes have frequently not been certified as Money Bills, because they deal with other matters besides 'charges'. At the same time, other bills, which are not supply bills, may be certified as Money Bills; such are generally brief bills, the specific purpose of which concerns public expenditure. It is the Speaker of the Commons who alone decides what qualifies as a Money Bill (see Table 5.2 for examples from the 1981–2 session).

It is sometimes erroneously stated that the House of Lords refrains from debating Money Bills, but in fact such bills usually are debated at second reading and very occasionally at later stages as well. In 1985 the Lords debated, and only narrowly rejected (by 110 votes to 91), a reasoned amendment to the second reading of a Money Bill, the London Regional Passenger (Transport) Bill, with some peers expressing concern at the allegedly retrospective character of this bill, and other peers arguing it was inappropriate on constitutional grounds to debate such a motion at all. This was unusual. In fact the House is extremely cautious about its handling of Money Bills.

Moving away from Money Bills, the Parliament Acts also provide for a Commons bill brought forward in one session to go for Royal Assent in the following session notwithstanding disagreement by the Lords providing twelve months has elapsed since the bill had its second reading in the Commons. The bill must be reintroduced in the second session substantially in the same form as it was when first brought from the Commons. In 1975 the Trade Union and Labour Relations (Amendment) Bill was delayed by the House of Lords, and in the following session the Aircraft and Shipbuilding Industries Bill was delayed (see Chapter 9, p. 206). On both these bills the Parliament Act procedures were activated, but in neither case did these procedures run their full course because compromise between the House of Lords and the Labour Government was eventually attained, though only after the bills concerned had been delayed by the Lords.

The language of the Parliament Acts is entirely in terms of Commons bills, so it would be impossible to use these procedures to ensure the passage of bills introduced into the Lords. The 1911 Act specifically exempts any bill to extend the life of a parliament beyond five years (upon which the Lords' veto remains absolute). Nor do the Parliament Acts apply to private legislation or to statutory instruments, upon which the Lords' power of veto remains.

Legislative Stages in the House of Lords

Although bills can be introduced in either House, most major and controversial bills must, in practice, be introduced in the Commons. This is because Opposition leaders in the Commons, as well as other MPs, feel it is their right as the people's elected representatives to be the first parliamentary discussants of major bills. Senior ministers usually want to introduce their prize departmental offspring personally, and since almost all senior ministers are in the Commons, this necessitates the introduction there of bills about which ministers have strong feelings of paternal jealousy.

The stages a bill goes through in the Lords are, in outline, the same as in the Commons, though there are differences in the detailed procedures and in the use made of these. As in the Commons, the first reading of a bill is almost always a formality. Sometimes a Lords' private members' bill has been debated and even rejected on first reading, but this only occurs if the peer concerned exasperates the House by persistently introducing bills which have no hope of success. After first reading a bill is printed, and an explanatory memorandum is usually made available.

The second reading debate is generally taken as an opportunity to consider the principle of a bill. The Government spokesman frequently makes a speech very similar to that made by his Commons colleagues on a bill which has already passed that House, though he may, in particular, indicate alterations made to the bill by the Commons, and perhaps areas where the Government itself intends to amend the bill during its passage through the Lords. Again the main Opposition spokesman is likely to make a speech reiterating many of the points already made by his colleague in the Commons. But while the Commons' debate has almost certainly been dominated by Government and main Opposition party spokesmen, in the Lords contributions from peers less closely involved with the party political struggle can be anticipated. In some cases these will be reflective speeches from retired ministers; others will be speeches from experts of various kinds, for example, trade union leaders or industrialists — who may take a party whip, but who, nevertheless, speak very much as individuals knowledgeable of the subject concerned. Speeches from members of minor parties, as well as from crossbenchers and, in some cases, from law lords and bishops will be made, and some of these may contain powerful attacks on the legislation concerned. Peers also make frequent second reading speeches, which act as trailers for amendments they would like to see made to a bill at later stages. For a bill first introduced in the Lords, the second reading debate affords the Government spokesman the first opportunity to explain the purpose of the bill and to expound its contents.

Whereas, in the Commons, a vote against a government bill at second reading is taken as a normal part of the Opposition's attack, such a vote in the Lords would inevitably constitute a direct challenge to the Government, and indeed to the Lower House in the case of a bill which has already been passed by MPs. This creates difficulties for the Opposition in the Upper House. For a bill introduced by a Conservative Government, opposed at every stage in the Commons by the Labour Opposition, it can be difficult for Labour leaders in the Lords to explain to the party faithful outside the House why they have not even bothered to force a division at second reading. On the other hand, while a Labour Opposition might do this, secure in the knowledge that any such division would be lost and the will of the Government not thereby frustrated by the unelected House, the danger remains that such an action could be held to set a precedent which if followed by a Conservative Opposition, would almost certainly have a very different outcome.

There are two procedures by which peers hostile to a government bill have forced divisions at second reading stage without risking loss of the bill itself. One is to move a reasoned amendment which can specify what aspects of the bill are deprecated by the Lords. For example, when the Local Government Bill (abolishing the GLC and Metropolitan counties) was debated at second reading on 15 April 1985, the Labour front-bench spokesman moved an amendment which stated 'this House regrets the failure to provide a local and democratic framework for the strategic services essential to the capital city and the metropolitan area'. This challenged the basic principles of the bill. The amendment was voted on (and lost) prior to the second reading of the bill being approved.

The other procedure is to move a resolution at the same time as the second reading debate takes place, which is then voted on after the bill has been formally given its second reading. This procedure was pioneered by Lord O'Hagan (at the time a cross-bench peer) on the 1971 Immigration Bill. His motion, spelling out reasons for regret at the bill, was debated simultaneously with the second reading, but then voted on after the second reading had been approved (24 June 1971).

While both these procedures have been used with some frequency by Labour Oppositions, never have such motions yet been carried because the Conservative Government has taken enough trouble to ensure their defeat. Never (yet) has the Conservative Party in Opposition adopted this procedure. If it did so, it could expect to win such a division, and though formally a bill might still be accorded a second reading, it would be inconsistent thereafter not to amend it in a sufficiently drastic way to ensure that the features deprecated in the resolution carried at second reading were removed. In practice a Conservative Opposition can content itself with passing whatever 'wrecking' amendments it considers appropriate at committee or report stage.

After second reading the presumption is that bills will have a committee stage for detailed debate and amendment. But the House does not go into committee on supply bills, and almost never does so on money bills. For such bills the committee stage is negatived immediately after second reading, and remaining stages may be taken formally forthwith. For other bills the committee stage can be cancelled (the order of commitment discharged) if no amendments are put down, and no peer indicates a wish to speak at that stage on any motion concerned with a particular clause remaining in the bill.

The committee and report stages for the detailed amendment of a bill vary very much according to the character of the bill. Controversial bills can attract large numbers of hostile amendments with many divisions taking place. Complex bills may require much detailed amendment, not least by the Government adjusting earlier proposals, and the draftsmen improving their handiwork. Other bills may have brief straightforward treatment. For bills brought from the Commons these stages in the Lords present opportunities for further consideration of proposals for change already made in the Commons, and *vice versa* on Lords' bills.

There are several important differences between committee stage in the Lords and in the Commons. First, while most bills in the Commons go to an *ad hoc* Standing Committee consisting of between sixteen and fifty members, almost all bills in the Lords are dealt with on the floor of the House. While in the Commons party whips can take steps to exclude backbenchers whose contributions might be unwelcome, in the Lords no such opportunity is afforded. Lords' whips never know who may turn up at committee stage, and even if the proceedings tend to be dominated by a few peers, divisions are much less predictable than in Commons standing committees.

Further contrasts between the two Houses in relation to the stages for detailed discussion of a bill derive from the absence of a Speaker in the Lords capable of exercising power to select amendments, or to rule on the admissibility of amendments. This is a matter left to the Lords as a whole. Amendments which would not be allowed in the Commons because they would be considered irrelevant to the purpose of a bill can be debated in the Lords. As on other procedural questions, the Leader of the House may ask for an amendment to be withdrawn on the grounds that it is irrelevant to a bill (see for example HL Debs, 29 October 1979, cols. 484–93). Behind the scenes considerable efforts are made by clerks and then — if these are unavailing — by party whips, to dissuade peers from tabling irrelevant amendments, though if this does happen the Lords may still take a fairly relaxed and flexible attitude. Thus, on a bill dealing with agriculture, amendments about fish farming may be debatable in the Lords but not in the Commons and, on a bill dealing with the protection of aircraft, amendments to include airports may be out of order in the Commons but not in the Lords.

At committee stage a bill is considered clause by clause, with amendments being dealt with according to groupings (proposed by the government department concerned with the bill). The names of up to four peers may be put down as sponsors to an amendment (or five if the peer in charge of a bill chose to add his name). Close observers of the House of Lords suggest that, in recent years, much more careful consideration has been given to the question of amendment sponsorship, with important amendments being drafted in such a way as to secure cross-party support, reflected in the names of sponsoring peers.

Following committee stage a bill is reported to the House. Given that almost all bills are dealt with on the floor of the House at committee stage, the report stage affords an opportunity for exactly the same people to go through the bill again. Procedure is slightly different (no 'clause stand part' debate for example), but the main value of this stage is to debate amendments drawn up in the light of committee stage discussions. The third reading follows but, unlike the Commons, this provides a further opportunity for substantive amendments. Though the *Companion to the Standing Orders* states that repetition should be avoided, in practice very similar amendments may be debated at committee, report, and third reading stages. In the Commons the Speaker can rule out of order amendments at one stage which repeat the substance of earlier amendments. Some ex-MP peers complain of the laxity of Lords' procedures in this regard (see Bruce-Gardyne, 1980).

When amendments are moved at third reading, the House of Lords has a final consideration of the bill on the motion 'that the bill do now pass'. This is usually brief, the opportunity for a quick summary of the changes made to a bill, often linked with collective self-congratulation, and the exchange of compliments among peers active on the bill. Occasionally, at the final stage of a bill, a hostile or critical motion is moved. If the Government has resisted all amendments at every stage, the Opposition may register its disapproval in a motion deploring this fact, as happened at third reading of the European Communities Bill in 1972 and at the final stage of the Transport Bill in 1983. Where amendments have been made a motion spelling out reasons for regret at the passage of a bill may still be moved; Labour did this at the end of proceedings on the British Nationality Act in 1981.

When a bill has completed its passage in both Houses it is returned for the first House to consider amendments made by the second House. In the case of a Commons' bill, if MPs reject any amendments made by peers, then the bill is returned again to the Lords with the Commons' reasons for disagreeing to the amendments in question attached to the bill. Such reasons are usually expressed very briefly in a single sentence. A full explanation for the disagreement can be found in the record of speeches printed in Commons *Hansard*. The Lords usually acquiesce at this stage, though peers may make speeches — some in sorrow, some in anger — deprecating the Government's foolishness in rejecting Lords' amendments. Sometimes one or other House will propose amendments in lieu of amendments already made, or amendments to amendments, and in this way some to-ing and fro-ing may take place before an agreed version of a bill can go forward for Royal Assent. If at the end of the session no agreed version has been attained, the bill concerned fails.

It is clearly conducive to careful consideration of a bill that sufficient time should be available between successive stages to allow for consultations and preparation of amendments. SO44 stipulates that no two stages of a bill should be taken on a single day. This Standing Order is suspended, sometimes in order to deal rapidly with a particularly urgent bill, but on other occasions to allow government business managers freedom to arrange business how they please at times of congestion. In 1977 the Lords agreed to a procedure committee report recommending minimum intervals between successive stages for lengthy and complex bills; these were two weekends between first and second reading, fourteen days between second reading and committee, fourteen days between committee and report, and three sitting days between report and third reading. Though not incorporated in Standing Orders these intervals are stipulated in the *Companion,* which also states that notice should be given on the order paper if they are departed from in relation to any bill. This has been by no means infrequent, especially when the business of the House becomes heavily congested late in a session.

The Problem of Legislative Congestion

Given the fact that all legislation must complete all its parliamentary stages in both Houses within a single session, the introduction of most major bills in the Commons first can lead to a legislative bottleneck in the Lords towards the end of the session, and this can so seriously impair the thoroughness of the work of the House in scrutiny and revision of bills that the problem deserves separate discussion. The very fact that such problems have occurred regularly under governments of both major parties indicates their intractable nature.

In the 1971–2 session, under the Conservative Government of Mr Heath, difficulties were acute. Peers returned after the summer recess four weeks before MPs. One task before them was to debate over 1,000 amendments to the Local Government Bill, of which over 600 were passed and sent back to the Commons. A motion calling for more legislation to be introduced in the Lords was passed without a division (25 October 1972) and in the following session the major bill reforming the National Health Service was introduced into the House of Lords, an arrangement which pleased peers and seemed satisfactory to MPs also.

In 1975 and 1976 difficulties were again considerable, especially in the latter year, aggravated by the Government's loss of its Commons majority during that session. When the Lords rose for the summer recess in 1976, the committee stage of ten bills, including six major ones (five of which had been guillotined in the Commons) had not begun. As well as bringing peers back early, the Government extended the parliamentary session, which meant that for eight weeks in the Autumn peers sat five days a week, usually till after 10.00 p.m. Again, it was not simply the long hours, but the deleterious effect on the quality of the legislative work of the Lords which angered peers. In some cases time schedules were so tight that it was impossible to get amendments made to a bill at one stage printed before the next stage commenced. The Opposition front-bench moved a motion formally expressing the regret of the House at the inadequate time to deal with legislation, which was carried by a large majority.

In the first session of the following parliament, with the Conservatives back in office, the legislative timetable again became seriously congested. One bill which caused particular difficulty, the Companies Bill, had actually been introduced in the Lords, but after going to the Commons, the Government had introduced forty-three new clauses, some at a very late stage in that House. The Upper House was then asked to deal with 246 amendments on a Tuesday which had only been published the previous Friday, forty-eight pages of complex proposals with much cross-referencing to other legislation. Opposition leaders protested and moved a motion deploring the way the Government had handled the House which, though lost by 119 votes to 80, did give rise to critical speeches from all quarters. Lord Boyd-Carpenter, the senior Conservative backbencher, referred to the timetable as 'making a mockery of the revising function of this House' (HL Debs, 27 October 1980, col. 922). During this debate Lord Denham, Government Chief Whip, argued that more notice had been given of amendments on this occasion than had been given in 1977 when the Lords had hurriedly to consider 252 amendments to the Patents Bill, or in 1975 when 300 amendments to the Children's Bill had to be dealt with. (Whereas, in the Commons, front-bench spokesmen cite precedents exemplifying previous governments' mismanagement of business when debating guillotine motions, in the Lords such exchanges take place when the House is asked quickly to dispose of large numbers of recently tabled government amendments!)

The most satifactory solution to the problem would be to introduce more of the major bills in the Lords. All governments have attempted this, but the obstacles to so doing have already been described. However, in the 1985–6 session, the end of which was again heavily congested, a major bill was introduced in the Lords, but ironically this was the Shops Bill (on Sunday Trading) which the Upper House spent seven days dealing with, but only as a prelude to its outright rejection at second reading by the Commons. When the House of Lords returned after the summer recess it faced repeated late sittings throughout a five-week 'overspill' period during which the detailed stages of five major bills had to be undertaken. A question in the House elicited the information that over 700 government amendments had been put down to these bills, one of which in particular, the Financial Services Bill, was a very complex measure largely rewritten at the tail end of the session. Again Opposition peers protested, especially when they felt that the Government had broken a private undertaking not to table amendments incorporating quite new material to this Bill. In his response the Leader of the House, Viscount Whitelaw, argued that the House 'had a much greater role as a revising chamber' than it had known in the past. This was both an explanation for the extra work involved, and also an assurance to the Lords that it had become quite simply a more important place and was doing more work (HL Debs, 14 October 1986, col. 687). This prompted the question whether the House of Lords could cope with its larger workload without adapting its procedures in some way.

Reform of Legislative Procedure

Proposals for reform in the way Parliament deals with legislation have frequently been made. Generally attention is focused on the Commons, though some proposals — for example a sessional carry-over of legislation — would involve both Houses. The Lords has considered some reforms involving the Upper House alone.

From time to time the idea of taking the committee stage of bills off the floor of the House has been considered. In 1968 this was done on an experimental basis with one bill, the Gaming Bill, and over the next eight years the experiment was repeated five times. The committees were composed in such a way as to favour the party in office, but without giving it an overall majority. Peers not appointed to public bill committees were allowed to attend their proceedings, to speak and to move amendments — which several did — but not to vote. Bills chosen for this treatment were ones upon which party political controversy was not anticipated.

How much time did such committees save? Borthwick (1973) estimated that the Gaming Bill committee saved two to three days, but that subsequent committees saved less time. After an interval of ten years, this procedure was used again following the difficulties over congestion in the 1985–6 session. The Pilotage Bill in the 1986–7 session was sent to a public bill committee, which spent eleven hours spread over five days dealing with it, but subsequently the same bill took ten more hours on the floor of the House. The use of such a committee was not judged a success (HL Deb, 5 March 1987, col. 807, 812; see also HL 9, 1987–8, para. 26). It seems doubtful that a reform of this kind on its own can make any significant difference.

More fundamental reform of the legislative procedure was advocated by the 1976 Select Committee on Practice and Procedure. This recommended that the Lords establish committees to commence work, while bills were still before the Commons, reviewing the proceedings there, and noting commitments given by the Government. Such committees would be given evidence-taking powers, like select committees. These proposals were not simply designed to save the time of the Lords, but to improve the quality of consideration given to bills. A sessional carry-over for bills was also recommended. However, when this report was debated in the House on 5th July 1977 its proposals did not receive any clear endorsement, and some peers, notably Lord Carrington (Conservative Leader), were highly critical of its suggestions. These were not taken up.

A Labour peer, Lord Northfield, himself a member of the select committee, described its recommendations as 'modest proposals', and in an interesting article he argued that experience gained in the work of the European Communities Committee should be applied in the area of public bill procedure (Northfield, 1978). This would entail the widespread use of pre-legislative select committees. It is not a reform which government or parliament generally shows much inclination to accept.

In 1983 Lord Diamond initiated a debate on public bill procedure, but his proposals, which involved standing committees composed with regard both to expertise and 'to the proportion of the votes cast for the main political parties at the last general election', implied the recognition of wholly new principles for the composition of parliamentary committees — and seemed more like an argument for electoral reform. They were given short shrift by peers (HL Debs, 3 November 1983, col. 642–60).

Amendments to Government Bills

Table 5.1 gives statistics for the number of amendments made by the House of Lords to government bills during the first three sessions of each of the last three parliaments. The inclusion of sessions terminated early by the calling of an election can produce a distorted picture because arrangements are made in such circumstances for the rapid enactment of some legislation and the abandonment of other items.

These figures need elucidation and qualification. The number of amendments made is a very crude index of the legislative impact of the House of Lords. (On this, see especially Griffith, 1974, Ch. 7). Yet the figures do provide a starting point for an assessment. Many bills are not amended at all in the Upper House. Money and supply bills have already been excluded from this analysis, but of the eighty other bills indicated in this table as having been introduced between 1979 and 1982, the House of Lords amended only thirty-nine. The figures for the 1981–2 session may be used to illustrate this point in more detail (Table 5.2). In that year, of twenty-two bills brought from the Commons (excluding money and supply bills) only eight were amended leaving fourteen to which the Lords made

Table 5.1 (a)   Government Bills Brought from the House of Commons (Excluding Money and Supply Bills)

Sessions	Total number of bills	Number of bills amended by House of Lords	Number of amendments made by House of Lords
1974–7	68	49	1,866
1979–82	82	39	2,231
1983–6	69	43	4,137

Table 5.1 (b)   Government Bills Introduced into the House of Lords (Excluding Consolidation Bills)

Sessions	Total number of bills	Number of bills amended by House of Lords	Number of amendments made by House of Lords
1974–7	58	38	1,594
1979–82	33	20	1,604
1983–6	42	28	1,373

Source: Calculated from figures supplied by the Public Bill Office, House of Lords. (See also HL 9, 1987–8, Tables VI and VII.)

no alteration. Of these fourteen, five were bills, the main object of which 'was to create a charge on the public purse' (introduced under a Standing Order specifying this in the House of Commons), and on only one of these did the House of Lords go into committee, and that for a mere half-hour. The Upper House can amend such bills (which may even be introduced into the Lords). But, equally, it is not surprising to find it refraining from doing so because such bills are mainly concerned with 'charges'. Of the remaining nine bills not amended in the Lords, five were not amended in the Commons either, and three of the remaining four received very brief Commons discussion and only slight amendment. The exception was the Northern Ireland Bill, debated for some 90 hours in the Commons (including a committee stage on the floor of the House with hours spent 'filibustering') but for only nine hours in the Lords. If we look at bills introduced in the Lords in the same session, we find five of ten such bills were unamended by peers, but four of these five were also unamended in the Commons.

Thus most bills which did not receive amendment in the Lords were either not amended in the Commons or received very slight amendment there. This illustrates the point that public bills vary enormously in importance and complexity. Table 5.2 shows that in the 1981–2 session the Currency Bill took 48 minutes for all its stages in the Commons and 19

Table 5.2 Government Bills Introduced into Commons, 1981–2*

Title of bill	Total time in Commons (hours)	Total time in Lords (hours)	Number of Lords' amendments	Time in Commons considering Lords' amendments (hours)
Canada Bill	21.45	7.14	0	—
Civil Aviation	12.06	1.33	0	—
Coal Industry	11.30	1.49	0	—
Criminal Justice	88.30	52.06	300	0.14
Currency	0.48	0.19	0	—
Derelict Land	5.30	0.46	0	—
Duchy of Cornwall	6.48	0.19	0	—
Employment	91.00	62.00	41	6.48
Finance[a]	127.00	—	—	—
Housing Amendment (Scotland)[b]	2.12	0.23	—	—
Industry[b]	4.40	0.10	—	—
Local Government Planning (Scotland)	101.15	0.52	16	0.26
Local Government Finance (No. 2)	77.45	26.36	32	5.38
Local Government (Miscellaneous Provisions)	23.15	31.31	225	2.48
Merchant Shipping (Liner Conferences)	14.00	1.51	0	—
New Towns	7.30	0.30	0	—
Northern Ireland	90.00	9.00	0	—
Nuclear Industry (Finance)[b]	4.00	0.26	0	—
Oil and Gas Enterprise	87.00	36.00	67	3.27
Shipbuilding	6.30	0.26	0	—
Social Security and Housing Benefits	68.30	12.40	27	0.11
Social Security (Contributions)	7.30	7.18	0	—
Stocks Transfer	2.06	1.07	0	—
Transport	83.00	31.45	134	4.26
Transport (Finance)	14.45	0.41	0	—
Travel Concessions	8.45	1.55	0	—

Notes: [a] Supply Bill
        [b] Money Bill

Table 5.3 Government Bills Introduced into the House of Lords, 1981–2

Title of bill	Total time in House of Lords (hours)	Total time in House of Commons (hours)	Number of Lords' amendments	Number of Commons' amendments
Administration of Justice	15.30	12.15	93	58
Civic Government (Scotland)	33.00	66.00	188	367
Civil Jurisdiction and Judgments	4.45	4.52	47	62
Fire Service College Board (Abolition)	0.15	0.04	0	0
Harbours (Scotland)	0.30	1.24	0	0
Hops Marketing	1.30	0.42	0	0
Legal Bill	4.45	14.00	20	18
Mental Health (Amendment)	32.15	75.00	119	123
Reserve Forces	0.02	0.19	0	0
Taking of Hostages	0.45	2.30	0	2

minutes in the Lords. This simple bill, passed without amendment, redefined 'new penny' as 'penny', so that the shortly-to-arrive twenty-penny piece could be described officially as it would be colloquially, namely as the twenty-penny piece rather than as the twenty-new-penny piece. In the same session the bill taking the longest parliamentary time was the Employment Bill, debated for almost 100 hours all told in the Commons and over 60 hours in the Lords; this was both a complex and politically controversial bill, introducing restrictions on picketing and strike action.

The fact that public bills vary so greatly and yet all go through the same basic parliamentary processes can be expressed as a criticism of these processes. But it can also be taken as an indication of their flexibility. The stages a bill must go through are the same, but the use made of these stages varies greatly (Drewry and Burton, 1980, discuss this point).

While in both Houses time is heavily concentrated on major and controversial bills, Tables 5.2 and 5.3 show that the House of Commons spends more time than the House of Lords on almost all bills, including those first introduced in the Upper House. In 1981–2 the only Commons bill on which peers spent longer than MPs was the Local Government (Miscellaneous Provisions) Bill. A similar analysis of time spent on bills in 1975–6 (not given here in detail) again found only one bill on which the Commons spent less time than the Lords. Generally MPs spend at least twice as long as peers on any bill, and sometimes ten times as long. The reasons for this have already been discussed (p. 104).

Table 5.1 gives figures for the total of Lords' amendments made to government bills. Some of these were subsequently rejected by the Commons, and in other cases amendments were proposed in the Commons in lieu of particular Lords' amendments. The proportion of Lords' amendments accepted or rejected by the Commons has varied greatly according to whether the Conservative or Labour Party has been in office. When Labour was in office the Lords made many more amendments against the Government's wishes, but these were mostly reversed by the Commons. Thus in the period 1974–7 of the 1,813 amendments made by the Lords, over 400 were rejected by the Commons, and in almost every case the House of Lords agreed not to insist on its amendment. Between 1979 and 1983 only six of the 2,283 amendments made by the Lords were rejected by the Commons.

One may generalise by saying that when Labour has been in office it has experienced frequent defeat in the Lords, and therefore as a matter of routine seeks the cancellation of large numbers of Lords' amendments in the Commons, which, providing its majority there is secure, does not normally present any difficulty. When the Conservatives are in office comparatively few amendments are carried in the House against the

Government's wishes, though when this does happen, a Conservative Government is much more hesitant about simply asking the Commons to reverse such amendments. This is because their acceptance by the Lords has frequently depended on support by some Conservative peers, if not by substantial cross-bench support, and may well have been foreshadowed by rebellion in the Commons as well. There may well be political embarrassment for the Government in the Commons if it simply insists on trying to reverse the defeat already suffered in the Lords. Therefore, the pressure to compromise can be considerable.

If one looks at the number of legislative defeats suffered by governments in the Lords it may appear as if the House had greatest impact on Labour legislation. But if one looks at the extent to which bills are actually amended in ways contrary to the wishes of the Government by the House of Lords, the impact is probably just as great on Conservative legislation. When Nicholas Baldwin asked active peers whether the Lords carried on to the statute book many more amendments against the wishes of a Labour government than against the wishes of a Conservative government, fewer than 7 per cent said 'yes', the great majority reckoning that the end result was very similar (Baldwin, 1985, App. 10).

The statistic showing the total number of amendments made fails to distinguish amendments of greatly differing importance. Some can be described as 'purely drafting' amendments, which means they involve no intention to alter, in any way, the substance or impact of the bill, but simply seek to clarify its wording. Some are 'technical' amendments which are intended to improve the bill by making its impact more precise; others are 'substantive' amendments which may concede important points without altering the basic purpose of the bill, while still others can be described as 'wrecking' amendments because they do change the basic nature of the bill, and may indeed result in the whole bill having to be abandoned.

Nor does the statistic of total amendments made reveal anything about the source of amendments. It is possible to identify the immediate source by consulting *Hansard* and seeing who moved the amendment concerned, but even the names of peers sponsoring an amendment do not, by any means, necessarily reveal its origin. This is most clearly seen in the case of government amendments, which constitute the bulk of all successful amendments. Frequently these are put down by the Government as concessions made in direct response to criticisms made at earlier stages of a bill's passage, sometimes even as a result of a defeat the Government has suffered, after which it brings forward amendments to clarify the change it has been forced to accept. Many government amendments to bills in the Lords are the result of undertakings given during the bill's passage through the Commons. Often these result from pressure brought to bear on the

Government by groups outside of parliament altogether, though in such cases spokesmen within both Houses will generally move amendments on behalf of outside groups as part of the whole process of exerting pressure on the Government.

It is therefore impossible to be precise about the origin of all amendments. Nicholas Baldwin found that almost half of all amendments moved in the Lords to government legislation between 1970 and 1983 were moved by government spokesmen, but he then sought to identify from within this group the proportion which were actually initiated by the Government and found this to be something under three-quarters, the remainder being government responses to undertakings given at earlier parliamentary stages or as the direct result of an identifiable undertaking given to an interest group.

When a bill is going through parliament, groups with interests in the subject matter of the bill are likely to be continuously active. Depending on the kind of bill and the nature of the group concerned, part of this activity will be continuing discussions with ministers and civil servants. But even when these are taking place, contact with MPs and peers is also likely to be sustained to ensure that the group's point of view is put forward in parliament during detailed discussion of the bill. Lobbying of this kind has always taken place, but there is good reason to believe it has increased in recent years. Furthermore, the House of Lords has undoubtedly become a more frequent object of attention by group leaders than it was in the past. Some peers in interview expressed the view that it was the 1980 Wildlife and Countryside Bill which first alerted professional lobbyists to the potential usefulness of Lords' proceedings for securing alterations to legislation. This was a major conservation measure introduced into the House of Lords, where countryside interests have traditionally been strongly represented. The 'usual channels' found debate on this bill almost impossible to control, and eventually the Lords spent eight days in committee dealing with it, making, in all, 520 amendments.

Whatever the importance of this particular bill, it also became evident in the early 1980s that as far as actually getting detailed changes made to bills was concerned, the House of Lords could be at least as useful as the Commons. Interest groups responded accordingly, and peers on all sides reported increases in their postbags. But stereotyped lobbying material, distributed to all members, is generally acknowledged as ineffective. More significant has been the increased attention given to the House by groups concerned to organise support for particular ends. Thus when an important bill is before the Lords, groups will usually arrange meetings to which interested peers are invited. Here draft amendments may be distributed and detailed explanations on particular points given. Thereafter group spokesmen will make themselves available throughout the passage of a bill, perhaps holding regular meetings at successive stages to provide ready-drafted amendments to interested peers. A well-resourced group such as a trade union may provide a near-full-time researcher to assist Opposition spokesmen to a bill. In other cases the assistance may be much more spasmodic, and Opposition spokesmen may bemoan the unwillingness of groups to offer greater assistance.

One way in which some groups seek to advance their cause is through private members' legislation. This chapter concludes with a brief discussion of such bills, after which return in Chapter 6 to examining the rôle of the House of Lords in relation to government bills since 1979.

Private Members' Bills

While government may be dominant within parliament, it does not monopolise parliament's law-making rôle. Backbenchers in both Houses have opportunities to bring forward bills at their own initiative, and every session sees quite a number of such bills — private members' bills — enacted. Mostly these are minor measures enjoying the benevolent neutrality (if not open support) of government. Some are significant changes in areas of law where parties traditionally fear to tread, issues left to the consciences of individual members. Such bills must — like other public legislation — go through all stages in both Houses before reaching Royal Assent. It is therefore necessary to consider both the treatment of private members' bills introduced into the Lords, as well as those brought to the Upper House following their passage through the Commons.

As regards the latter, the difficulties that face MPs who wish to introduce private members' bills are well known. The time available for debating such bills is strictly limited, which means that for all but the most innocuous of bills a precondition of success is that the MP introducing the bill draws a high place in the ballot of private members' time.

Almost all private members' bills which complete their Commons stages are passed by the House of Lords (between 1978 and 1986 of eighty-six bills brought from the Commons, only five failed to reach Royal Assent, and each of these was in some sense exceptional). The greater procedural flexibility in the Upper House ensures that all private members' bills receive some debating time, so that those bills passed entirely without debate in the Commons are always accorded at least a brief explanation in the House of Lords. Since few private members' bills arrive from the Commons before Easter (and some not until July) their consideration does add to the pressures the Upper House usually faces late in the session, though most take relatively little time. Of seventeen private members' bills brought from the Commons in 1985–6, only one took more than two hours for all its Lords' stages. This was the Disabled Persons (Services,

Consultation and Representation) Bill, which peers debated for five hours and to which the Lords made 102 amendments, a quite exceptional number for a private members' bill. Only because this measure enjoyed wide support, was it safe for peers to give it such close time-consuming attention.

Any amendments made to Commons' bills by peers must of course be approved by the Lower House. Usually the last private members' Friday of each session is devoted to taking Lords' amendments, but some may be dealt with earlier. Governments in the 1950s and 1960s were, in general, much readier to provide time for the later stages of private members' bills than more recent governments. (According to a Commons written answer published on 26 January 1987, (col. 106–23) virtually no government time had been provided for any private members' bill at any stage since 1979; whereas between 1954 and 1970 government time was provided for consideration of Lords' amendments to forty-nine bills.) This has had the effect of severely inhibiting the House of Lords from exercising its revising rôle in relation to private members' bills brought from the Commons. To insert any changes may be tantamount to killing a bill, and several times peers have complained about this. In 1985–6 only three out of seventeen were amended in any way.

The difficulties involved in securing time in the Commons explains the low success rate for private members' bills first introduced in the Lords. Table 5.4 shows that since 1979 only 40 per cent of bills which completed their Lords' stages also got through the Commons. This was a higher proportion than in the 1974–9 Parliament, but a good deal lower than earlier Parliaments, notably 1966–70. A Lords' private members' bill taken to the Commons can be taken up by any MP, but only if the bill is given an unopposed second reading on a Friday afternoon is it likely to be successful. However, mere statistics are in this case slightly misleading because some private members' bills passed by the House of Lords in one session were taken up in the Commons in a later session and their passage as Commons private members' bills may well have been facilitated by their prior debate in the House of Lords.

Table 5.4   Private Members' Bills Introduced into the House of Lords

Parliament	Total number introduced	Number of bills completing HL stages	Number of bills gaining Royal Assent
1966–70	49	15	12
1970–4	48	16	10
1974–9	77	28	9
1979–83	91	27	11
1983–6	49	25	10

This was undoubtedly the case with some very significant private members' bills in the 1966–70 Parliament, especially the so-called permissive society legislation. Twice the House of Lords passed bills legalising homosexuality (previously always a criminal offence) before such legislation was successful in the Commons. The legalising of abortion was likewise heralded in the Lords, again with the House both pushing public opinion along on the subject and showing how some of the difficulties inherent in legislating in such an area could be overcome. For a time it seemed that the Upper House was the 'place for all social reform to be first discussed' as Lord Gardiner — Labour Lord Chancellor at the time — claimed (HL Debs, 23 November 1966, col. 251). The presence of bishops, law lords, eminent doctors and other experts, as well as the freedom from constituency pressures, were all factors which made the Lords well-suited to the difficult task of producing viable legislation on complex issues (see Richards, 1970).

The impetus for reform of this kind appeared to decline in the 1970s, though frequent attempts at relaxing restrictions on Sunday observance were made, and abortion continued to be a highly controversial subject with more emphasis in the 1980s on the need to restrict the availability of abortion and introduce legislation on the 'beginnings of life' issues reported on by the Warnock Committee in 1985. On such questions an attempt at major reform in the Commons failed, and debates in the House of Lords revealed deep divisions of opinion, inhibiting any attempt at comprehensive reform by private members' legislation, even though some minor proposals for change in the law were attempted. A recent example of a matter upon which legislation was eventually passed, but which proved extraordinarily difficult to get right, was female circumcision, a subject on which the House of Lords worked hard before a Commons' private members' bill — the 1985 Prohibition of Female Circumcision Bill — was enacted.

A number of private members' bills introduced in the Lords in recent years have been referred to select committees. These are discussed in Chapter 8, but we may note here that no similar recent practice giving opportunities to both the advocates and opponents of a proposed bill to assemble evidence in support of their views has developed in the Commons.

Most successful private members' bills introduce minor changes, possibly removing anomalies in earlier legislation — or introducing small alterations recommended by committees of inquiry — but ignored by governments. Several all-party campaigning groups within parliament have used private members' bills to try to achieve their ends. In the 1970s an all-party group was formed to help the racing industry. Several peers have been prominent in this group and several Lords' private members' bills have been directed to this end. Lord Newall, Chairman of the British Greyhound Racing Board, introduced a bill in 1980 to allow an increase in the number of races at meetings, and another in 1985 to relax, in a minor way, restrictions on betting at dog races. Both these attained Royal Assent.

Animal welfare and conservation is another area where private members' bills have proliferated, again success being much more likely for bills with specific and limited aims. Eight successive private members' bills introduced in one or other House on scientific experiments on animals failed, until eventually in 1985 the Government sponsored legislation on this subject. Three bills introduced by Lord Janner in the early 1970s sought to regulate zoos. This culminated in the Zoo Licensing Act of 1981 which, though a Commons bill, entered into an inheritance prepared by the Upper House.

Sometimes all-party groups are rather more partisan, an example being the so-called 'All-Party' Repeal Group which in the early 1980s set about introducing bills to repeal statutes which imposed restrictions of various kinds. A Rent (Abolition of Control) Bill was introduced by Lord Vaizey in 1982 which sought to abolish all controls on rents; needless to say this didn't proceed. Lord Spens, Chairman of the Group, introduced a Wages Council (Abolition) Bill in 1984, a subject taken up in modified form by the Government's 1986 Wages Act. In 1982 Lord Rugby introduced a bill to remove the monpoly enjoyed by opticians, which he withdrew after a three-and-a-half-hour second-reading debate (described by the Government spokesman as 'extraordinarily interesting' (HL Debs, 18 February 1982, col. 727)) and again this subject was later taken up by the Government. So was Baroness Trumpington's bill about Sunday trading of the same session. The 'Repeal Group' was a kind of ginger-group of crossbenchers and Tory backbenchers, eager to encourage the Thatcher Government along the path of liberalisation.

Constitutional reform is another subject frequently ventilated by private members' bills. As well as a bill of rights, the House of Lords has debated electoral reform, with a bill allowing district councils to opt for a single transferable vote system for elections being introduced first in 1983 (when it was defeated) and again in 1985, when Lord Blake, Conservative peer and formerly Chairman of the Hansard Society Commission on Electoral Reform successfully took a bill through the Lords, with the only opposition coming from the two front-benches. Such sources of hostility were of course sufficient to ensure the bill a rapid burial in the Commons.

Private members' bill procedure is used in both Houses to give prominence to debate on certain subjects, without any very serious legislative purpose being evident. In the Commons many so-called ten-minute rule bills fall into this category. In the Lords peers concerned simply to initiate a debate generally use other procedures. But sometimes private members' bills are introduced which do not appear to be serious attempts at legislation. If the House feels this to be the case such bills may be refused a second reading. Two bills on Namibia introduced by Lord Hatch of Lusby in 1985 and 1986 were obvious examples. In 1984, Lord Sudeley introduced a Prayer Book Protection Bill, but after a four-hour debate, he withdrew the bill (rather than risk its rejection on a division); his main aim appeared to be the establishment of a select committee of the House of Lords, but opinion was against this. In 1983 Lord Jenkins of Putney introduced a bill to allow trustees of the British Museum to return objects to countries of origin (such as the Elgin Marbles), but the Chairman of the Trustees, followed by the ex-Chairman, followed by two more trustees and the Minister for the Arts, all roundly condemned the bill, which not surprisingly expired there and then, a fate Lord Jenkins must have anticipated.

Private members' bills are introduced in the Lords by peers from all parts of the House, including occasionally the Opposition front-bench. In 1974 Lord Hailsham of Saint Marylebone introduced a bill to remove any doubt about the possibility of a Roman Catholic becoming a Lord Chancellor. Serving Law Lords, including the Lord Chief Justice, have introduced bills, as have bishops and the Archbishop of Canterbury (the latter a bill to facilitate the sharing of Church buildings, enacted in 1969).

Given the unwillingness of governments to legislate in some areas, and the apparent reluctance of ministers to introduce minor bills, usually — so it is said — because they are untimely in advance of more general legislation (which, however, can seem interminably delayed), private members' legislation is an important safeguard. The role of the House of Lords is circumscribed by the procedural rigidity of the Commons. But this is also a factor which contributes to the usefulness of Lords' proceedings.

6

THE TREATMENT OF GOVERNMENT LEGISLATION 1979–87

The purpose of this chapter is to examine the impact the House of Lords had on government legislation in the period 1979–87. This is potentially a vast subject, and some degree of selectivity is inevitable. The approach adopted here is to begin by giving particular consideration to occasions on which the Government suffered defeat in the division lobbies; next to consider the effect of the Lords on legislation in a number of specific areas, notably the 'right to buy' council housing legislation, and measures relating to local government. Finally we will examine more closely the legislation of a single session, that of 1985–6, to illustrate both the effectiveness and the limitations of the Upper House's legislative activities.

Government Defeats

Of the total of 106 defeats suffered by the Government in the Lords' division lobbies between 1979 and 1987, ninety-nine involved amendments being made to Government bills (the remainder involved defeats on motions or procedural matters). Analysis of these ninety-nine defeats shows that in fifty-four cases the change thereby made to a bill was accepted in principle by the Government (though further amendments to tidy up the details were often necessary); in twenty-eight cases amendments were rejected (though in a few cases after a second defeat in the Lords, the Government accepted the will of the House); while in the remaining seventeen cases a definite compromise was reached.

These amendments varied greatly in importance. Some were minor to the point of triviality, while a few were very significant indeed. In between were many which made changes to bills which could be described as minor from the perspective of the Government's overall legislative programme, but which, nevertheless, were important to particular groups. The frequency of defeat on more significant amendments was certainly greater between 1983–7 than in Mrs. Thatcher's first parliament.

It so happens that the first three defeats suffered by the Thatcher Government in the 1979–80 session illustrate rather well the varied circumstances and importance of government defeat in the Upper House. In chronological order these were: a defeat of a very minor kind on the Bees Bill in February; defeat on the Criminal Justice (Scotland) Bill also in February; and third, a major defeat on the Education Bill over school transport charges in March 1980.

The Bees Bill had been introduced by the Government in response to pressure from bee-keepers. It concerned the threat posed by a lethal bee disease — varroasis. Under the bill, hives found infected would be compulsorily destroyed. In the Commons the question of compensation for commercial bee-keepers who lost hives in this way was raised, but the Government resisted amendments on this point, and did so again when the same change was advocated in the Lords, arguing that it had only agreed to bring the bill forward because no public expenditure was involved. Eventually peers voted by thirty-three votes to twenty-five to amend the bill to make possible the payment of compensation without obliging such payments (18 February). Back in the Commons the Government Minister indicated willingness to accept this amendment, but at the same time he emphasised that the Government had no intention of using the permissive power it had thus been given. The amendment therefore made no practical difference to the implementation of this bill. Had peers altered the bill more drastically, for example to require the payment of compensation, their amendment would have been rejected. This was a hollow victory, but perhaps one considered at the time to have some symbolic value, the putting down of a marker of opinion to which a subsequent government might choose to respond more sympathetically.

A further example of a minor defeat with cosmetic rather than substantive implications occurred when peers amended the 1980 Health Services Bill. The bone of contention here concerned the salaries reimbursement scheme operated for GPs' employees, which disallowed reimbursement to GPs who employed their relatives, because, according to the Government, it would be impossible to prevent abuse in such cases. Peers protested that a system which compelled two doctors married to two nurses to employ each other's wives (rather than their own) or forgo salary reimbursement was ludicrous. Again the amendment did not require the Government to act on this matter, but established that a change could be made at some point in the future by statutory instrument. The Lords carried the amendment against the Government's wishes by seventy-one votes to forty-one (10 July). The Government made no effort to reverse the change, but made clear it had no intention of bringing forward the necessary order. Nevertheless the fact that the Lords voted by so large a margin for this change ensured continuing pressure on the Government in coming years, and further questions on the subject were regularly asked in the House (for example 20 February 1985, col. 567–9).

The second Government defeat, chronologically speaking, occurred in 1980 on the Criminal Justice (Scotland) Bill. Again this was a minor affair, but it was different from those just discussed in that it illustrated the rôle of the House in an area where it feels a high degree of self-confidence. The bill followed recommendations of the Emslie Committee in stipulating that when sentencing a convicted murderer a trial judge should, in open court, give reasons for the sentence imposed together with his recommendation concerning the minimum term to be served. Lord Keith of Kinkel, a law lord with Scottish judicial experience, opposed this, arguing that the purpose behind the proposal was simply to ensure that the views of the trial judge would be available subsequently to the Parole Board, an objective by then routinely secured by other means. The minister made an unconvincing reply and the Lords supported the amendment by forty-seven votes to thirty-nine (26 February). When the bill went to the Commons, the Government allowed a free vote, in which the Lords' view was upheld.

On matters to do with the courts and the administration of justice, the presence of senior judges as well as the Lord Chancellor and former occupants of the Woolsack, enhances the authority which the House of Lords feels entitled to exercise. On the 1982 Criminal Justice Bill, peers passed minor amendments against the Government's wishes, dealing with bail conditions and the sentencing of young offenders, neither of which the Government overturned (22 June). More significant examples occurred when the Lords inflicted three defeats on the Government during the passage of the Police and Criminal Evidence Bill in 1984. One of these restricted police powers to stop and search to constables in uniform, and this was rejected by the Commons (31 July). Another, moved by Lord Scarman and carried against the Government by seventy-one votes to sixty-five on 19 October, required that racially discriminatory behaviour by the police would be a disciplinary offence, and this the Government eventually accepted, while the third — also moved by Lord Scarman — concerned the rules of evidence, and resulted in a government compromise.

A further example of government defeat on matters judicial occurred when the Lords voted by 140 votes to 98 to delete a clause from the 1985 Prosecution of Offences Bill, which would have enabled the Attorney-General to refer to the Court of Appeal any sentence, imposed by a Crown Court for an indictable offence, which appeared to him to be too lenient. Such a reference would have been for an opinion, which would have constituted authoritative guidance for the courts in subsequent cases, but without altering the particular sentence in question. On this occasion the Lord Chancellor found his views rejected in debate by at least eleven peers who had substantial judicial experience, and supported only by Baroness Phillips 'speaking on behalf of various women's organisations' (26 January

1985). The Government accepted the defeat, though after further public outcry about apparent leniency in sentences for some rapists, it announced this whole matter would be included again in new legislation, and at least one peer, Lord Denning, who had spoken against the Government in 1985, declared two years later that he had changed his mind on the issue.

The third defeat inflicted in 1979–80 was entirely different again. This was the much-publicised rejection by peers of the clause in the 1980 Education Bill which would have allowed local education authorities to impose school transport charges for children in rural areas. The Government was eager to facilitate expenditure savings of some £20–30 million by this means. But the proposal offended both rural and religious interests (because children travelling to denominational schools would be particularly affected). Some local authorities announced the kind of charge they proposed to make while the bill was still before parliament, and in so doing catalysed opposition to this proposal. In the Commons thirteen Conservative MPs voted against the Government on this issue, and a further sixteen abstained. To try to head off defeat in the Lords the Government offered a compromise package (limiting charges to two children per family and so on), but to no avail. The Duke of Norfolk, a Conservative back-bench peer and well-known as a leader among Roman Catholics, led the assault (13 March 1980). He was supported by strong speeches from two former Conservative Secretaries of State for Education, Lord Butler of Saffron Walden, and Lord Boyle of Handsworth. Public interest had been aroused, and many peers spoke of their heavy mailbags on this subject. The Government went down to a convincing defeat, by 216 votes to 112 (with forty Conservatives rebelling). An attempt to reverse such a defeat in the Commons would probably have led to further humiliations for the Government, so instead ministers gave way.

This was a crucial episode in revealing the importance the House of Lords could have under the new Conservative Government. The greater readiness of back-bench MPs to rebel — a noticeable change in the Commons during the 1970s — meant that the reversal of Lords' defeats could certainly not be taken for granted by the Government. Furthermore the mail received by both peers and MPs indicated widespread resistance to the proposed change, not least among grass roots Conservative Party supporters. In most subsequent cases where the Lords inflicted significant defeats on the Government it is plausible to argue that the Conservative Party in the country was at least as sympathetic to the Lords' view as it was to the Government's.

Such an example occurred on the British Nationality Bill in 1981 over proposed treatment of Gibraltarians. By 150 votes to 112 the Lords accepted an amendment moved by Lord Bethell, a Conservative back-bench peer and a member of the European Parliament, to alter the status of Gibraltarians (22 July 1981). During the final stages of debate on this bill in the Lords, reference was made to the possibility of the Government rejecting this amendment and a constitutional crisis ensuing, but Lord Boyd-Carpenter argued that if the Government did reject the change no such crisis would occur because all the Government had to do was to wait a year and invoke the Parliament Act in order to secure the passage of the bill (HL Debs, 20 October 1981, col. 731–2). But the Government had already been under pressure in the Commons on this issue, and decided its better course was to give way to peers, which it did. By contrast on another matter upon which the Government suffered a defeat on this bill, an amendment to make discretionary decisions taken by the Home Secretary subject to appeal to the courts if an applicant alleged discrimination, the Government sought and obtained approval in the Commons to reverse the Lords' amendment. When the bill returned to the Lords, Lord Elwyn-Jones from the Labour front-bench urged peers to insist on their amendment despite its rejection by the Commons, but the Government successfully resisted this by 116 votes to 96. It is worth noting that thirteen of twenty-two Conservative peers who voted against the Government on this matter of appeals in July 1981 voted with the Government (thus reversing their former position) in October; the remaining nine stayed away. But this was an issue upon which the Government had much more solid support from its Commons backbenchers.

'Right to Buy' Legislation

A jewel in the crown of the Thatcher Government was its right-to-buy legislation, enacted for the benefit of tenants of public sector housing. To begin with the basic principle of this policy was strongly contested, but as far as the House of Lords was concerned debate focused on where the precise boundaries of this policy should be drawn. How far should central government go in enforcing such a policy, especially in areas where the only housing within the financial means of many was local authority owned? What discount should be allowed to tenants who purchased their homes? Should all accommodation, including that purpose-built or specially adapted for the elderly or disabled, be included? If local authority tenants enjoyed the right to buy, should this be extended generally to all tenants of those housing associations which had received public funds?

Three major bills were enacted, the 1980 Housing Bill, the 1984 Housing and Building Control Bill, and the 1986 Housing and Planning Bill. On each of these measures the Government suffered important defeats in the Lords which it was unable to reverse. Peers generally were inclined to impose limits on the individual's right to buy. Pressure groups such as

Shelter and Help the Aged were behind some of the more important amendments made by the Lords.

Take first the question of accommodation suited to the needs of the elderly. The 1980 Bill originally excluded from the right to buy only the tenants of 'sheltered' accommodation, that is, houses or flats with warden services or the like provided. By 109 votes to 74 the House of Lords extended this exclusion to all dwellings designed or specifically adapted for the elderly, and habitually let to them, an estimated additional 220,000 homes (21 July, 1980). The argument for such extension lay in the need to preserve such housing for occupation by the elderly; the argument against centred on the desirability of making as uniform as possible the individual's right to buy, without discrimination on the grounds of age.

Even before the 1980 Bill had completed its Lords' stage, a Government minister announced in the Commons (30 July) that this amendment would not be accepted. Peers took umbrage at this tactless treatment of their House, and marked their displeasure by initiating a further defeat on the Government in voting to adjourn their House in protest. A week later, however, the Government changed its mind and accepted the Lords' amendment, motivated to do so by a desire to see the legislation on the statute book before the summer recess.

The alteration, thus forced by the Lords, involved difficult decisions about what precise accommodation qualified as being adapted for elderly tenants. The Department of the Environment was clearly unhappy about administering the resulting rules, and the suspicion quickly arose that some unsympathetic local authorities simply advised elderly tenants that they had no right to buy their houses or flats. Should the Government seek to define the criteria used in assessing accommodation adapted for the elderly more precisely, and chase up recalcitrant local authorities? Or should it go for a radical solution, namely to extend the right to buy to all elderly persons (save those in sheltered accommodation)? After the 1983 election a new bill was introduced which initially contained no proposals on the subject. However, late in its Commons passage — at report stage — the Government introduced amendments going for the radical solution, namely extending the right to buy to all elderly tenants. Commons scrutiny of these changes was inevitably perfunctory, but in the brief debate which took place several Conservative MPs expressed disquiet. *The Times* (23 December 1983) criticised the Government, saying: 'It has slipped in important changes at an obscure stage', and urged the House of Lords to examine the bill very carefully. On 28 February 1984, an all-party initiative in the Lords led to the rejection of the Government's proposal by 113 votes to 90. Ministers then put forward a compromise — involving enhanced local authority rights of repurchase — but this was again rejected by peers, who voted 101 to 100 (10 May) to insist on their version of the bill, thereby continuing the exclusion from the right to buy of accommodation purpose-built or adapted for the elderly. A four-week hiatus followed before the Government announced its acquiescence.

Under the 1984 Act local authorities had to seek approval from the Secretary of State if they wished to retain accommodation which an elderly tenant wanted to purchase. Only in a small minority of cases did the Secretary of State withhold approval for a sale. When the 1986 Housing and Planning Bill came forward proposing further extension of the right to buy, peers sought to amend this to maintain the principle established — albeit against the Government's wishes — in the earlier legislation. Once again the Commons reversed a Lords' amendment (5 November 1986), but peers voted the following day (by 148 to 124) to insist on their amendments, and a day later, up against the sessional deadline, the Government asked the Commons to acquiesce to the Lords' views. On this occasion several back-bench Conservative MPs expressed their anger at the Upper House's intransigence: one even suggested this was 'a very black day for the constitution' (HC Debs, 5 November 1986, col. 974).

On three different occasions the House of Lords had thus prevented the Government carrying through its avowed aim of obliging local authorities to sell properties to pensionable age tenants, and twice this had involved peers voting a second time to insist on their amendments in the face of clearly expressed opposition from the Commons. It would have been possible for the Government to have used the Parliament Act to secure the passage of this legislation in the form ministers wished. But to do so would have involved delay, and in 1986, in particular, the Government was very eager to see its legislation placed quickly on the statute book because another part of the same bill involved further incentives (in the form of higher discounts) to the tenants of flats, the sale of which the Government was anxious to complete.

A similar conflict took place over accommodation for disabled people. While the 1980 Act had excluded dwellings purpose-built or adapted for the disabled, the 1983 Bill sought to extend the right-to-buy principle in this area. However, an amendment moved in the Lords by a disabled peer, Lord Ingleby, to exclude most such accommodation was carried against the Government (by 136 votes to 104 on 28 February, 1984), and this the Government decided not to try to overturn, while making clear in the Commons, on 12 April 1984, its disagreement with the Lords' decision. On this matter the Government's decision was perhaps surprising because the disabled lobby was far from united on the question, with two disabled peers speaking against the change made in the Lords.

Other aspects of the 'right to buy' legislation were impeded by the House of Lords. In 1982 the Government decided to extend the right to buy to two groups of tenants not covered by its earlier legislation, namely those whose landlords were charitable housing associations and those whose landlords owned the leasehold, but not the freehold, of their properties. Its bill to this effect, the Housing and Building Control Bill, received an almost unprecedented verbal mauling at second reading in the House of Lords, on 11 April 1983, when only one of the twenty-six non-ministerial speeches made offered any support at all for the Government. In particular it was the implied threat to charitable bodies which worried peers. The Government argued that under the 1974 Housing Association Act much public money had been put into charitable Housing Associations, and tenants of such bodies should be able to purchase their dwellings in the same way as local authority tenants. But to the Government's opponents its proposal involved the compulsory expropriation of assets held by charitable bodies, since any accommodation sold would be at a heavy discount. Lord Goodman, a prominent cross-bench peer and former Chairman of the Housing Corporation, 1973–7, argued that the bill was symptomatic of a deep-seated hostility within the Government to voluntary and charitable work. If it were passed bodies such as Guide Dogs for the Blind or St John Ambulance Brigade might be well-advised to decline help from public funds because, if such were accepted, a future government might intervene claiming the assets held by these charities really belonged to the state. At committee stage the Lords voted overwhelmingly (182 votes to 96 on 26 April 1983) to remove from the bill the right to buy for tenants of charitable housing associations, and shortly afterwards the Government announced it would not attempt to restore this proposal. The early dissolution of parliament then led to the bill's demise.

A successor bill introduced in the new parliament did not refer to charitable housing association tenants. But the Government made clear its intention to find a means to give such tenants a right to buy. Not until the day the bill — again the Housing and Building Control Bill — got its third reading in the Commons did an announcement appear, as a written parliamentary answer (21 December 1983). This outlined a scheme whereby the Government would provide to tenants of such associations funds equivalent to the discount they would have obtained if they had possessed the right to buy, which the tenants concerned could then use towards the purchase of a property on the open market. Thus the Housing Associations would not be compelled unwillingly to sell, but their tenants would not be disqualified from receiving a financial discount equivalent to that available to local authority tenants, though in this case to spend on a property of their choice on the open market.

This wholly novel scheme received its first parliamentary examination when the Lords debated government amendments at the bill's committee stage. On division at report stage the Lords narrowly approved the scheme (by 99 votes to 94) which then duly received Commons endorsement when the bill returned to the Lower House for consideration of Lords' amendments. The House of Lords had thus obliged the Government to adopt a wholly different method, from that which had originally been envisaged, to extend the right to buy to some 80,000 or so housing association tenants. In so doing it had arguably safeguarded an important principle of charity organisation.

The same bill also sought to extend the 'right to buy' to tenants whose landlords were public bodies owning the leasehold but not the freehold of their properties (some housing associations and a few local authorities were in this position). A complication arose here in that under the 1967 Leasehold Reform Act it had become possible for certain occupiers to purchase the freehold of their property against the freeholder's will. Thus, the 1983 bill in giving tenants the right to purchase their property would carry with it, ultimately, the right to purchase the freehold, and the consequences of tenants exercising these rights would, in some cases, be very considerable. At committee stage in the Lords, peers voted to exclude from this extension of the right to buy all tenants whose freehold was owned by charitable trusts (by 157 votes to 77 on 28 February 1984). The Government resisted this amendment and overturned it in the Commons, proposing instead a financial solution to the problem through increased compensation to freeholders who lost freehold property rights in this way. Back in the Lords the substance of this amendment was accepted (on 10 May) but a further defeat was inflicted on the Government when peers insisted on protection for universities as freeholders of land leased to charitable trusts (by 128 votes to 99). The Government accepted this change, though it made further detailed amendments on the point. In this the House of Lords again showed a particular concern to protect the interests of charitable trusts, though ultimately these interests were focused on a few hundred dwellings only, particularly some built on land owned by Cambridge University colleges, but let on long leases to housing associations.

The House of Lords defeated the Government in nine other divisions on its 'right to buy' housing legislation between 1979 and 1987. In some cases the Government simply reversed amendments thus made: for example, an amendment made in 1980, to reduce the discount payable to tenants. In other cases a compromise was reached: for example, on an amendment facilitating the possibility of elderly tenants taking option mortgages, also in 1980. Finally, some were accepted, notably amendments made in October 1986 to both the Housing and Planning Bill and the Housing (Scotland) Bill regarding the responsibilities of local authorities towards the homeless. In this latter case disquiet had been caused by a legal judgment in February 1986 — the *Puhlhofer* case — in which the House of Lords as Court of Appeal had found that local authorities, while responsible for housing the homeless, were legally entitled to do this in completely unsuitable accommodation (even though it was suggested in pig sties or chicken huts!). An amendment drafted by Shelter was debated in the Lords at committee and report stages of the Housing and Planning Bill, but withdrawn because ministers indicated they were considering the matter. Finally at third reading Opposition peers decided to press the amendment which was carried by 109 votes to 102 on 28 October 1986. On the following day peers were due to debate the rejection by the Commons of a similar amendment they had made earlier in the session to the Housing (Scotland) Bill, but the Government announced its willingness to climb down and accept the change the Lords had made earlier.

Notable in the treatment of legislation on housing was the determination, indeed intransigence of peers, including Conservative backbenchers. The general principle of selling public-sector housing was not in question, but what the House of Lords did was to insist on definite limits and exceptions to that principle. Lord Simon of Glaisdale, a former Lord of Appeal and a crossbencher (also a former Conservative MP and minister) expressed well the tensions felt between the House of Lords and the Government on this matter, supporting the principle of the 'right to buy' policy, but disagreeing with the 'passionate logic' which sought to carry that 'good principle into every corner of our social and legal life in the face of commonsense, humanity and all experience' (HL Debs, 10 May 1984, col. 1040).

Local Government Legislation

During the 1983–7 Parliament the House of Lords came into greater public prominence through its hostility to certain aspects of the Government's legislation affecting local authorities. Given the unitary character of the British constitution, local authorities derive their powers ultimately from Parliament, and legally these may be altered at any time by Parliament. But unwritten conventions of the constitution have customarily spoken in terms of partnership between local and central government, a mutual recognition of states and spheres of competence. Mrs Thatcher's Government took the view that some local authorities had themselves broken the terms of this partnership by, for example, failing to co-operate with government expenditure plans: her Government's response was to tighten central control over all local authorities. This process provoked strong objections from many involved in local government, Conservatives included, who felt that their problems were needlessly multiplied through continuous and thoughtless Whitehall interference. Local authorities generally found some able spokesmen for their interests in the Upper House, as well as a large number of peers with some experience of local council activity, sympathetic to their viewpoint.

The Greater London Council and the metropolitan county authorities were particular targets of Government displeasure. The Conservative manifesto of 1983 promised their abolition, but the legislation necessary for this complex process could not be brought forward until 1984. In the preceding session the Government introduced a Local Government (Interim Provisions) Bill, a 'paving' bill concerned with transitional arrangements. As part of these, the legislation included provision to cancel elections due in 1985 and to set up, in their place, bodies nominated by the relevant lower-tier authorities to run the affairs of these doomed authorities during their final year of existence. This proposal was open to criticism, not only because it involved the cancellation of elections, but because in London at least it would have entailed the replacement of a Labour-controlled GLC by a Conservative body nominated by London boroughs. The proposal was heavily criticised in the Commons (nineteen Conservatives voted against the Government at second reading on 11 April 1984). In the Lords the Government narrowly avoided defeat — by 237 votes to 217 — on a critical amendment at second reading (11 June), but then was decisively defeated (by 191 votes to 143) on a 'wrecking amendment' at committee stage (28 June), the effect of which was to prevent the cancellation of elections until the main abolition legislation had completed its parliamentary passage. This would have imposed too tight a timetable for the Government, which therefore decided to offer a compromise by allowing existing councils to run on for an extra year (rather than seek their replacement) while still cancelling elections due in 1985. Peers accepted this compromise by 248 votes to 155 on 16 July.

For the Government the ironic consequence of this was to allow the GLC leader, Ken Livingstone, a further year in office without the need for him to submit to re-election. It involved the Government seeking a whole new strategy for actually carrying through the abolition of these authorities, and one that involved much greater complexity. But the House of Lords had safeguarded what was widely perceived to be a constitutional principle, even if in so doing it had proved itself highly inconvenient to the Government. The House of Lords found itself the bemused recipient of plaudits from the Labour left (a banner on the GLC headquarters over the Thames proclaimed 'Thank you peers for saving London') and from such an organ of the establishment as The Times which declared the episode 'a triumph for the principles of constitutionalism, and specifically for the principle of a bicameral parliament' (30 June 1984).

In the following session the substantive abolition legislation appeared. On this the Government suffered four defeats in the Lords, and though none of these were matters of major importance, they did result in some quite significant changes to the legislation. In general, peers sought to strengthen the rôle of London boroughs and metropolitan districts and to limit the power of central government to regulate the subsequent activities of authorities established under the bill. For example the requirement to review the new Inner London Education Authority by 1991 and the power to make subsequent changes by parliamentary order was replaced by a power only to make a discretionary review. The Government also made some important concessions in circumstances where it might otherwise have suffered defeat, for example replacing an advisory London Planning Commission (to be appointed by Central Government) with a joint planning committee composed from the London boroughs, and also making provision for residual bodies to endow charitable trusts out of money received from the disposal of land, which was a way of enabling some continuing support to be available for voluntary organisations.

One aspect of the GLC campaign against abolition was a lavish advertising campaign. Government annoyance at the use of public funds by local authorities for 'political advertising' led to the introduction of a further Local Government Bill in 1985, the main purpose of which was to ban such material. The House of Lords made two important changes to this bill, both as a result of Government defeats. The first narrowed the scope of the prohibition proposed in the bill by removing the ban on material which 'can reasonably be regarded as likely to affect' political support, leaving a ban on material which 'appears to be designed to affect such support', a change which the Government minister argued 'would seriously undermine the effectiveness of the prohibition on party political material as a whole' (HL Debs, 18 February 1985, col. 537). The second altered the status of the code of practice to be issued by the Department of the Environment, making clear that this would be for guidance only and not obligatory for local authorities.

Because this bill also contained provisions requiring local authorities to fix their rates by 1 April each year, the Government was very anxious to see it on the statute book before the Easter recess. In the Commons there had been difficulties over the bill which had already resulted in Government concessions in order to get the bill out of standing committee early enough in the session to meet this deadline. When the bill returned again to the Commons with the Lords' changes the Government accepted them, but at the same time made clear its reluctance and its determination to return to the point again in the future (HC Debs, 25 March 1986, col. 881).

Several other bills had direct effects upon local government, and many more indirect effects. By 1987, the readiness of the House of Lords to be awkward and even intransigent over such legislation had become a definite calculation in ministers' minds as to precisely what proposals to bring forward. An example of this was the Government's decision not to bring in a major bill obliging local authorities to put their services out to competitive tender as foreshadowed in the 1986 Queen's Speech. Commenting on the announcement that the planned bill was being postponed, *The Economist* (21 February 1987) pointed to the prospect of the bill being 'ignominiously savaged in the Lords' as one factor. The same measure was supposedly to return to the subject just discussed limiting local authorities' freedom to publish political material, but this proposal also was deferred, otherwise 'the Lords would have made several breakfasts of it' (*ibid*). After securing a third election victory a bill dealing with competitive tendering was introduced in the 1987–8 session.

The Government's considerably more circumspect handling of the House of Lords (compared with its handling of the Commons) on the Teachers' Pay and Conditions Bill of 1986–7 was also noticeable. This 'emergency' measure brought forward to enable the Secretary of State to impose a pay settlement on teachers by the expedient of abolishing their right to negotiate their own salaries through their unions, was rushed through all its Commons stages in three days in December 1986. The House of Lords debated it over a four-week period in early 1987. After the bill's second reading in the Lords, the Government announced a number of concessions which (as a *Times* headline stated) appeared designed 'to head off Lords' revolt'. One issue of concern was the fact that though spoken of as a temporary measure, the bill would have allowed an interim advisory committee set up to advise the Secretary of State about teachers' pay to continue in existence indefinitely after 1990, subject only to parliamentary order by negative resolution; in other words the temporary machinery could continue until Parliament specifically voted for its abolition. Some peers wanted to amend the bill so that it would lapse completely after three years. The Government offered as a compromise that continuation would depend on a definite vote in Parliament, that is, affirmative resolution procedure (see Chapter 8, pp. 179–80). A former Clerk of the Parliaments, Lord Henderson of Brompton, remained highly critical of the bill's supposed temporary nature (embodied in the use of the word 'temporary' in the long title of the bill) alongside provision for its indefinite continuation in the body of the bill.

A second area of concern lay in the initially undefined composition of the Interim Advisory Committee. Again, before the Lords' committee stage began the Government announced its decision to amend the bill so that the committee would contain representatives of the teachers' unions and of the local authorities' association. Another amendment which had been resisted in the Commons, but which was made in response to peers' pressure, ensured that Advisory Committee reports would be published and, in response to pressure from the churches, an amendment was made ensuring participation in the consultation process by representatives of voluntary schools.

These changes were made without government defeat in the lobbies, though several other more significant amendments were resisted only through a large turn-out of Conservative loyalists. When these were debated back in the Commons the Opposition spokesman described them as 'relatively trivial', although he also paid tribute to the high quality of debate in the Upper House (HC Debs, 26 February 1987, col. 438). The changes were slight compared with the stark view taken by most of the teachers' unions and the Opposition parties of the enormity of what the Government was doing in removing teachers' negotiating rights, temporarily up to 1990, but possibly well beyond that date. Nevertheless in terms of alterations to the bill, the impact of the Lords was definitely greater than that of the Commons.

The 1985–6 Session

Finally, we take a more detailed look at the 1985–6 session. By considering every bill amended by the Lords (listed in Table 6.1) and trying to identify the source of amendments, an attempt is made to assess the impact of the House of Lords on the totality of government legislation. (In doing this use has been made of notes supplied by the Government Whips' Office which specified *all* changes made to bills in the Lords and identified the sources of amendment where possible.) In 1985–6, the House of Lords amended fifteen of the twenty-nine bills brought from the Commons, altogether making 2,165 amendments. In addition 265 amendments were made to nine bills introduced directly into the House of Lords. Each of these twenty-four bills is discussed briefly in this section, but the focus of attention is on substantive changes made to bills rather than amendments as such.

First we take Commons bills on which the Government suffered defeats in the Lords. The Housing and Planning Bill and the Housing (Scotland) Bill have already been discussed, as has the Local Government Bill. On the latter, as well as suffering the two defeats which it did not reverse (see above, p. 141), the Government made three minor concessions, all partly in response to pressure from peers, as well as fourteen other substantive changes not arising out of pressure from within the Lords.

The Government was defeated three times on the Social Security Bill, a complex and contentious measure making wide-ranging changes. An Opposition amendment providing that the full amount (rather than four-fifths) of a person's domestic rates should be taken into account when calculating entitlement to income support was narrowly carried (89 votes to 86), but the Government reversed this, and because Commons' financial privilege was asserted, peers let the matter drop. The second defeat

Table 6.1 Government Bills Subject to Amendment in the Lords, 1985–6

	Number of amendments	Number of government defeats
Commons bills		
Agriculture	68	–
Airports	118	–
Building Societies	246	–
Dockyard Services	11	1
Drug Trafficking Offences	222	–
Financial Services	784	1
Gas	34	–
Housing and Planning	339	3
Housing (Scotland)	19	4
Local Government	27	2
Museum of London	1	–
National Health Service (Amendment)	11	1
Public Order	40	–
Social Security	195	3
Wages (Confirmation of Orders)	50	–
Lords bills		
Animals (Scientific Procedures)	26	–
Commonwealth Development Corporation	1	–
Education	80	2
Family Law	3	–
Legal Aid (Scotland)	33	1
Patents, Designs and Marks	19	–
Salmon	81	–
Shops	6	1
Sex Discrimination	16	3

occurred when the Lords voted by 116 to 87 to increase financial support for some severely disabled persons living in the community, a matter raised by Alfred Morris for the Opposition in the Commons, and taken up by a cross-bench peer, Lord Henderson of Brompton, in the Lords. The Government compromised a little on this, but Lord Henderson continued to press the case for greater financial assistance whereupon the Government secured a huge attendance (458 peers at the House) on 24 July to crush his proposal by 213 votes (208 Conservatives and five Crossbenchers) to 143 (71 Labour, 36 Alliance, 34 Crossbenchers, one Bishop and one Conservative rebel). The third defeat was on an amendment moved by Lord Wigoder, a Liberal peer, which sought to maintain a supplementary benefit claimant's right of appeal to an independent tribunal, a right abolished by the bill. Though the Government compromised slightly, it refused to grant a right of appeal to an independent body. Lord Wigoder (like Lord Henderson) moved that the House should insist on its amendment, but his motion to that effect was also voted down (by 202 votes to 113).

At least four other minor, but substantive, changes were made to this bill in the Lords, three of which were attributable to parliamentary pressure in both Houses and one to pressure from local authorities. A few other miscellaneous amendments agreed by the Government were also made.

A change that the Opposition had tried but failed to make to the National Health Service (Amendment) Bill in the Commons was carried by 110 votes to 86 in the Lords, and accepted by the Government. The presence of some leading Conservative peers in the Opposition lobby and the fact that time was short because this occurred late in the session (15 October) were probable factors that encouraged ministerial acquiescence. The amendment in question extended the removal of Crown immunity so that not just hospital kitchens were affected, but other hospital premises. Two other minor changes were made to the bill in response to parliamentary pressure, as well as some technical government amendments.

The Financial Services Bill was a lengthy and complex measure imposing a new legislative framework on the City and viewed as a necessary prerequisite for deregulation — the so-called 'big bang' — which occurred as the bill was completing its parliamentary stages. The Government was under pressure from the Opposition and from numerous city interests. Difficulties and government defeats occurred in the Commons, and in the Lords a very large number of government amendments had to be debated in a very short space of time. Many government concessions were made as a direct result of the need to secure Opposition co-operation to get the final stages of the bill dealt with quickly. For example, an ombudsman-type procedure to examine complaints against the newly-established Securities and Investment Board was accepted despite earlier resistance. Extensive new provisions were introduced dealing with investor compensation, and with enforceable contracts. These were issues on which the Government definitely gave ground in order to safeguard its timetable for this bill. There was only one defeat in the division lobby when an Opposition amendment to ensure adequate independent representation on the governing bodies of new self-regulatory organisations charged with overseeing the City's financial institutions was carried. Because of time pressure, the Government decided not to try to reverse this. All told the House made 582 amendments to the bill, debated and accepted over two days in the Commons.

The final Commons bill on which the Government suffered defeat in the Lords was the Dockyard Services Bill. Lord Denning moved an amendment which provided trade unions with an avenue of complaint to the courts if they felt the Secretary of State had failed to consult them as required by the

Act. The Government accepted this change, though with some apprehension about its possible effect. In December 1986, it was reported to be the cause of embarrassment to ministers in their negotiations to 'privatise' the Rosyth Naval base.

No government defeat took place on any other bill brought from the Commons, though many amendments were made to several. For example, the Building Societies Bill went back to the Commons with 246 amendments, but only twenty of these were really attributable to peers themselves, and these twenty together made five minor changes to the bill. Perhaps the most important was an amendment altering from negative to affirmative procedure any order imposing a duty on auditors to provide information to the Building Societies Commissioners (see pp. 179–80).

A total of 222 Lords' amendments were made to the Drug Trafficking Offences Bill, but only two were the result of points raised in the House, both useful improvements agreed by the Government after first being raised by Opposition or cross-bench peers.

Of 118 amendments made to the Airports Bill, 109 resulted from either promises previously given in the Commons, or were the result of policy changes or were technical or drafting improvements. The remaining nine could be attributed to peers, mainly in this case government backbenchers. They made four small changes to the bill which basically had the effect of expanding the obligations and powers of the Government in minor ways.

A total of fifty-two amendments were made to the Agriculture Bill of which some fourteen were attributed in whole, or in part, to the influence of peers themselves, the remainder resulting from undertakings given in the Commons, or simply to second thoughts within government. Among the matters covered by the Bill to which amendments were made, at least in part due to the initiative of peers, were the detailed arrangements for the transfer of milk quotas, the statutory basis for the continuation of the Agricultural Advisory Service (commercialised by the bill) and the monitoring of environmentally sensitive areas.

Though none of the Opposition amendments pressed to divisions on the Wages Bill were carried, some significant concessions were made by the Government on this measure, the basic purpose of which was to abolish the powers of wages councils. For example, amendments were passed protecting the rights of workers to holidays and holiday pay entitlement accrued before the protection of wages councils was withdrawn. Opposition pressure in the Commons was responsible for another set of amendments introduced in the Lords which specified that employers must notify homeworkers of their minimum legal entitlement, as well as workers on employers' premises.

Peers made forty amendments to the Public Order Bill, some of which also involved government concessions on substantive points. For example, an Opposition amendment moved by Lord Elwyn-Jones reducing the maximum sentence for riot from life imprisonment to ten years was accepted. Government back-bench peers pressed for more effective controls on aggravated trespass (following hippy convoy incidents which took place while the bill was before the Lords) and were partially rewarded. However, the Opposition failed to have the new offence of disorderly conduct removed from the bill, and was no more successful in its attempts to have an appeal system set up to allow for appeals against conditions imposed by senior police officers on assemblies and processions.

Opposition pressure to amend the Gas Bill also met with little success. All told 630 amendments were debated at various stages but only thirty-four were agreed by the Lords. The main changes concerned the interests of Gas consumers. In the Commons the Government had resisted proposals to include regional and small business representation on the new Gas Consumer Council, but in the Lords, ground was given on these points. Another change was intended to provide extra safeguards for the elderly and disabled. But attempts at more meaty changes, for example, concerning the basic structure of the regulatory framework for the gas industry or the provision of a formula to constrain the price of gas, were unavailing.

The final Commons bill amended in the Lords was the Museum of London Bill. A government undertaking made at Commons committee stage was honoured when an amendment making obligatory the publication of regular reports on the activities of the museums was included.

Among bills unamended by the House of Lords, the most notable was the European Communities (Amendment) Bill, which incorporated in UK law provisions agreed by the EC heads of government in a treaty known as the Single European Act. In the Commons, the bill was guillotined and no amendments were made. In the Lords, Lord Denning threatened to precipitate a crisis by moving amendments supposedly safeguarding British sovereignty, the effect of which would have been a repudiation of the Single European Act Treaty. The Government successfully crushed his 'wrecking' amendment by 176 votes to 52.

Of the nine government bills introduced into the Lords to which amendments were made, four involved government defeats. One of these was the Shops Bill, upon which the Government successfully resisted amendments aimed at placing limits on retail trading on Sundays, but suffered a one-vote defeat on an aspect of shop-worker protection. This was not seen as vital, but since the bill was subsequently lost at second reading in the Commons, change became otiose.

The Sex Discrimination Bill removed various statutory restrictions on women's hours of work and altered previous legislation to conform with judgments made by the European Court of Justice. Opposition amendments carried on division resulted in two new clauses. One of these (carried by 99 votes to 95) resisted the straightforward repeal of legislation protecting women's working conditions, stipulating instead that equal conditions for men and women should prevail. Another (carried by 95 votes to 92) gave employees affected by the bill a right to claim for unfair dismissal. A third government defeat in the division lobby was on an amendment moved by a back-bench Conservative, Baroness Platt of Writtle (Chairman of the Equal Opportunities Commission), which imposed on employers a duty to consult over substantial changes in hours of work, and to safeguard the health, safety and welfare interests of all employees (especially those, of either sex, with domestic and family responsibilities). All these amendments were rejected by the Government in the Commons, much to the disappointment of Baroness Platt. Some other Lords' amendments were accepted by the Government, including one moved by Baroness Platt, which removed the exemption from sex discrimination legislation of partnerships of five or fewer persons in their treatment of partners.

A further important bill introduced into the Lords in this session was the Education Bill, originally concerned with school governing bodies and teacher effectiveness. This bill was eventually likened to a Christmas tree because it became festooned with extra provisions as it progressed through parliament. Baroness Cox, who had been briefly a member of Mrs Thatcher's Government, led a Conservative rebellion which resulted in government defeat on an amendment forbidding partisan political activities in primary schools. Another defeat occurred when the House voted, albeit narrowly to 94 votes to 92, to forbid corporal punishment in state schools and thus comply with a 1982 European Court of Human Rights judgment. In the previous session the Government had abandoned an Education Bill following a Lords' defeat on this subject. This time ministers decided to allow a free vote in the Commons, in which abolition was upheld by a majority of one.

Sex education was another subject upon which the Government was forced to give ground, bringing in an amendment at third reading which stipulated that sex education must be given within a moral framework; in the Commons, substantial further changes were made transferring control over sex education to governing bodies. The Government was forced to withdraw an amendment at third reading in the Lords, the purpose of which was, supposedly, to safeguard free speech in universities. Peers expressed anger that the new clause was only published on the Friday preceding their debate on it on Monday 2nd June. Some university vice-chancellors publicly expressed dismay at the Government's failure to consult on the details of this proposal. The Government withdrew the clause, but reintroduced it when the bill was in the Commons. Peers then held an anxious two-hour debate on it as a Commons amendment, with the balance of vice-chancellorial opinion going against the Government. Baroness Young ended her defence of the clause by appealing to peers not to send the 'wrong signal' from the Lords, but most of those with experience of university administration were less concerned with sending out signals than having a basically unenforceable statutory provision placed upon them. In the background was the knowledge that if the Lords rejected the clause, time for compromise was short, and the Prime Minister was reported to be personally determined to see the clause enacted (*The Times*, 31 October 1986). Peers approved the change by 129 votes to 78.

Altogether the House made eighty amendments to the Education Bill, but on several points the Government gave undertakings in the Lords to bring forward changes in the Commons, which contributed to the total of 130 amendments made by MPs, to all of which peers agreed.

The only other Lords' bill on which the Government suffered a defeat was the Legal Aid (Scotland) Bill when an Opposition amendment deleted a clause limiting the availability of legal aid in certain criminal cases. The clause was restored in the Commons, and peers did not contest the matter further. Again, as well as some twelve minor changes being made to the bill in the Lords (involving thirty amendments), several further government amendments were introduced in the Commons as a result of undertakings made to peers.

A bill dealing with a highly-sensitive subject was the Animals (Scientific Procedures) Bill. This measure was the product of much inquiry and discussion before the bill was drafted (see Chapter 8), but seven significant, if minor, changes were made during its parliamentary passage, two in the Lords and five in the Commons, though again the Commons amendments were all foreshadowed during peers' debates on this bill.

Remaining legislation introduced in the Lords included the Salmon Bill (debated very thoroughly), the Patents Bill (to which only drafting amendments were made), and the Family Law Bill (to which the Government made a single change in response to Labour and cross-bench pressure). None of the amendments to these bills were important.

Conclusion

What can be concluded from this somewhat cursory examination of the treatment of government legislation? First we do well to remind ourselves of the sheer complexity of the legislative process. Almost any proposal made by government has repercussions for numerous groups and identifiable interests within society. Many of these become involved in the legislative process, not infrequently dealing directly with government departments. Some also alert MPs and peers to their concerns, who in turn may press these upon government. Part of this activity takes place within parliament, during the formal legislative stages of a bill. But the parliamentary stages may be likened to the visible tip of the iceberg, nine-tenths of which lies beyond public view. Nevertheless a study of what is public and visible can help develop our appreciation of what goes on elsewhere.

The fact that the initiative for most successful amendments to bills lies outside of parliament does not diminish the importance of parliamentary proceedings. Where these are accepted by government (and frequently then introduced as government amendments), a public explanation of the change made has to be given in parliament, and this is subject to debate and criticism. Where government resists amendments, and these are pressed upon it during parliamentary proceedings, the arguments both for and against proposed changes are ventilated. The fact that most of such debate is of no interest to the public (and often beyond the comprehension of all but a few experts in that field) does not invalidate its importance. Interest group leaders interpret what goes on to their members, just as government seeks to develop a favourable view of the position it takes among the interested and informed (the 'specific publics' involved). But this must not be taken as implying too ordered and rational a view of the whole legislative process. Interest groups sometimes completely fail to notice the possible effect of a bill within their area of concern, and much of what goes on in parliament, especially in the part-time House of Lords, is a matter of accident or luck rather than deliberate plan or foresight.

Paradoxically the value of the House of Lords in the legislative process appears to lie precisely in its complementarity to the Commons, based as this is on the former's non-elected (and undemocratic) character. It is the less party-political character of the House which is the single most important fact differentiating its legislative rôle. On any item of legislation some peers at least approach it devoid of a party stance, while many who basically subscribe to government or main opposition party views do so with considerably greater flexibility than their Commons counterparts. The expert, the political and the truly lay contributors all mingle in the House of Lords, and in so doing almost invariably seek to exert influence over legislation rather than contest power.

The House of Lords has a value to the government first, because it enables parliamentary debate on some bills to start elsewhere than in the Commons, and this offers a helpful flexibility, especially in relation to bills the party-political significance of which is slight or non-existent. Second, the House is useful to the government as a kind of legislative long-stop, enabling ministers to introduce amendments fulfilling undertakings given in the Commons, or at least brooding on arguments and counterarguments put forward at earlier stages, and having the time for further opportunities for discussion and consideration of the interests involved. In 1969, Richard Crossman suggested that if no second chamber existed the Commons would need at least two further stages for dealing with legislation. There seems little reason to dissent from that judgement today.

But the House of Lords is also useful to the Opposition, and indeed to many outside groups of all kinds. It is true that debate in the Lords can be repetitive of what has already been fully discussed in the Commons. But frequently debate in one House does, so to speak, clear the ground in relation to a particular bill, and enable debate in the second House to focus more sharply on particular provisions and possible changes. Exploring possible options for change, and their various consequences, is arguably an activity best carried out by two separate bodies over an extended period of time, with several opportunities being given for possible amendments to be made. It is often parliamentary debate which first alerts outside groups to the potential effect of a bill on their interests, and the opportunity to raise issues through the second House is important to them. Most changes made to bills appear very minor, but their importance to particular groups can easily be under-estimated. At the same time some significant changes are made, and appear to be made as a result of pressure focused on and through the House of Lords. This has clearly been the case with the 'right to buy' housing legislation.

The whole legislative process is far too subtle to permit any simple quantifiable index of the comparative influence of the two chambers (or of outside bodies) to be constructed. But detailed examination of the rôle of the Lords in getting particular changes made to bills shows that this has grown significantly in recent years. By 1987 the impact of the Upper House in amending the actual content of bills was widely recognised to be greater than that of the House of Commons.

7

THE DELIBERATIVE WORK OF THE HOUSE

One of the main functions which the Bryce Commission, in 1918, considered to be appropriate to the House of Lords was the discussion of general subjects connected with the Government's stewardship. Repeatedly since then this aspect of the work of the Lords has been emphasised. The White Paper on Lords' Reform in 1968 identified six main functions, the first of which was 'the provision of a forum for full and free debate on matters of public interest'. As a check upon the Executive, a body which discusses what the Government is doing, or is failing to do; has done or has not done; ought to do or ought not to do, the House of Lords has functions which closely parallel those of the House of Commons. The House of Lords spends something over one-third of its time debating motions and dealing with questions. What kinds of subject are dealt with? How important is this activity and who is influenced by it? Does the House of Lords deserve the high reputation it is often accorded for the quality of its debates? These are matters dealt with in this chapter.

Parliamentary Debate

In some fundamental respects the activity of debate is similar in both Houses of Parliament. Crucial is the fact that the government is obliged to define its attitude to the subjects raised in motions or in questions. It is this obligation on government to state its view, to argue its case, to defend its policy, which is the distinctive feature of *parliamentary* debate. Outside of parliament, government has no such direct obligation, and while within parliament government spokesmen may evade or vacillate or even contradict each other, none the less the fact remains that their responses are taken as authoritative indications of the government's attitude to an issue. To an important extent, speeches made during a debate serve to provide the context within which the adequacy, or otherwise, of the government's position can be assessed. That is a major purpose of debate. In preparing to reply to a debate a minister — and perhaps even more important his advisers — are required to consider arguments brought to bear against the government's position. The realisation that there are relevant facts unthought of by government, implications of policies unanticipated by government, perhaps policy ideas which deserve more serious attention by government — any of these can result from debate.

Beyond parliament and government the influence of debate is exceedingly hard to determine. Only a tiny fraction of the public pay any continuing attention to what goes on in either House of Parliament, but this fact must not be taken as proof that parliamentary debate has no influence on the electorate. Particular interest groups and specialised media do give attention to what is said there on specific subjects, and these in turn influence a wider public. Furthermore, the mass media's coverage of political news is to some extent shaped by parliamentary activity. It is not simply a matter of how much news about parliament is reported, but also a question of the extent to which journalists, feature writers, producers of documentary programmes and so on make use of parliamentary proceedings in researching topics. While the whole process of influence is difficult to analyse, just as the nature of public opinion is hard to define, it is reasonable to argue parliamentary debate is not without some influence on the electorate.

If the House of Lords, in principle, shares with the Commons the fact that through debate the government must publicly define its view of subjects discussed, and that in doing so both government and public may be influenced by the activity of debate, there are also important differences between the two Houses. Crucial is the fact that the Commons may still aspire to the exercise of political power, while the Lords can only hope to exert influence. The government is responsible to the Commons in the sense that it must retain its majority in the Commons in order to survive. A motion of no confidence in the government has a place in the Commons, but such a motion would be meaningless (and offensive) in the Lords. While in a formal sense the government may not be obliged to comply with a motion specifying some action by the Executive passed in the Commons, it nevertheless finds a motion of this sort passed by the Lords much easier to ignore than one passed by the Commons. While the government is responsible to the Commons because it is ultimately removable by the Commons, it is in effect only answerable to the Lords.

The junior status of the House of Lords in political terms inevitably results in its debates being accorded very much less public attention than those of the Commons. But so long as it exists it cannot be ignored, and in recent years it has almost certainly been gaining rather than losing importance. Among the distinctive characteristics of the House which, it can be argued, enhance its rôle as a debating chamber are the presence of a wide range of expertise and a degree of procedural flexibility unparalleled in the Commons.

Table 7.1   Non-Legislative Debate and Questions, 1984–5

	Total number	Total time (hours)	Time as a percentage of total time in session
Motion for address (Queen's Speech debate)	1	20	2.0
Motions to 'take note'			
Government (see Table 7.5)	3	20	2.0
EC committee reports	9	21	2.0
Science and technology committee reports ⎱ see Table 7.4	2	7	0.6
Motions for resolution			
Government (see Table 7.5)	1	5	0.5
Other (see Table 7.5 and Table 7.2)	4	20	2.0
Motions for papers	37	132	12.8
of which 'balloted motions' (Table 7.3)	14	32	3.1
Unstarred questions	45	68	6.6
Motions on subordinate[a] *legislation* (excl. motions for approval and prayers)	7	15	1.5
Ministerial statements[b]	104	43	4.2
Starred (oral) questions	576	61	5.8
Total		411	40.0

Notes: [a] Motions on subordinate legislation included debate on one motion on the Statement of Charges in Immigration Rules (25 October 1985) which was not technically a statutory instrument.
[b] Ministerial statements; three further statements were not made orally, but were printed in *Hansard*.

The procedures available for debate and for the asking of questions have already been outlined in Chapter 4. Table 7.1 categorises all non-legislative debate and questions in the 1984–5 session. Debate can take place on motions, and also on unstarred questions at the end of the day's business. Though debate as such does not take place on ministerial statements, comment and questions are allowed, and in practice a kind of 'mini-debate' in effect takes place. Both ministerial statements and private notice questions have been discussed in Chapter 4. Peers sometimes wish to debate a statutory instrument without in any way threatening the use of the formal power the House of Lords possesses to kill such instruments; in such cases motions may be put down and votes can take place which register the opinion of the House on an instrument. In a formal sense this is non-legislative debate, and so is included here, though discussed in Chapter 8.

Debate on Motions

Tables 7.2 to 7.5 give information about all debates on motions in the 1984–5 session. Taking first motions debated in time allocated to the parties, these are usually full-day debates (with no time limit) held on Wednesdays and formulated as motions for papers. However, parties may decide to use their 'Wednesday' to hold two separate debates, in which case a 2½ hour time limit will apply to both. They may also decide not to use the supposedly neutral 'motion for papers' form, but instead to put down a motion for resolution, in which case the debate will terminate with a vote (unless the Lords accepts the motion without a division). A procedure allowing a five-hour time limit to debates is also available, which has the advantage of fixing the finishing time for a debate. This can be of particular value if a vote is anticipated. In the 1984–5 session the Labour Opposition used its second Wednesday (12 December) for a debate on unemployment for which it put down a motion for resolution. A five-hour time limit was applied, and when the debate ended shortly before 8.00 p.m. the motion was lost by 105 to 134 votes (the motion stated 'This House recognises the human misery and waste caused by current unemployment of labour and resources; deplores the lack of urgency shown by HMG in tackling this problem, and calls for a statement of the positive steps to be taken to enable available labour to be used to meet undoubted national needs'). In this case the Government clearly felt it necessary to resist the motion, but when a Liberal peer's motion calling for the repeal of Section 2 of the Official Secrets Act was debated on 20 March, ministers did not resist and the motion was accepted without a division.

How the 'Wednesdays' are used and the choice of subjects debated are matters decided by the parties. When the Conservative Party was in Opposition prior to 1979 the front-bench decided; since 1979 the Association of Conservative Peers (see pages 72–3) have decided on a draft motion, which is then always shown to the Chief Whip who may then consult the Government department concerned and subsequently lean a little on the ACP Committee to try and ensure a form of wording congenial

Table 7.2 Motions Debated in Time Allocated to Parties, 1984–5

Date	Party	Peer	Subject of motion	Time (hours)	No. of speakers
11 Nov.	Lab	Birk	Central and local government	6	23
21 Nov.	Cross-B.	Sherfield	Research councils	4½	17
5 Dec.	Cons	Boyd-Carpenter	Civil Service	5½	19
12 Dec.	Lab	Cledwyn of Penrhos	Unemployment*	5	30
23 Jan.	Lab	Beswick	Social and economic policies	10¼	43
30 Jan.	Lib/SDP	Harris of Greenwich	Drug trafficking*	2½	24
		Mayhew	Strategic Defence Initiative (SDI)	2½	11
6 Feb.	Cons	Renton	Civil Defence	5	21
13 Feb.	Lab	Jeger	National Health Service	6½	23
20 Feb.	Cross-B	Henderson of Brompton	A disability council	2½	18
		Hunter of Newington	Pharmaceutical industry	2	9
6 March	Lab	Jenkins of Putney	Arts and broadcasting	6½	24
20 March	Lib/SDP	Wigoder	Official secrets legislation*	5	20
3 April	Lab	Barnett	Budget proposals and unemployment	5	21
10 April	Cons	Boardman	Wealth creation and employment	5	20
23 April	Cons	Home of the Hirsel	USSR and the West	6½	27
1 May	Lab	Lockwood	Women in public life	2½	12
		John Mackie	Rural areas policy	2½	14
8 May	Cross-B	Allen of Abbeydale	Compensation for personal injuries	2¼	10
		Shannon	Industry Year, 1986	2½	14
15 May	Lib/SDP	Rochester	Trade union ballots	2½	12
		Kennet	SDI and NATO	2½	10
5 June	Cons	Thorneycroft	Privatisation and wealth creation	4½	14
19 June	Lab	Jeger	Social Security review	5½	19

Notes: These debates were all held on Wednesdays, except that on Monday 23 April, the debate held on that day having been postponed from 13 March because of the death of the Soviet Leader Chernenko on 10 March.
    * Motions for resolution (all others were motions for papers).

to the Government. On the Labour side the front-bench decide after discussion at the weekly party meeting, but when the party is in office, the Labour Peers' Co-ordinating Committee is responsible for the choice. Clearly many subjects are chosen with an eye to the anticipated political mileage the debate may offer to one or other party. Sometimes this is a matter of timing, for example, the two debates in April 1985 were held very much in the shadow of the budget, and provided peers with opportunity to debate the Government's economic strategy.

Some motions are worded in such a way as to express a definite point of view, for example Lord Beswick's motion on 23 January (which was also longer than most); it called 'attention to the need for HMG to develop economic and social policies which unite the nation; which aim at directly creating employment rather than reducing taxation; which give new life to national pride in our welfare state and encourage motives of social responsibility rather than self-interest'. This was in fact the first fully televised debate, and that fact no doubt accounted for the unusually large number of speakers. More often motions are quite neutral in form, for example 'to call attention to the relations between central and local government' (Baroness Birk, 14 November). Sometimes a motion is debated prior to the introduction of a bill, in an effort to develop opinion about a subject with a view to amendments being made to the expected legislation. Baroness Cox introduced a debate on politicisation in education shortly before the arrival of the 1986 Education Bill, which was subsequently amended heavily by the House (see Chapter 6).

It is noticeable that on a Labour motion there are usually fewer Conservative than Labour speakers, and *vice versa*. Sometimes the imbalance is very marked, as for example when only two Conservatives (one a Government minister) spoke compared with eleven Labour speakers on Baroness Jeger's motion on Social Security review on 19 June. When Lord Boardman (an ex-Conservative minister) moved a motion calling attention 'to the obstacles imposed by legislative and administrative action which inhibit the creation of wealth and opportunities for employment' on 17 April, thirteen Conservative peers contributed but only three Labour peers.

Table 7.3 lists all balloted motions debated in the 1984–5 session. The ballot is one for motions already placed on the order paper, so peers enter it simply by putting down a motion. As can be seen a very wide range of subjects were thus debated. The shortest 'short' debate of the session was held on Lord Massereene and Ferrard's motion on 'recent developments in natural medicine' on 27 February, with only six other peers taking part. No time limits for speeches were necessary on that occasion. Sometimes, however, so many peers wish to speak in 'short debates' that each speech can only be four or five minutes in length.

Table 7.3   Balloted (Two and-a-Half-Hours) Debates, 1984–5

Date	Peer	Party	Subject of motion	No. of speakers
28 Nov.	Balfour of Inchyre	Cons	Unemployment: factors of special disadvantage	9
28 Nov.	Annan	Cross-B	Books: production and sale	14
19 Dec.	Houghton of Sowerby	Lab	Rôle of House of Lords	12
19 Dec.	Lloyd of Hampstead	Cross-B	Films policy	12
16 Jan.	Molloy	Lab	World disarmament	8
16 Jan.	Jenkins of Putney	Lab	UK–USA relationship	11
27 Feb.	Buckmaster	Cross-B	Refugees and Third World	12
27 Feb.	Massereene and Ferrard	Cons	Natural medicine	7
27 March	Somers	Cross-B	The railway system	12
27 March	Hatch of Lusby	Lab	Third World starvation	16
24 April	Fisher of Rednal	Lab	Housing investment and the homeless	11
24 April	Reay	Cons	Chemical weapons	9
22 May	Parry	Lab	Tourism and the economy	11
22 May	Chelwood	Cons	Arab–Israeli dispute and EC	13

Table 7.4   Debates on Select Committee Reports, 1984–5

Date	Peer	Party	Subject of debate	Time (hours)	No. of speakers
15 Nov.	Gregson	Lab	Health and hygiene[a]	2¾	10
15 Nov.	Kings Norton	Cross-B	Road Transport[b]	1¼	6
29 Nov.	Scarman	Cross-B	EC Commission's Power[b]	2½	7
11 March	Plowden	Cross-B	Common Fisheries Policy[b]	2¼	11
25 March	Gregson	Lab	New technologies[a]	4	15
25 March	Seebohm	Cross-B	Parental leave[b]	1½	7
22 April	Nathan	Cross-B	Lead in petrol[b]	1½	8
25 July	Rochdale	Cons	Air transport[b]	2¾	10
21 Oct.	Kearton	Cross-B	European Union[b]	4	15
21 Oct.	Plowden	Cross-B	Common Agricultural Policy	4½	16

Notes: [a] Science and Technology Committee Report.
           [b] European Communities Committee Report.
           All on motions to take note.

Motions for short debate tend to be worded in a way that indicates the particular concern of the peer who has put down the motion, and are therefore frequently more specific than motions for unlimited-time debates. In this respect they are more like unstarred questions. These procedures do give back-bench peers the chance to raise subjects which their party leaders or more senior colleagues would definitely not choose.

Debates are usually arranged on all major select committee reports without much difficulty (Table 7.4). The Chairman of the committee (or subcommittee) concerned customarily introduces the debate, and several other members of the committee usually take part. The holding of such debates gives an opportunity for other peers, knowledgeable on the subject, to add their weight to — or make their criticism of — the report concerned, and of course, the Government must provide a reply in the form of a front-bench speech. About a quarter of all speeches made in these debates in 1984–5 were from the cross-benches, a much higher proportion than in other debates. This is indicative of the significant rôle crossbenchers play in select committees.

Other motions debated in the same session are listed in Table 7.5. The Lords always debates the defence estimates though usually on a single day rather than over two days. Most major government reports will be debated on take-note motions. In 1982 the House of Lords debated the Falklands situation on government 'take note' motions four times. Amendments to such motions have been moved and voted on, though this is unusual and probably contrary to practice (for example on 5 February 1973, when the House rejected by 92 votes to 52 a Labour amendment to a Government motion on 'The Programme for Controlling Inflation').

The forty-five unstarred questions debated in 1984–5 are too many to list. In scope they varied widely. Sometimes quite specific questions are asked, for example on the state of repair of piers on the Firth of Clyde (22 November 1984) or the case of Annie Maquire's conviction and sentence (Lord Fitt, 17 May 1985). Other are very broad, for example, 'Are HMG satisfied with the consequences of their Aid Policy'? (28 March 1985). This latter resulted in the longest debate on an unstarred question of the session, almost three hours with thirteen speeches; the shortest debate lasted 30 minutes and dealt with import of books from Argentina. Always unstarred questions come last in the day's business. Peers anxious to initiate a debate under this procedure will discuss with the Chief Whip's office the possibility of finding a suitable day when other business can be expected to finish at a reasonable hour. In 1984–5, on only six occasions did debate on an unstarred question commence after 9.00 p.m.

This procedure does allow debates to be arranged at short notice so the Lords can respond quickly to some new event or controversy. It is a highly flexible procedure. Among the topics debated in 1984–5 were the

Table 7.5 Other Motions Debated, 1984–5

Date	Peer	Party		Subject of motion	Time (hours)	No. of speakers
7 Nov.	Young	Govt	Queen's	Foreign affairs	7¾	29
8 Nov.	Elton	Govt	Speech	Home and social affairs	4½	17
13 Nov.	Gowrie	Govt	Debate	Economy and industry	6¾	24
10 Dec.	Young	Govt		Future of Hong Kong[a]	5¼	18
11 Feb.	Trefgarne	Govt		Airport inquiries[b]	5¼	25
22 April	Shackleton	Lab		Falkland Islands[c]	3¾	13
26 June	Trefgarne	Govt		Defence estimates[b]	9¼	37
3 July						
5 July	Trefgarne	Govt		Airports policy[b]	4¼	17
22 July	Soames	Cons		Televising House of Lords[a]	3½	23
29 Oct.	Canterbury	Archbishop		UN: 40th Anniversary[c]	4	16

Notes: [a] Motion for resolution.
[b] Motion to take note.
[c] Motion for papers.

withdrawal of the pound note; the Commons Public Accounts Committee Report on de Lorean; Custodial Provision for Female Offenders; and Nicaragua. Labour peers initiated fifteen such debates, including seven from front-bench spokesmen, Conservative and Alliance peers thirteen apiece and cross-bench peers four. Compared with Commons daily adjournment debates the obvious differences are the varied length and timing of such debates and the relative (though not complete) absence of constituency-type subjects.

The Character of Debate

Under all these procedures the word 'debate' is in some ways a misnomer. Typically a motion (or unstarred question) gives rise to a series of speeches, each carefully prepared and often read almost verbatim. Succeeding speeches may deal with wholly diverse aspects of a subject. References made to other speeches are as likely to be personal — congratulations, reminiscences and so on — as to be substantive arguments. Peers seldom interrupt each other's speeches, much less often than in the Commons. A quite irrelevant or highly provocative speech may pass without comment, though if criticism is made this can be all the more effective in the Lords for the scrupulously polite way in which it is put.

The House of Lords in general appreciates speeches that are brief, relevant and based on real knowledge of the subject under debate. Among active peers many take a kind of professional pride in making original and pithy speeches, but by no means all are so disciplined. Much is made of the expertise the House possesses, and on many subjects the Lords can boast several 'authorities' among its membership. Most debates contain speeches from two or three peers recognised as experts, and perhaps from several more with some kind of direct personal experience of the subject. Equally, however, most debates attract speeches from some peers who are recognised in the House as bores with nothing significant to say. Sometimes it is noticeable that those peers best-informed about a certain subject do not speak on that topic in a debate.

It is the initiator of a debate whose contribution is generally of greatest significance regarding the quality of that debate. He will usually contact a number of other peers from all political groups in the House who are recognised as particularly knowledgeable in the area concerned. He may discuss with such peers particular points which might be raised in the debate, and include in his opening speech some kind of lead for peers who are to speak later. He will very likely contact the government spokesman concerned giving some advance warning of questions he will be posing, as indeed may other participants. Extensive contacts with outside groups may all be part of his preparation too.

Compared with the Commons the significantly less party political character of the Upper House gives its debates a very different flavour. Even where subjects have been chosen by parties anxious to use a debate to advance a party cause, contributions will usually be made from cross-benchers, many of whom are genuinely apolitical. Speeches are always made from the party front-benches, but party spokesmen often give themselves more latitude than their Commons' counterparts, and back-benchers may blatantly contradict party policy. The House of Lords contains peers recognised as spokesmen for various groups, who will receive detailed briefing prior to a debate, and perusal of specialised media suggests increased attention being given to the reporting of Lords' debates. Peers do attend debates in which they are not participants in greater numbers than MPs attend Commons' debates. The relatively junior ministerial status of most Government spokesmen who reply to debates may in part be counter-balanced by the presence of ex-cabinet ministers, permanent secretaries, judges, eminent scholars or captains of industry, a feature which contrasts sharply with the Commons' Chamber. The fact that debates can be televised, and that extracts from speeches are regularly shown in edited programmes on the work of the House adds a new dimension to Lords' debates.

Assessment of Debates

But how influential are such debates? The major target of influence must be the Government. To this end the fact of Government answerability in the Lords is important. Peers are different from other citizens in that they have unique opportunities to engage the Government in public debate. By no means all choose to do this, and by no means all have the skill or knowledge to do this effectively. But some do. A former service peer explained in interview that he values his membership of the Lords because 'If I were not a peer they (the Government) could fob me off'. A former Permanent Under Secretary (Lord Allen of Abeydale) has campaigned in the Lords on a number of issues which fall in the ambit of his previous department, the Home Office. His questions and speeches on some topics have undoubtedly had repercussions within the Government, for example, the provision of regional secure units. Other individual peers use Lords' procedures to worry away at the Government over the years on particular subjects with some measure of success. Examples would include: Baroness Burton of Coventry on civil aviation and consumer matters generally; Lord Houghton of Sowerby on animal welfare; Lord Melchett on certain environmental and planning issues; and Baroness Masham of Ilton on the disabled.

Success may depend, to a considerable extent, on how a peer follows up a debate. The mover of a motion may be asked to go and see the senior minister concerned. One peer, after what he felt was a rotten response from a Foreign Office Minister of State to a debate on World Hunger, went to see the Minister for Overseas Development and felt he got much further. Another peer, feeling he had a similar poor response, wrote to the Lords minister concerned and asked for a more considered reply. After interminable delay he got what he described as a 'hopeless' letter back, so wrote again sharply saying his points had obviously not been understood, but that rather than prolonging the correspondence he would put down further questions in the House. He then received a much more satisfactory letter from the Secretary of State.

If a motion specifying some action is carried against the Government, ministers are not thereby obliged to carry out that action. On the other hand to fail to do so may expose the Government to further unwelcome public criticism. Some examples may help. The Government's decision to establish a trading fund basis for the Ordnance Survey was criticised in the House, and on 9 February 1983 a motion moved by Lord Shackleton 'urging HMG to refer this proposal to the new advisory board for the Ordnance Survey before laying the relevant order' was carried by 104 votes to 74. The following month the Government announced that it would do this, and in due course a report was received which recommended against the Government's proposals, following which the Government announced, in January 1984, that it would not proceed with them.

Another example concerns cuts in external services of the BBC. Proposals for such cuts were (again) announced on 25 June 1981; a debate on an adjournment motion took place in the Commons on 23 July, but without a division. On 30 July, after a five-hour debate in the Lords (during which only five out of over thirty speakers supported the Government) the House voted by 82 to 45 'calling upon HMG to reconsider its instruction to the BBC to impose cuts'. Back in the Commons, on 26 October, a further debate took place on an Opposition motion during which the Government announced a compromise, and in so doing won the support of some wavering Conservative MPs, and won the division by 278 to 224. In the Lords on 26 November, Lord Byers initiated a further debate on an unstarred question, asking HMG, 'why in view of the opinion expressed in this House on 30 July they decided to proceed with damaging cuts . . .?' He claimed that the Government's compromise was 'horse trading or window dressing' but the extent of the cuts had been halved (from £3m to £1½m) and the Government compromise had clearly gone some way to satisfy peers.

On some subjects the House of Lords may be said to have a particular authority because of the expertise of some of its members. The judicial system is one such example, a point exemplified in the debate on the Fraud

Trails Committee report which took place one month after the report was published on 10 February 1986 (see above, page 49). A debate in the Lords on the Central Policy Review Staff proposals for a run-down of the foreign service 'killed these proposals stone dead' according to Lord Boyd-Carpenter (1980, p. 256). There are always a few peers whose political seniority ensures that they can command attention through speeches if they so wish. Examples would include Lord Stockton's speeches on the policies of the Thatcher Government and Lord Avon's speech on the Middle East at the time of the six-day war in 1967. Viscount Radcliffe's speech, also in 1967, on Mr Wilson's rejection of his report (the Radcliffe Report) on D-notices was described by Richard Crossman as 'the most effective quiet rebuke of a prime minister by a public servant of modern time', though Wilson himself made no mention of the speech in his memoirs (Crossman, 1976, p. 414; Wilson, 1971, p. 417–18).

In some cases the object of a debate is to influence other bodies besides the Government. For example a debate was held on the Press Council report on the 'Yorkshire Ripper' case in July 1983. Among peers who spoke were former journalists, ex-members of the Press Council and Royal Commissions on the Press (though none of the three former Chairmen of the Press Council in the House). In replying to the debate, the Home Office junior minister, Lord Elton, made clear that he felt the real purpose of the debate was to concentrate the minds of those with responsibility in the press on the issues of concern. After a debate on Internal Drainage Boards in November 1981, the minister who replied was surprised over the following months at how much notice had been taken by Drainage Board members of what was said in the debate. In 1982, Lord Nugent of Guildford emphasised in a speech the failure of the BBC and IBA to publish in their annual handbooks details of action taken on complaints received; the minister replying said no doubt the relevant authorities would take note of this, and in 1983, when Lord Nugent again initiated a debate on the subject he was able to express satisfaction that the handbooks did contain details of complaints.

Quite apart from any question of influence or power, debate in the Lords may serve a quite different purpose because of its cathartic value. Some peers make very pompous and boring speeches; others give vent to real anger and bitterness at times. Replying to a sour debate on the National Health Service in 1975, a Labour minister said he felt as if he was a passive bucket into which people were being emotionally sick, and added that 'no doubt the debate had provided an opportunity for people to discharge a reasonable amount of emotion and the cathartic effect must have been of immeasureable value' (HL Debs, 3 December 1975, col. 735). The same peer ten years later during aother debate on the NHS referred to the fact that he had been involved with a fair number of such debates over the years, but had come to the conclusion this was 'a most depressive, useless and pointless exercise' (HL Debs, 20 November 1985, col. 582).

Almost everyone involved with Lords' debates acknowledges that a great deal of what is said is worthless. 'Ninety per cent is puff' said one former minister in interview, but he then added 'ninety per cent of Commons debate is puff too — only a different kind of puff'. The title of a book by a former *Hansard* assistant editor in the Lords, '*A Hard Core of Wind*' (Braham, 1986), exemplifies the sceptical attitude some close observers take to the value of Lords' debates. But others offer markedly different views. Some two years after entering the Lords, Viscount Tonypandy, former Speaker of the Commons, wrote 'My short experience of the House of Lords has convinced me that there is not the slightest doubt that the debating level . . . is much higher than in the Commons . . . there is not the same vested party interest. . . There is an independence of mind and scholarship that serves the nation well' (Thomas, 1986, p. 226).

Oral Questions

The device of the parliamentary question has often been cited as a distinctive British contribution to the art of parliamentary government. In the Lords as in the Commons Question Time assumes a prominent part in each day's proceedings. It was apparently in the Lords that the first 'question' was asked, irregularly, in 1721 (Chester and Bowring, 1962, p. 12). Subsequently the Commons took up the practice and formalised it, with the Lords following suit. In essence the procedure is the same in both Houses, with ministers providing government answers to questions put down by members. But within this simple framework the way the procedures for questions have developed in the two Houses has been very different.

In the first place while the Commons decided to apply a time limit for oral questions, with the minister answering as many as possible in the time allocated, the Lords decided to limit the number of questions to which oral answers could be given on any single day. Since 1959 this limit has been fixed at four per day. Typically the Commons may get through thirty or forty questions in the 45–55 minutes available, while in the Lords four questions usually take about 25 minutes. Thus the Lords spends less time on oral questions but considerably longer on each question.

A second major contrast with the Commons lies in the fact that in the Lords there is no ministerial rota for answering questions, and no equivalent to the twice weekly contests between party leaders which occur at 'Prime Minister's Question Time'. Furthermore given the fact that not all departments have ministerial representation in the Lords, replies to questions frquently must be given either by ministers in departments dealing with quite different policy areas or by Lords-in-Waiting.

A third contrast between the two Houses derives from the absence of a Commons-type Speaker in the Lords. This is seen in the character of proceedings on the floor of the House at Question Time, and with regard to responsibility for the actual admissibility of questions. With no time limit and no Speaker, and with many peers frequently endeavouring to participate in exchanges on a question, proceedings can become somewhat chaotic, though perhaps the degree of orderliness which does prevail is the more remarkable. It is the Leader of the House to whom peers look to guide them through this period of daily turbulence.

As to the admissibility of questions, peers are urged to take advice from the Clerks (*The Companion*, p. 48) but unlike MPs they cannot be obliged to do so. A question may thus occasionally appear on the order paper which is primarily a statement of fact or an expression of opinion, or in some other way breaches guidance which has been given by successive procedure committees. Ultimately the Lords can refuse leave to a peer to actually ask a question put down in his name on the order paper but this is very unusual (for example, HL Deb, 19 January 1983, cols 1407–11). A minister may, of course, decline to answer an inadmissible question, and in the opinion of Lord Henderson of Brompton, formerly Clerk of the Parliaments, ministers should more readily exercise this right (HL Debs, 18 April 1985, col. 809).

The whole character of Question Time is therefore very different in the two Houses. The fact that ministers answering questions in the Commons invariably have direct responsibility for the subject involved, together with the more intense party political character of the House, has made Question Time primarily a set piece activity for party politicians. At the same time the brevity of exchanges and the speed with which questions are taken serve to protect ministers from any kind of searching examination. While most ministers do find Question Time in the Commons a considerable ordeal, it is primarily the intensity of the party struggle which brings this about.

In the Lords party politics is much more muted, a fact illustrated by the character of Question Time. But it is by no means entirely absent. Opposition spokesmen listen carefully from their front-bench when a question within their own area of responsibility is being answered, and have in recent sessions noticeably developed the practice of their Commons counterparts of 'riding in' with supplementary questions aimed at exposing some weakness in the Government position. The fact that much longer is spent on each question in the Lords than in the Commons may also add to the demands made of a minister, because there is more time for peers to find any weak points in the answers given. Furthermore, a minister never quite knows who may pop up (from behind or in front of him), nor how the considerable experience and expertise potentially available in the House may suddenly be brought to bear on the subject-matter of the question concerned. For these reasons some ministers believe that answering questions in the Upper house is a considerbly greater ordeal than doing so in the Commons.

All government spokesmen dealing with questions do, of course, have civil service briefs available. But again contrasts between the two Houses should be noted. Because of the rota system in the Commons, ministers know that only on certain days — for most only once in every three weeks or so — will they have to answer questions. In preparation for dealing with questions a Commons' minister may therefore set aside several hours earlier that day to 'mug up' relevant facts, quotations and so on. Furthermore, senior civil servants in the department know that, if necessary, they must put aside other tasks to help prepare their minister for his Question Time ordeal in the House. If he fails to perform well the repercussions are likely to be damaging for the department as well as for the minister. A Lords' minister, however, has no set question days, and can expect to have to answer questions a good deal more frequently than his Commons' colleagues. Furthermore he is unlikely to find civil servants as aware of, or as sensitive to his needs as they are to those of a Commons' minister. He will receive a file with a draft answer (together with answers to possible supplementaries) and have the opportunity to discuss this with civil servants beforehand. But if he is not a minister in the department concerned, this can well mean a hurried few minutes being spent shortly before Question Time with a group of civil servants he has never met before. One former civil servant, later a peer, recounted in an interview how abruptly he had dealt with a Lords' minister who once interrupted him during a lunch appointment to seek advice about answering a question in the House later that afternoon, an incident he looked back on with some regret after he himself had some experience as a member of the House of Lords!

Sometimes the inadequacies of hurried preparation become all too apparent at the Despatch Box. Occasionally the wrong answer will be read out (e.g. 17 June 1985, col. 1) or basic ignorance on some fundamental point become evident (e.g. 8 Feb 1984, col. 1140). However in general the Upper House is very understanding about such things; most peers privately praise government spokesmen for doing their difficult job as well as they do, and direct any anger they feel at civil servants for inadequate briefing.

Where a senior minister is available in the Lords, the above points do require qualification. For example, Labour peers made a particular point of pressing questions to Lord Young of Graffham after his appointment as

Secretary of State for Employment in October 1985. In two successive weeks he was absent from the House, and employment questions were dealt with by another minister (the Minister of State for Defence Support). This brought protests from the Leader of the Opposition, and a promise from Viscount Whitelaw that Lord Young would be present in the House of Lords for the next question on employment. When this was taken, two days later, exchanges on a single starred question lasted twenty minutes, with the Leader of the House doubtless reluctant to curtail the questioning lest he be thought to be shielding the newly appointed Secretary of State (see HL Debs, 15 October; 22 October; 24 October 1985). In the following months a stream of questions on employment were tabled by Labour peers, driving Lord Young at one point to contrast his position as a minister in the Lords unfavourably with that of a Commons' minister (HL Debs, 4 March 1986, col. 87).

The *Companion to the Standing Orders* emphasises that 'Question Time should normally be concluded in twenty minutes'. Such brevity has however become the exception rather than the rule. In the 1984–5 session, questions were contained within the twenty-minute limit on fewer than a quarter of the sittings. Sometimes questions in the Lords take 40 minutes. If the main reason for such longevity is the greater number of supplementary questions which are tolerated in the Lords (as compared with the Commons) a contributory factor is also the lengthier ministerial replies considered appropriate to the Upper House, where conventions of courtesy and politeness demand that government spokesmen appear as helpful as possible to questioners.

Among MPs there are wide variations in the use made of Question Time, with a relatively small number asking a highly disproportionate number of questions. In the Lords disproportionality is even more noticeable. In both 1983–4 and 1984–5 fewer than twenty peers asked over half of all the starred questions, with six peers being responsible for a

Table 7.6 Starred and Written Questions, 1984–5

	Starred (oral) questions		Questions for written answers	
	No. of peers who tabled questions	Total no. of questions	No. of peers who tabled questions	Total no. of questions
Conservative	57	203	77	331
Labour	30	231	51	430
Lib/SDP	23	107	24	239
Cross-bench	17	35	25	132
Total	127	576	177	1,132

Source: Derived from House of Lords' *Hansard*.

quarter of the questions in each session. At the same time in 1983–4 (a longer than usual session) only 147 peers asked any starred questions, and in 1984–5 only 127 peers did so (see Table 7.6). Unlike the Commons, the Opposition front-bench in the Lords do ask oral questions (though individual practice varies a good deal). The proportion even of 'active' peers who ask oral questions is therefore under half, and of the total eligible to do so, only about 15 per cent in fact do.

No peer may put down more than two starred questions for any single day, or have more than three starred questions on the order paper at any one time. But a really determined peer can still ask a large number of questions. Lord Hatch of Lusby asked more oral questions than any other peer in 1983–4 (thirty-seven questions) and 1984–5 (forty questions). Such proclivity provokes resentment elsewhere in the House; on 29 January 1985, when Lord Hatch's eleventh question of the session was being dealt with, a Conservative back-bench peer moved that 'the noble lord be no longer heard' and this motion was carried handsomely on division by 103 votes to 59.

Former MPs predominate among the most frequent questioners; of the thirteen who asked more than ten questions in 1984–5 nine had been MPs. While some degree of specialisation is evident in this group, the very regular questioners tend to ask about varied topics. If there is a common theme it is the advancement of the party political struggle. Lord Hatch of Lusby's forty questions mainly concentrated on foreign affairs or defence matters (though never an MP he was for twenty years Commonwealth correspondent of the *New Statesman*). Lord Molloy (thirty-four questions) asked about the National Health Service, foreign affairs matters, and other miscellaneous topics. Both these peers were back benchers, but Lord Dean of Beswick (twenty questions) spoke from the Labour front-bench on Treasury matters, and most of his questions fell in this area. Three-quarters of Lord Jenkins of Putney's sixteen questions concerned nuclear weapons or closely related matters. The latter three were all former MPs. Three Conservative peers asked fifteen questions each: Lord Boyd-Carpenter, Orr-Ewing and Gainford, the former two but not the latter being ex-MPs. Their questions overed a miscellany of subjects.

A peer among this group of frequent questioners who clearly did specialise was Baroness Burton of Coventry; she asked twenty-nine questions all dealing with consumer affairs. Ever since her entry into the Lords in 1962 she has been one of the most frequent questioners, persistently pressing ministers of all governments on consumer issues. Her sustained shrewd questioning has earned the admiration of many peers, and several of her campaigns, spearheaded through Question Time in the Lords, have had an impact on government or nationalised industries.

Among less frequent questioners were Lord Hunter of Newington, an eminent doctor and Cross-bench peer, whose six questions all dealt with medical matters; Lord Rugby, an optician, also a Cross-bencher, who asked three questions on spectacles; Baroness Lockwood, a Labour supporter and former Chairman of the Equal Opportunities Commission, who asked several questions about the rôle of women in education, employment and so on; Lord Nugent of Guildford, a Conservative back-bench peer; who asked mainly about road safety matters, and Lord Ezra, a Liberal peer and former National Coal Board Chairman, who asked several questions on energy policy. These are all examples of peers who know a great deal about a particular subject, and who use Question Time in the Lords as one means among others, to advance arguments or ideas which they wish to press upon the Government. Party politics may not be absent from their thinking, but neither is it likely to be their primary consideration. They are unlikely to be out 'to get' a particular government minister. If they have a clear target in mind when asking their questions it is more likely to be civil servants who deal with the subject in the relevant government departments.

As Table 7.6 shows, slightly more questions came from the Labour Opposition than from the Government back-bench peers in 1984–5. When the Conservatives were in Opposition in 1975–6, Conservatives asked almost twice as many questions as did Labour backbenchers. There were many more Conservatives available, even if some Labour peers tried to make up for their lack of numbers by their assiduity. Clearly many party-minded peers would be reluctant to see a situation in which few questions were forthcoming from 'their' side. On the other hand, given the readiness with which mini-debates develop at Question Time, it is possible for a partisan questioner to emerge bruised rather than victorious when his question has had an obvious party-political intent. Within the Lords a group of Conservative peers who sought to help their front-bench by asking friendly questions was established in 1982, but rapidly acquired the epithet 'own-goals group' for exactly this reason. Sometimes totally ignoring a partisan question may be the most appropriate response; when a Conservative back-bench peer in 1986 asked a particularly silly question — 'What levels of radiation were recorded in the Local Authority nuclear free zones during the period of fall out from the Soviet nuclear reactor at Chernobyl? — no other peer attempted to intervene: a rather rare occurrence on any question.

Some questions are very broad in scope and can therefore become pegs on which to hang mini-debates on some aspect of Government policy. For example: 'To ask HMG whether they consider they have made effective use of the surplus earnings of North Sea oil' (23 Jan 1985); or 'What action HMG intends to take in view of the statement by the USA Secretary for Defence that Armageddon is real, specific and imminent' (21 October

1985). Compared with the Commons a significant contrast is the relative absence of constituency questions. But the absence is relative rather than absolute. Some peers do ask about local issues. For example: Lord Jenkins of Putney asked about Putney Bridge station on 14 July 1982; and Lord Dean of Beswick asked about a statement made by Lord Young of Graffham on Radio York about unemployment in that city (16 February 1987); he did this at the prompting of Labour's prospective parliamentary candidate for the constituency of York, and his answer was given publicity in the local press. Occasionally peers with territorial titles ask questions relating to their 'territory'; for example, Viscount Mersey on 8 July 1985 asked 'Whether the Mersey is still the dirtiest river in the country?' and in the ensuing exchanges the Bishop of Liverpool joined in, illustrating the concern Bishops display for diocesan problems. The same Bishop asked a question on the Liverpool Philharmonic Orchestra, and in the 1981–2 session the Bishop of Rochester asked about Chatham Dockyard and the Bishop of Carlisle about training facilities in West Cumbria.

How worthwhile are starred questions in the Lords? As in the Commons it is at Question Time that the Chamber is most likely to be crowded, and the House at its liveliest, even unruliest. But much of what takes place seems like shadow-boxing between political opponents whose significance in the national party context is really very marginal. That is probably the least valuable aspect of Question Time. But peers use starred questions to keep some unpopular subjects or half-forgotten reports on departmental agendas. A Baroness Burton of Coventry, by sheer dogged persistence, may force reconsideration to be given to some decision convenient to bureaucrats but disadvantageous to the public. Another peer may, through a question, effectively serve warning on the Government that he is likely to pursue a subject through a full scale debate unless some appropriate action is taken. Overall, given the extent to which Commons' Question Time has become dominated by the scoring of party points, the Lords' procedure may be regarded as a mildly useful complement.

Questions for Written Answer

Peers, like MPs, may put down Questions for Written Answer. Such questions together with the Government's answers appear in *Hansard* at the end of each day's record of proceedings in the House of Lords. No limit exists on the number of questions which may be asked, and in recent years, in both Houses, their number has greatly increased, though the 1,200 or so per year in the Lords remains small by comparison with the 40,000 or so such questions in the Commons. Table 7.6 shows that as with starred questions, a relatively small proportion of peers actually do ask questions for written answer — a total of 177 in 1984–5, though 508 peers took part in debates in the Lords in that year. Again, within this total, there is a similar concentration of activity on a very small number of peers: in 1984–5 seven peers together asked one-third of all written questions, and a total of seventeen asked over half.

Looking for a moment at the very frequent questioners it is possible to derive some idea of the purpose to which this procedure is put. The most prolific questioner in 1981–2 was Lord Avebury, formerly Mr. Eric Lubbock, Liberal MP for Orpington from 1962 to 1970. His 163 questions for written answer in that session were particularly concerned with two categories of people, namely prisoners and immigrants (or would-be immigrants). Efforts on behalf of such folk resulted in an ever-increasing volume of inquiries and problems being directed his way. By 1983 he began to wilt under the strain and his activities in the House diminished, though in 1984–5 he still tabled forty-five questions for written answers (but only one for oral answer). The peer who asked the most written questions in 1984–5 was Lord Melchett, the young Labour hereditary peer (born in 1948) whose concern for environmental matters is well known (he was president of the Ramblers Association in the early 1980s). His eighty-eight questions dealt with many aspects of wildlife protection, areas of special scientific interest, use of pesticides, road building schemes and so on. Some were very specific, for example concerning the condition of a particular piece of footpath (25 June 1985), others highly technical, for example a question about the A34 at Whitway in Hampshire (31 March 1982) which was complemented by a starred question, and then an unstarred question with accompanying debate, all on the same subject, urging the Government to reconsider its decisions.

In the 1984–5 session, the peer who followed Lord Melchett in the frequency of use of questions for written answer was Lord Kennet, a leading figure in the Social Democratic Party, also a hereditary peer, and a former Labour minister of the 1960s. His seventy-seven questions for written answer concentrated on defence and maritime issues. Other peers who frequently used this device were: Lord Jenkins of Putney, forty-two questions, mainy on nuclear related questions: Lord Harris of Greenwich, SDP, thirty-three questions, many on wild-life; Lord Graham of Edmonton, a Labour whip in the Lords, thirty-two questions on various topics, mainly environmental; Lord Brockway, a veteran Labour peer, who has for many years in both Houses sought to expose possible inconsistency or hypocrisy in the Foreign Office, which department answered most of his thirty-two questions.

In addition to regular questioners, the device of the written question does permit any of the 900 or so peers who, from time to time, sit in the House of Lords, to raise particular issues which interest them. No fewer than 59 of the 331 peers putting down questions for written answer in 1984–5 asked a single such question in the entire session. The eminent scientist, Lord Flowers, asked a single question about the Sizewell Nuclear Power Station; Lord Bancroft, former Head of the Civil Service, asked about the membership of the Museums and Galleries Commission; the Bishop of Rochester asked about grants for stadium safety precautions; Lord O'Brien of Lothbury (former Governor of the Bank of England) asked about the reserves banks were required to hold; Lord Aldington (formerly Toby Low, Conservative minister in the 1950s) asked about first class travel; and Lord Home of the Hirsel (formerly Conservative prime minister) asked about a particular training barracks.

Such examples illustrate the variety of questions put down for written answer. Most appear to be straightforward requests for information. Some seek a general statement from the Government concerning its policy or attitudes to a specified matter. The information so gained may be used in debates or other proceedings in the Lords. As in the Commons, some questions are 'inspired'. In such cases government sources suggest to a friendly backbencher the wording of a question which can then be used to make public some government announcement or statement of information. A comparison of Lords and Commons *Hansard* for July 1985 indicates that approximately one-quarter of Lords' questions for written answer have identical simultaneous parallels in the Commons; these questions clearly were 'inspired', though undoubtedly there were many more 'inspired' questions in the Commons in the same period, but probably only very few others in the Lords.

Written questions can be used in an effort to expose inconsistencies or apparent stupidities in government administration, and this can assume a definite party-political character, especially where very large numbers of questions are asked. Some MPs use written questions in this way in the Commons, but such use among peers is rare. Certainly in the Lords the most frequent use of this device is to enable peers to probe departments and to permit governments to publish information quickly and in an easily accessible form. Questions for written answer is a procedure which has a clear rationale and usefulness to all parliamentarians.

Conclusion

Non-legislative debate has a rather ephemeral character. It is difficult to be precise about the influence of such proceedings, just as it is difficult to be precise about how informed opinion or many policy ideas have been developed within society. Both within the Lords as well as outside it opinions sharply diverge as to the value of its debates. Disagreements arise in part because of the different criteria applied in making an assessment. Some emphasise the qualifications of those who take part in such debates, and not infrequently the *curriculum vitae* of speakers is highly impressive. Their listeners and readers may admire the quality of speeches made.

But that doesn't necessarily mean the House is having much effect on government, nor indeed on any of the other centres of power in society. The mere fact that peers taking part in a debate have an impressive list of qualifications is not in itself evidence for the political importance of those debates. A debate may be no more than a kind of elite academic seminar on a subject, engaging with the forces that direct government activity in only the most superficial way. Lucid, original and sparkling speeches may have no more influence than boring and repetitive ones. As far as influence on the executive is concerned both alike may be merely the release of wind.

That would certainly be too harsh a conclusion. Indications have been given in this chapter of occasions when proceedings in the Lords — on questions or in debates on motions — do appear to have had an influence on government. Most peers can quite readily give examples of where they believe this to have been the case: and most also nurture the belief that the proceedings of the House have a wider influence within society, even if this is usually both small and indirect.

8

SELECT COMMITTEES
AND SECONDARY LEGISLATION

The rôle of Parliament in passing public bills and in debating government activity is comparatively well-known. Less public attention is generally given to other aspects of parliaments's work, which are nevertheless of considerable importance. Some of these may be thought of as a kind of second tier of legislative activity. In this may be included private bills, statutory instruments and European Community legislation. Work on private bills has declined throughout this century, just as work on statutory instruments has grown and, particularly in recent years, work on European instruments. For much of this activity considerable use is made of select committees, which are also used by the Lords to examine particular subjects, and sometimes particular bills, especially private members' bills. This chapter surveys the work of the House of Lords in all these areas.

In some respects this may seem a field of miscellaneous activities, and in part this is true. But there are common themes which can be mentioned now, and discussed later. Among these is the obscure nature of much of this work, especially that which deals with private legislation, and here the work of the Lords is much more nearly co-equal with the work of the Commons than is generally the case with public legislation.

Another theme which links much of this discussion is an institutional one, namely the use of select committees. Such committees have become more prominent in both Houses in recent years, particularly with the establishment of the departmentally focused select committees in the Commons in 1979. This prompts the question, to what extent has the Upper House been rivalling or duplicating the Lower House, or has it primarily been seeking to complement the work of the Commons, filling in the gaps, as it were? Discussion of developments which have taken place should offer us some help in answering this question, which will be taken up again in the conclusion. Finally, we may once again take note of the degree of flexibility which has been shown by the Lords in adapting itself to both its own changing membership and to the new tasks being imposed upon parliament.

175

Private Bills

Private bills enable individuals, groups or bodies to do something which
the law of the land — as enacted in past public legislation — does not
otherwise allow. In the nineteenth century, private bills were both
numerous and important. Throughout the twentieth century the trend has
been to provide, by means of public legislation, procedures which enable
bodies who hitherto achieved their ends through private bills to obtain the
legal powers they need by other means. Thus the building of reservoirs, the
digging up of churchyards, the construction of highways can usually be
achieved today without resort to a private bill. Nevertheless, there are
typically some thirty or so new private bills introduced every session, and
in respect of these the House of Lords has co-equal powers to the House of
Commons and in practice does a similar amount of work as the Lower
House.

Parliamentary procedure on private bills is superficially similar to that
for public bills. A first and second reading is followed by a committee
stage, then a third reading takes place. But in fact the use made of these
stages is quite different. The 'promoters' of a bill petition for the right to
introduce it, and this is only granted after 'Examiners' (who are
parliamentary clerks) have satisfied themselves that the elaborate standing
orders concerned with the presentation of such bills have been observed.
The purpose of these is chiefly to ensure that all interested parties have due
notice of the bill. Bills are allocated for introduction evenly between the
two Houses; bills which major on financial matters are taken first in the
Commons, while a tradition favours the Lords taking most local authority
legislation first. After passing one House bills must go through the other,
though unlike public bills, private bills may be carried over from one
session to the next. In the Lords the second reading is usually moved
formally by the Lord Chairman, but if opposition to a bill is likely, the
promoters must find some other peer to introduce the bill, so that the Lord
Chairman preserves his neutrality. Unlike a public bill the granting of
second reading does not imply approval of the principle of a bill, only that
the House feels the bill may properly proceed to a committee. Sometimes
an 'instruction' to such a committee is approved by the Lords; if so this
usually requires the committee to give special emphasis to some factor.

Opponents of a bill may lodge petitions against it, in which case the bill is
referred to a select committee, usually consisting of five peers, specifically
appointed to deal with that particular bill. The proceedings in such
committees are quasi-judicial, with promoters and petitioners arguing their
case through counsel, sometimes for days on end. But only about half-a-
dozen bills per session have, in recent years, been opposed in this way.
Quite frequently petitions are lodged against a bill, but then withdrawn, in

many cases because the two sides have reached agreement before incurring the considerable legal expenses of a full select committee hearing. Bills which are not formally opposed (by petitions) are referred to an Unopposed Bill Committee which consists only of the Lord Chairman (assisted by his counsel) though he may ask other peers to attend.

The activity of the Lords on such bills has been at least as important as that of the Commons. In particular the House has done much work on bills promoted by local authorities. The 1972 Local Government Act stipulated that existing local legislation would lapse unless re-enacted by 1984. This was considered desirable in order to ensure that newly-established local authorities were equipped with all the necessary powers to apply by-laws and carry out other functions and that the statute book was not cluttered with out-dated legislation. The first such bill presented was the County of South Glamorgan Bill which took twenty-six mornings and fourteen full days before a Lords select committee in 1975–6. Fears that parliamentary machinery would be choked trying to cope with all such bills within the ten-year deadline were expressed. A Local Government (Miscellaneous Provisions) Bill introduced by the Government in 1976 obviated the need for some clauses in local authority bills by giving similar powers to all local authorities, and ultimately the ten-year deadline only had to be extended slightly.

Private bills can be very time-consuming: the Lloyd's Bill of 1982 involved a select ommittee in nineteen days of hearings. The Hampshire (Lyndhurst By-pass) Bill occupied a select committee of peers for fourteen days in 1987. This was a controversial bill, inherently so because it involved road building in part of the New Forest, but additionally because the promoters, the Hampshire County Council, used private bill procedure to obviate the need to seek approval from the New Forest Verderer's Court. This does illustrate the point that on some matters promoters may have a choice between proceeding by means of a private bill or by some other route. In the case of the Lyndhurst-by-pass bill two of its most vigorous opponents, the official verderer of the New Forest and his predecessor, were both members of the House of Lords. Despite their objections the bill was approved by the select committee, and the House.

Occasionally the two Houses disagree over their treatment of a private bill. The most notable example was when the Lords threw out at third reading the bill to nationalise Felixstowe Dock in 1976 (discussed above, p. 22). In 1980 a bill to give certain powers to the Dartmoor Commoners was rejected in the House of Commons after it had passed the Lords.

The possibility of using joint select committees for private bills has frequently been mooted. Such committees, it is said, could cut down expense to promoters in cases where bills are formally opposed, but against this it is argued that opponents of a bill are in a stronger position once they have heard the promoter's case fully deployed. Savings in parliamentary man-hours are another consideration. In the 1986–7 session it proved impossible to find MPs willing to serve on a select committee dealing with a particularly contentious private bill. The modern MP typically does not rate highly among his duties the spending of many days listening to barristers presenting arguments, often on very technical matters, which may be planning issues in a part of the country far removed from his own constituency. A joint select committee was established in 1987 to inquire into the whole subject. It is a reasonable guess to say that any resulting reform is likely to enhance rather than diminish the relative importance of the House of Lords in this area. It is almost certainly easier to find peers than MPs willing and able to give the time involved to dwell on the minutiae that frequently preoccupies such committees. It may be argued that all such activity should be remitted to planning inspectors or to the courts. But against this it is suggested that that section of the public who become involved in such matters appreciate direct contact with legislators, not simply officials, or lawyers (HL 146, 1986–7, esp. pp. 17ff). A second chamber may have a particular value in making available for such work legislators who have a certain detachment from party politics and from electoral considerations.

A particular kind of private bill is one that deals with the affairs of a specific individual; these are known as personal bills, and are always introduced into the House of Lords, from which, if approved, they proceed to the Commons. In the Lords they are referred to the Personal Bills Committee, which consists of the Lord Chairman and six other peers, two of whom must be law lords. No personal bill may be given a first reading until this committee has reported to the Lords. Its basic task is to ensure that such a bill is necessary to achieve the objective of the person involved, and that this objective is not inconsistent with public policy. Hence bills to relieve individuals of penalties for traffic offences imposed by the courts, or to confer academic awards where these have been withheld, have been excluded! If the bill is approved for introduction, it then proceeds in a way very similar to any other private bill. Such bills are few; typically they deal with estates, naturalisation claims, or, most notable in recent years, marriage enabling bills, occasioned by the desire of particular individuals to become legally married in circumstances in which existing UK law forbids this. Because debate at second reading on marriage bills has sometimes brought the discussion of personal details to the floor of the House, a new procedure was agreed in 1986 whereby after a formal second reading such bills are dealt with in a small committee (the initial composition of which was the Lord Chairman, a Bishop, a Labour Baroness and a Conservative life peer). Several attempts have been made to relax the law on affinity by public bills (introduced by private members) but these all failed until a slight change — relating to step-relatives — was made in a successful bill introduced by Lord Meston in 1986. The House of Lords has a creditable record in dealing with matters in this sensitive area.

Some bills, while altering the general law of the land as public bills do, also have some of the characteristics of a private bill because they affect specific private interests in a way different from other interests of the same kind. These are known as hybrid bills, and may, in respect of the clauses which affect private interests, be referred to a select committee (which deals with the bill in the same way as an opposed private bil), after which the bill is re-committed to a committee of the whole House (in the Lords) and goes through the usual public bill procedure. The most obvious recent example of a hybrid bill is the Channel Tunnel Bill, which after going through the Commons, was referred to a select committee in the Lords which sat for thirty days dealing with petitions, eventually recommending over 100 amendments to the bill (alleviating particular concerns). In this case some uncertainties were expressed about the *locus standi* of petitioners, because several bodies representing interests in the north of England — such as local councils — wished to petition against a bill which they believed would intensify regional division. The committee decided that it would hear petitioners whose interests in the bill were indirect in this sense, as well as those directly affected by proposed construction works.

Secondary Legislation

The long-term diminution of private legislation, to which reference has already been made, has been accompanied by an upsurge in secondary legislation, also described as subordinate or delegated legislation. In Chapter 6 we considered the primary legislative process by which bills become Acts of Parliament. Many primary (or parent) Acts themselves confer legislative powers, which can be exercised by ministers subject to varying forms of parliamentary control. Most delegated legislation is carried out by means of statutory instruments, and before discussing the rôle of the House of Lords in relation to these, some general explanation is desirable.

Statutory instruments (SIs) are basically of three kinds. First are affirmative instruments, so called because they require the positive approval of both Houses of Parliament. In both Houses a motion must be moved, and accepted, or carried on division, otherwise the instrument concerned falls. Generally speaking the most important instruments are in this category. A much larger number are known as negative instruments because these, once laid before Parliament, come into force automatically unless within a specified time limit (usually forty days) one or other House carried a motion (technically known as a 'prayer') calling for their annullment. Finally there are general instruments which are not necessarily laid before Parliament at all, though on comparatively rare occasions, such may become the subject of parliamentary proceedings, for example through debate on a motion. The neatness of this categorisation is spoilt somewhat by the fact that primary legislation sometimes stipulates varied and unusual forms for SIs. Some instruments — concerned with financial matters — only require to be laid before the House of Commons.

This categorisation by no means exhausts the rule-making mechanism which exists. In particular in recent years increasing use has been made of codes of practice which have proliferated without any systematic forms for such codes being adopted, a development which was criticised in a Lords debate on the subject on 15 January 1986. In addition to codes, which may or may not be statutory, and may or may not be enforceable through the courts, other forms of 'quasi-legislation' can be identified — such as government circulars — all helpfully discussed in Ganz (1987). Such forms of 'legislation' have become more important as successive governments have assumed more far-reaching responsibilities in the life of society, or at least have attempted to influence behaviour in such areas as industrial relations, health and safety, race relations, the treatment of livestock and so on.

Although the number of statutory instruments has not grown particularly in recent years (from around 1,000 per year) their length and complexity appears inexorably to have expanded. Furthermore, as the Chairman of the joint select committee on statutory instruments recently commented 'a lot of SIs today no longer deal with means but with principles' (HC 350, 1986–7, Q4). Matters which, a few years ago, would have been included in the parent Act, because they really deal with policy, are now being dealt with by SIs. In so far as this reduces the complexity of primary legislation, it enhances the importance of secondary legislation, and the consequent need for Parliament to provide a satisfactory means for scrutiny of the latter.

However, parliamentary procedures can be criticised because these allow for only a relatively perfunctory scrutiny of statutory instruments. Even the most important SIs are effectively subject to only a single stage in parliamentary proceedings. Furthermore no SI can be amended; it can only be accepted or rejected. And the pressure on parliamentary time is such that in the House of Commons at least the opportunities to debate SIs are now seriously curtailed.

Prior to 1973 both Houses had their own select committees to scrutinise instruments (in the Lords this was known as the Special Orders Committee) but since that date a joint select committee has existed for this task. This consists of seven members of each House; it is an apolitical committee because its concern is not with the merits or policy implications of instruments, but rather with their technical propriety. In other words, it considers such questions as: whether the instrument is drafted properly; whether the power under which it is laid actually exists in the parent Act; and whether the instrument represents an unexpected use of that power. This committee reports on all instruments, but obviously it can only issue substantive reports on a tiny fraction of the six or so instruments tabled every sitting day. Only occasionally does it take evidence from government departments. However, the joint committee does have legal advisers who scrutinise all instruments carefully.

There are some differences in the detailed way in which the two Houses handle statutory instruments. A minor point is that affirmative instruments cannot be approved by the House of Lords until they have been the subject of a report from the joint select committee, whereas in the Commons such instruments may be debated and passed even before the Committee's report has been made. Occasionally, this has resulted in the Upper House alone being able to debate some aspect of a statutory instrument adversely commented on by the Committee. A more significant contrast lies in the circumstances in which debate takes place in the two Houses. In the Commons many affirmative instruments — as well as prayers — are now debated in standing committee, and where this is not the case, debate on the floor of the House is almost always limited to one-and-a-half hours, and usually very late at night. In the Lords all affirmative instruments (and those few prayers which are tabled) are taken in the chamber. In 1985–6 a total of 182 affirmative instruments were debated in the Lords, of which seventy-five were not debated in the Commons chamber (though MPs did debate twenty-four instruments which never came before the Lords because of their financial character).

Most debates in the Lords on affirmative instruments are relatively brief but the fact that they take place in the chamber does mean that a short explanation of the instrument concerned is given by the minister, and can easily be referred to in *Hansard*. Furthermore, such debates do afford Opposition spokesmen, and other peers, the opportunity to engage in a certain amount of probing, sometimes friendly, sometimes unfriendly, which can help to elucidate the instrument. Quite often the House spends only ten minutes or so on an instrument; most such debates last less than an hour, a very few extend to two or three hours, or even longer.

Because the House of Lords retains a formal power of veto on orders, peers in general are reluctant to press opposition to an order to a division in which an order might be rejected. Never has a prayer against a negative instrument been carried, and only once has the House rejected an affirmative instrument. This latter solitary example was the celebrated Southern Rhodesia Sanctions Order of 1968, which, however, was approved when relaid a short while later. The inhibition the House feels about using its power in this area means that the Opposition party in the House traditionally refrains from forcing votes directly against orders. Apart from the 1968 example, the Conservatives did not do so in the 1960s or 1970s. Between 1979 and 1981 Labour did divide the House on nine occasions against affirmative orders, but all these the Government comfortably won. Since 1981 Labour has reverted to the practice of not forcing such divisions. To do so could create precedents very unwelcome to any future Labour Government.

It might have been thought that given this inhibition on the use of power, the House of Lords would have allowed proceedings on statutory instruments to become purely formal, or at least if that were not the case (which manifestly it is not), the House might have ceased to have any real influence in this area. But this does not appear to be the case either. The House does sometimes force (or perhaps shame) the Government into withdrawing an instrument (or maybe not laying it in the first place). To this end peers do use procedural means, other than direct votes against an instrument, to record the view of the House. Motions, in the form of reasoned amendments, are sometimes moved at the same time as a motion to approve an instrument, or at the same time as a prayer. In such cases the prayer can be withdrawn after debate (or the motion to approve the instrument not formally opposed), while the motion expressing regret, or calling for the withdrawal of the instrument on some stated ground, can be voted on, and may even be carried against the Government. Some illustration of such activity will help to clarify what is involved.

In 1984 the Opposition considered the possibility of voting diectly against the order for the cancellation of the GLC elections. This was laid under the Local Government (Interim Provisions) Bill, which had stipulated that cancellation could only take place after the principle of abolition of the authorities concerned had been approved by Parliament. An answer to a parliamentary question in May indicated that the Government would see the rejection of this order as a breach of convention. (HL Debs, 14 May 1984, col. 1268). Eventually the Opposition in the Lords tabled a motion stating that the House viewed cancellation of the elections as prejudicial to peers' consideration of the substantive Local Government Bill (which was then still before the Commons), but this motion was handsomely defeated (by 145 votes to 72, 18 December 1984). Had this motion been passed it would not itself have prevented cancellation of the elections, though it would have added to government embarrassment on the issue. If such a motion is carried it simply records the view of the House.

In December 1983, a motion, stating that in the opinion of the Lords the Equal Pay (Amendment) Regulation did not comply fully with European

Community stipulations, was carried by 108 votes to 104, but at the same time the regulations themselves were formally approved. This was part of a lengthy campaign within Parliament to intensify pressure for equal treatment of the sexes. Another example occurred in July 1985 when a motion expressing regret at top public sector pay awards was approved by 140 votes to 135 in July 1985, at the same time as the Lord Chancellor's Salary Order was approved (the Lord Chancellor being the only minister whose increase required parliamentary approval). On this occasion Viscount Whitelaw, Leader of the House, explained that he would convey the views of the House to his Cabinet colleagues. No doubt he did so (in case they didn't read the newspapers!) but the Government had won a vote on the same subject in the Commons, and the Lords' vote had no practical effect, other than possibly adding a little to public embarrassment on this whole subject.

The Conservatives in Opposition in the 1970s sometimes used a motion for resolution to similar effect. For example, in 1975 a motion condemning the Government for laying an order providing for the withdrawal of funds from direct grant schools was handsomely carried (by 131 votes to 44), while the order concerned was not contested, despite the fact that in the Commons the Conservative Opposition had sought to defeat the order in a division. Sometimes, however, an adverse vote on such a motion does cause the Government to withdraw an order, even though the order itself has not been defeated. This happened when Lord Duncan-Sandys moved a motion calling for the withdrawal of a Town and Country Planning Order in 1977. In 1968 the Government White Paper on Lords Reform stated that some instruments had not been laid because of known opposition in the Lords. The most prominent example was probably the Cabinet decision not to proceed with the decision to build a third London airport at Stansted, which was made shortly after a Lords debate on the subject in December 1967 revealed strong opposition in the House.

On other occasions hostile motions have been tabled and debated, but withdrawn in the light of Government assurances. In May 1986 the Labour Opposition tabled a motion on the Hong Kong (British Nationality) Order which directly called for the withdrawal of the order, and its replacement by one which would give greater consideration to ethnic minorities. This was debated for three-and-a-half hours on a Friday, at the end of which the Opposition leader, Lord Cledwyn, stated that the Government minister had gone substantially further than any minister had done on any previous occasion in providing reassurance about minority groups, and the hostile motion was therefore withdrawn. The promise of concessions from the Government ensured that no vote took place (16 May 1986).

A hostile motion may be withdrawn even though no concessions have been promised. On 19 March 1985, the Labour Opposition tabled both a 'prayer' against an order restricting doctors' freedom to prescribe certain drugs and a motion deploring the decision; on this occasion a Liberal peer tabled an amendment to the Opposition motion, which was also hostile to the Government. After debate a vote on the amendment took place, then the main motion was negatived without a division, and the prayer withdrawn. The debate had lasted almost four hours, and was part of a campaign in the Lords on this subject (debates had taken place under other procedures on 15 January, 6 and 20 February). On 18 June 1986, a prayer opposing government plans to test four sites for possible disposal of radioactive waste was moved by a Conservative back-bench peer. The debate didn't begin until after midnight, but within an hour seven peers spoke, all critical of the Government's position. The following year the Government abandoned its plans, which had also been severely criticised in the Commons.

Occasionally, the motion to aprove an order may be withdrawn after being heavily criticised in debate. The Funds for Trade Union Ballots Order was withdrawn in July 1982 because the Government spokesman — a newly appointed Lord-in-Waiting — was unable to clarify ambiguities highlighted in two somewhat formidable Opposition speeches — from Lord Wedderburn of Charlton and Lord McCarthy. The motion for approval was moved the next day when the Government spokesman concerned had been better briefed. In the previous session the Building Societies (Authorisation) Regulations had been withdrawn in somewhat similar circumstances, to be relaid when a difficult point raised by an Opposition peer could be clarified.

Some statutory instruments may be classed as hybrid, and while the House of Commons has no procedure for distinguishing such instruments, in the Lords these (if opposed) may be referred to the Hybrid Instruments Committee, which in turn may recommend a full select committee hearing. Successive governments have at times sought to eliminate or curtail this procedure, but it has been jealously guarded by peers (see Jones, 1966; also HL Debs on the Offshore Petroleum Development Bill, 10 February 1975, col. 1109–36; 25 February 1975, col. 648–64). It is rarely used; only twice since 1973 have full select committee hearings taken place on such instruments, but one of these — a London Docklands Development Order in 1980 — involved a select committee sitting on forty-six days to hear petitioners.

Finally, mention can be made of special procedure orders upon which, under a procedure established in 1945, joint committees may sit; since then there has been, on average, one such committee per session. If the Government wishes to over-ride a joint committee report, then a Confirmation of Orders Bill is required. The best-known example in recent years concerned the Okehampton by-pass. This was a particularly complex twenty-year-long saga, which eventually culminated in such a bill to set aside the verdict of a joint select committee, which had in turn found by a four-to-two majority against the outcome of a ninety-six day public inquiry. Such bills proceed straight to third reading; in the Lords an eight-hour debate on 5 December 1985 represented the last opportunity for the Government's decision to be frustrated. The 'Okehampton Crisis Committee' published a large newspaper advertisement that day appealing for 'fair play' from the Lords. The bill's leading opponent was Lord Molson, an MP from 1935–61 (when he became a peer), and the man largely responsible for parliamentary pressure which led to the 1945 procedure being established. His speech was a *tour de force,* revealing still some of the qualities which won him a First in jurisprudence at Oxford in the 1920s, but despite his pleas, his motion to reject the bill was lost by 27 votes to 112. A more circumspect motion (regretting the bill) was moved from the Opposition front-bench — and lost by 32 votes to 108. As a result, sometime in the late 1980s, Okehampton will have a by-pass, running south of the town, and infringing the Dartmoor National Park.

Returning in conclusion to secondary legislation generally, it is worth re-emphasising the growing importance of this area and the increasing difficulty evident in securing adequate debate in the Commons. Because the House of Lords contains many peers who have considerable experience of statutory instruments — notably as ministers or senior civil servants — it is well-equipped to play a part in the parliamentary function of scrutiny. It probably does this most effectively on those instruments which are not of foremost political importance. The power it retains does not seem to have inhibited the Lords, even if it requires peers to adopt some slightly circuitous procedural routes on those occasions when they want, formally, to register the opinion of the House in opposition to an Order. A hidden but useful aspect of the debate the House holds on instruments is that departmental lawyers (who usually draft statutory instruments) know that their handiwork may be examined in this public and partially expert forum.

European Communities Committee

Membership of the European Community potentially imposed upon Parliament a new responsibility for scrutinising Community legislation. But the Community's legislative procedure focuses on the Council of Ministers, composed of representatives of the governments of the member countries. This has the task of approving or otherwise proposals put to it by the Commission, the 'civil service' of the Community. Hence national parliaments had (and still have) no automatic input into the legislative process. If they were to be involved at all, the most obvious way was through the scrutiny of draft legislation before this was put to the Council of Ministers for decision. As the date of British accession — 1 January 1973 — drew near both Houses of Parliament set up select committees to consider how this might be done. In the Lords this committee became known as the Maybray-King Committee, after its chairman, Lord Maybray-King, formerly Speaker of the House of Commons.

There were several reasons why the House of Lords was well placed to take a prominent rôle in this new parliamentary function. A much greater degree of consensus about UK membership of the Community existed in the Lords than in the Commons (peers had voted 451 to 58 in support of the principle of entry, MPs by 356 to 244), which meant that scrutiny of EC matters was less likely to be dogged by continued controversy over the principle of membership in the Lords. Arguably a chamber of influence, rather than of power, was better adapted to the actual scrutiny of draft legislation, given that the EC legislative process did not admit a formal rôle for national parliaments. Finally, and perhaps of greatest significance, was the simple fact that by the early 1970s the arrival of many life peers had swollen active membership of the House of Lords to the point at which it had surplus capacity to take on significant new work, which could hardly be said of the House of Commons.

Though the Maybray-King Committee initially recommended a joint select committee, this was not favoured by MPs, so the two Houses went their separate ways, though eventually fashioning scrutiny procedures which complemented one another rather well. The government of the day was very tardy in its whole approach, with ministers showing all their usual suspicion of a new parliamentary investigatory function. When the House of Lords debated the Maybray-King committee report in December 1973, Labour peers in Opposition criticised the Government's reluctance to act quickly on the recommendations made; Lord Crowther-Hunt in a maiden speech drew attention to the fact that over 250 regulations had been approved since Britain joined the Community, but no parliamentary means for scrutiny had yet been established. After further discussions between the procedure committee, and first the Conservative and then the Labour Government, a select comittee was set up in April 1974, largely in the form the Maybray-King Committee had recommended the previous July (Kolinsky, 1975).

The terms of reference of the House of Lords committee enjoin it to report on proposals which 'raise important questions of policy or principle' and on 'other questions to which the committee considers the special attention of the House should be drawn'. This allows the committee to be selective about what it does, choosing certain proposals for investigation as well as making reports on aspects of Community policy. Some of its reports are on items of draft legislation, others on commission discussion documents or reviews of policy in some areas. By contrast the Commons select committee reports briefly on every item of draft legislation, indicating whether or not it believes important questions of principle or policy are raised, but without entering into any discussion of the merits of such proposals. By avoiding such discussion it has no doubt been easier for the Commons committee to preserve its unanimity when making reports. While the Lords' committee tends to produce lengthy reports with relatively large quantities of accompanying evidence, by contrast the Commons committee produces brief reports which simply alert the House as to whether or not debate on the proposal is considered desirable. Only rarely does the Commons committee now take evidence: it did so twice in 1984–5.

The Lords committee evolved a method of working which suited the conditions of the House. A main committee initially of seventeen peers, later expanded to twenty-five, was established, with the actual work of investigation being carried on through sub-committees, initially five in number, but soon increased to seven (though reduced to six in 1987). The sub-committees have been subject orientated, like the European Parliament committees, rather than based on Whitehall departments. Each sub-committee, as well as containing a few members of the main Committee, co-opts other peers for particular inquiries, and peers not co-opted are invited to attend and take part in evidence taking sessions. This quite frequently occurs. In this way around 100 peers have, in recent sessions, had some part in the work of the EC committee (during the 1986–7 session 113 peers took part in EC committee inquiries). Thus the large part-time membership of the House, with its varied expertise, has been well utilised. For example, according to the House of Lords Information Office, in 1978 among the ninety peers then involved, seventeen were former ministers, nine former civil servants or diplomats, eighteen had held university posts, eleven were scientists, and eight farmers. Particular reports have sometimes been signed by a galaxy of peers, experienced and authoritative in the subject concerned. An inquiry into the European monetary system was undertaken in 1983 by a sub-committee chaired by a former Governor of the Bank of England. On the committee were: another former Governor; a former head of the Treasury; a former chief economic adviser to HMG; as well as several former ministers. The committee unanimously recommended that the UK should join the EMS at an early date, though not necessarily immediately (HL 39, 1983–4).

The chairmanship of the main committee was, from the start, a full-time salaried post, held successively by Lord Diamond, Baroness Tweedsmuir of Belhelvie, Lord Greenwood of Rossendale, Baroness White, and then Baroness Llewelyn-Davies of Hastoe, who was succeeded by Baroness Serota in 1986. All of these had held ministerial office in one or other

Table 8.1 European Community Committee Reports, 1985–6

Title of report	Date of report	Information or debate	Date of debate	Length of report (no. of pages)	Length of evidence and appendices (no. of pages)
Report by main committee The Single European Act and Parliamentary Scrutiny	8.5.86	D	31.7.86[a]	6	2
Sub-committee A: Finance, Economics and Regional Policy, Chm. L. Seebohm					
Indirect Taxation and the Internal Market	15.4.86	D	10.4.86	27	144
The Community Budget	29.7.86	I	–	20	72
Sub-committee B: External Relations, Trade and Industry, Chm. V. Rochdale					
European Maritime Policy	18.3.86	D	2.5.86	24	322
Disclosure of Significant Shareholdings	8.7.86	I	–	11	68
Standards for Simple Pressure Vessels	29.7.86	D	10.86	8	54
Sub-committee C: Education, Employment and Social Affairs, Chm. B. Serota					
Income Taxation and Equal Treatment for Men and Women	19.11.85	D	17.2.86	25	181
Consumer Protection Policy	17.6.86	D	10.4.86	17	293
Recognition of Higher Education Diplomas	29.7.86	D	10.10.86	29	525
Sub-committee D: Agriculture, Food and Consumer Affairs, Chm. L. Gallacher					
Examination of Animals and Fresh Meat for the Presence of Residues	17.12.85	I	–	13	71
Reform of EC Cereals Policy	18.2.86	D	21.5.86	23	156
1986–7 Farm Price Policy	19.3.86	D	21.5.86	23	132
Internal Markets for Foodstuffs Meat Products	} 20.5.86	D	20.5.86	33	131
Socio–structural Policy in Agriculture	29.7.86	I	–	30	213
EEC Forestry Policy	4.11.86	D	17.2.86	25	231

Table 8.1 *(continued)*

Title of report	Date of report	Information or debate	Date of debate	Length of report (no. of pages)	Length of evidence and appendices (no. of pages)
Sub-committee E: Law, Chm. L. Templeman					
Counterfeit Goods	3.12.85	I	–	9	55
Privileges and Immunities of MEPs	18.3.86	D	25.11.86	16	142
Delegation of Powers to the Commission (interim report)	15.7.86	I	–	14	58
Milk Production (outgoers' scheme)[b]	18.2.86	D	21.4.86	14	108
Sub-committee F: Energy, Transport, Technology and Research, Chm. V. Torrington					
Television Without Frontiers	17.12.85	D	3.3.86	22	275
Nuclear Power in Europe	15.7.86	D	20.11.86	67	497
Sub-committee G: Environment, Chm. L. Nathan					
Disposal of Waste Oils	17.12.86	I	–	8	78
Dumping of Waste at Sea	8.7.86	D	18.12.86	26	239

Notes: [a] Debated during 2R European Communities (Amendment) Bill.
[b] Jointly with sub-committee D.

House before becoming chairman. A professional legal adviser with special knowledge of EC law was appointed, followed later by an assistant legal adviser, several clerks seconded full-time to the work of this Committee, and others who helped part-time. Sub-committees can also appoint specialist advisers for particular inquiries, and this has become general practice.

A major task for the chairman of the main committee has been to decide which proposals merit scrutiny and which do not. About 800 proposals are made annually, for each of which the government department most immediately concerned produces an explanatory memorandum. With the assistance of this document the chairman lists proposals initially in two categories: list A being proposals not requiring special attention (approximately 75 per cent), and list B containing those thought to require consideration (approximately 25 per cent). Reports are published regularly by the main committee indicating the apportionment, and also showing to which sub-committee proposals in the second list (List B) have been sent, as well as giving information about the stage of scrutiny reached on each proposal. Some having been remitted for scrutiny are simply noted and not given further consideration. Others are investigated (sometimes by a special joint committee established between two sub-committees): a report is drawn up, for approval by the main committee, sent to the House and published. Each such report states whether it is for information only, or whether it is also recommended for debate. Occasionally the main committee itself draws up a report. It did this in 1986 on the implications of the Single European Act which it believed would, in the long run, weaken the position of the UK Parliament, though it saw no difficulty for the committee in adapting its procedures to the proposed alterations (HL 264, 1985–61). An innovation in 1987 was the publication of exchanges of correspondence between the committee and ministers on draft proposals upon which time prevented a full inquiry taking place (HL 6, 1987–88).

Where debate is recommended, this invariably takes place, and without any undue delay — a further contrast to Commons practice. During the 1983–7 parliament, of the seventy-six reports made, forty-eight were recommended for debate, and by June 1987 all but one had been debated, the exception being a report made only a month before dissolution. Sometimes more than one report is debated on a single occasion, and debates on reports occasionally take place alongside some other item of business, for example, the second reading of a relevant bill.

The total output of the EC Committee is considerable. Each sub-committee produces at least as many major reports as each of the departmental select committees in the Commons. The total number of reports in the 1985–6 session was 24, with 500 pages of report, a further 250 pages for appendices, and some 3,800 pages of published evidence. (See Table 8.1)

In seeking evidence, European as well domestic sources are tapped, with the sub-committees almost always inviting an MEP to give evidence for each inquiry, and often hearing from members of the EC Commission as well. Frequently sub-committee members travel to Europe and hold informal discussions on the topic of an inquiry.

The committee has developed close links with both the Commission and the European Parliament. One has the impression that informal contacts keep committee members abreast of the direction of thinking within Community institutions, and the likely, most worthwhile, area for inquiries. The contribution of clerks from the European Office of the House of Lords is not to be underestimated here; generally for example a clerk is present at plenary sessions of the European Parliament.

Committee reports usually receive publicity in the serious press. Within Whitehall departments and among interested MPs evidence suggests reports are regarded as extremely useful sources. Elsewhere in Community institutions, reports from the committee appear to be highly thought of and widely distributed. Tribute is frequently paid to the quality of the committee's work (see Bates, 1985, and Grantham and Hodgson, 1985).

The committee seeks to provide an informed and expert appraisal of Community proposals, as well as indicating their likely effect on UK interests. Very rarely do sub-committees, or the main committee vote to settle conflicts of view; instead reports are drafted so as to reflect differences which remain after the process of evidence-taking and deliberation has been completed. Some of the chairmen seem to revel in the intellectual challenge of producing a cogent and convincing report which is fair to the evidence received and the opinions held within the committee. Reports are usually apolitical, not naively ignoring politics, but rather approaching subjects with an independent-mindedness which treats the political aspects of a question as one factor along with others that demand attention.

Whether by accident or design (or a bit of both) the Lords committee has come to play a very different rôle to the Commons committee. To begin with the two committees were often investigating the same document, and in some cases civil servants gave evidence to one committee one day and the other the next. But steps were soon taken to avoid such duplication of effort, for example, through making evidence obtained by one committee immediately available to the other. Distinctiveness within a co-operative framework became a characteristic of these committees.

The Science and Technology Committee

The Prime Minister was apparently 'put out' when the House of Commons failed to reappoint its Science and Technology Committee at the time of the 1979 reforms (HL Debs, 10 February 1984, col. 1434). The House of Lords decided to fill the gap, which it did by appointing, in January 1980, a select committee simply 'to consider science and technology'. Like the EC Committee, this select committee is reappointed each session; it works through sub-committees (usually two as well as a general purposes sub-committee); in addition to its fifteen members, other peers may be co-opted for particular inquiries, and the sub-committees invariably appoint specialist advisers and frequently travel overseas in the course of their inquiries.

The membership of this committee brings together peers eminent in the world of science and technology — Fellows of the Royal Society and leading industrialists — with politician peers, not least former ministers. The first chairman of the committee was Lord Todd, a Cambridge University scientist and former chairman of the Advisory Council on

Table 8.2 Science and Technology Committee Reports

Title of report	No. of report	Debated in House	Government reply	Further reports
Electric Vehicles (July 1980)	First report HL 352 (1979–80)	11.11.80	–	Third report HL210 (1981–2) (July 1982)
Scientific Aspects of Forestry (Nov 1980)	Second report HL 381 (1979–80) 2 vols	23.2.81	Second report HL 83 (1981–2) (Feb 1982)	Fourth report HL 211 (1981–2) (July 1982)
Hazardous Waste Disposal (July 1981)	First report HL 273 (1980–1) 2 vols	17.11.81	Third report HL 126, 1984–5 (April 1985)	Sixth report HL 234 (1984–5) (July 1985)
Science and Government (Nov 1981)	First report HL 20 (1981–2)	15.2.82	Cmnd 8591 (July 1982)	
Water Industry (Dec 1982)	First report HL 47 (1982–3) 2 vols	25.5.83	Memo placed in House of Lords' Library (Nov 1983)	
Engineering R & D (Feb 1983)	Second report HL 89 (1982–3) 3 vols	4.7.83	First report HL 27 (1984–5) (Nov 1984)	
Occupational Health and Hygiene (Dec 1983)	Second report HL 99 (1983–4) 3 vols	15.11.84	Fifth report HL 289 (1983–4) (July 1984)	

Subject	Report	Debated	Government response	Follow-up report
Remote Sensing and Digital Mapping (Dec 1983)	First report HL 98 (1983–4) 2 vols	25.5.84	—	
Agriculture and Environmental Research (July 1984)	Fourth report HL 272 (1983–4)	—	Fifth report HL 233 (1984–5) (July 1985)	
Education and Training (December 1984)	Second report HL 48 (1984–5) 3 vols	25.3.85	Cmnd 9653 (Nov 1985)	
Science and Technology in Local Government (Nov 1985)	First report HL 11 (1985–6)	21.1.86	Third report HL 243 (1985–6) (July 1986)	Fourth report HL 127 (1984–5) (April 1985)
Marine Science and Technology (December 1985)	Second report HL 47 (1985–6) 3 vols	7.5.86	Cmnd 9861 (July 1986)	
Innovation in Surface Transport (Jan 1987)	Second report HL 57 (1986–7)	7.7.87		
Civil Research and Development (Jan 1987)	First report HL 20 (1986–7)	19.2.87	Cm. 185 (July 1987)	
UK Space Policy (December 1987)	Second report HL 41 (1987–8)			

Scientific Policy. In 1984 he was succeeded by Lord Sherfield, former permanent secretary at the Treasury and an ex-chairman of the Atomic Energy Authority. By 1987 the committee had published thirteen major reports (see Table 8.2 for a full list) several of which had been supplemented by further reports. All but one of these were debated in the House of Lords, usually within about three months of publication. Such debates provided an opportunity for a preliminary reply from the Government — given in a minister's speech — but further replies usually published by the committee have become the norm.

The Government was initially very tardy about its responses, and when these appeared it was sometimes reasonable to infer that rather casual consideration had been given to the report concerned. In February 1982 in its reply to a report on forestry the Government referred to the report as having been published the previous December, when in fact it had been published fourteen months earlier. The committee's third major report, on hazardous waste disposal, was published in July 1981, and debated in the Lords the following November, but no government reply was forthcoming until April 1985, despite questions in the House by the committee chairman. When the reply eventually came, the committee was highly critical, not only of the four-year delay, but also of the failure of the Government 'even yet to reach conclusions on three important recommendations' namely for registration of hazardous waste producers, quarterly returns of their waste and the licensing of handlers of such waste. The committee returned to the subject, having been invited to review arrangements for hazardous waste disposal by a Department of Environment minister, but it continued to be highly critical of the Government.

Some of the committee's reports have dealt quite specifically with matters of current policy or legislative decision. In 1983–4 an inquiry was held into remote sensing and digital mapping. During this the terms on which the Government was proposing to privatise the Ordnance Survey came in for considerable criticism, and were indeed eventually altered. These alterations were insisted on by a minister who, after he had appeared before the committee to give evidence, realised the difficulties the Ordnance Survey faced. In 1985 the committee undertook a major inquiry into science and technology in local government, and actually issued a special report in April urging amendments to the Local Government Bill then before Parliament. Earlier, in 1981 and 1983, amendments to the Forestry Bill and the Water Bill respectively had been based directly on recommendations included in committee reports (Bates, 1985, p.52).

Witnesses, including ministers and civil servants, who appear before the committee know that among its members are some who, on any reckoning, are authorities on the subjects concerned. On the whole, too, committee members have the time and persistence to keep worrying away at the Government on recommendations the committee makes. It has proved itself much readier than Commons select committees to follow up earlier reports and to do so by specifically inquiring into the implementation of recommendations which have been accepted. On topics the committee chooses to investigate it has raised the threshold of awareness within government and public bodies. Its report on civil research and development recommended a fundamentally new structure for coordinating funding, and this drew a very positive response from the Government in a White Paper in July 1987 indicating that the Prime Minister would head a Cabinet committee on the subject. On the other hand, despite the authoritative character of its reports, the Government has at times virtually ignored these, and if it does so the committee can do little other than publish a further critical report.

Ad Hoc Select Committees

Since 1970 the House of Lords has made limited but regular use of select committees to examine public bills on particular subjects. Seven committees have been established to examine bills and four to examine subjects. These committees have consisted of from seven to twelve peers; they have been appointed only to deal with a particular subject or bill, and have ceased to exist when their report has been completed.

All but one of the select committees appointed to examine bills have dealt with private members' legislation. The exception was the Hare Coursing Bill, which, though introduced by the Labour Government in 1975, had been a private members' bill the previous session. This was the first time a government bill had been referred to a select committee in the Lords since 1917. In some respects this committee was the least satisfactory. Its report recommended that the bill should not proceed, but the committee was divided, and this central recommendation was agreed by four votes to three. The bill made no further progress.

Of the private members' bills referred to select committees, the first three were all introduced by Liberal peers. Baroness Seear's Anti-Discrimination Bill in 1972 dealt with the difficult subject of sex discrimination. This was a matter upon which the Government was under some pressure in both Houses; a Commons bill had lapsed in 1971-2 and a parallel Commons committee was established in 1972-3. The Lords select committee first considered the extent of sex discrimination, then reported specifically on Baroness Seear's bill. Both Houses through select committees and private members' bills goaded the Government into introducing its own bill in the 1972-3 session.

In 1977 a select committee examined a Bill of Rights introduced by Lord

Wade. Though almost evenly divided on whether or not such a bill would be worth-while, the committee did marshall the arguments on the subject effectively. One of the peers involved later wrote that he commenced with a strong prejudice against such a bill, but he realised he was wrong, and became a supporter (Redcliffe-Maud, 1981, p. 145). No doubt the committee's report had a wider educative effect, and a bill based on the European convention on human rights subsequently passed the House, but made no headway in the Commons.

One select committee came down unequivocally against the bill it was set up to investigate; this was the 1978 committee on Lord Byers' Foreign Boycotts Bill, a proposal which, though cast in general terms, was clearly aimed against the Arab boycott of Israel. The object of the bill was to make compliance with the boycott illegal. It was clear that the Government had no intention of supporting such legislation, but at the same time it felt the whole subject could benefit from public ventilation. The evidence taken by the committee — from exporting firms, government departments and the Foreign Secretary — was overwhelmingly against the introduction of legislation. But the committee in its report strongly urged companies to show more courage in fighting the boycott, and urged the Government to be more vigorous in assisting companies, even using public funds to support boycott-related activity.

A subject which successive governments baulked at tackling was the welfare of animals used in laboratory experiments, even though during the 1970s at least seven private members' bills on this topic were introduced. In 1979 the House of Lords sent Lord Halsbury's Laboratory Animals Protection Bill to a select committee. Lord Halsbury, a cross-bench hereditary peer, an FRS and a former member of both the Medical and Science Research Councils, later explained how he had taken Lord Houghton of Sowerby — a veteran animal welfare campaigner — into his confidence, and that it was Lord Houghton who had suggested this procedure (HL Deb, 28 November 1985, col. 1025). The resulting committee received some 900 letters and memoranda and took oral evidence at six of its sixteen meetings, eventually producing a much revised draft bill, which the House of Lords duly passed, but which made no progress in the Commons. The Government was plainly reluctant to legislate in this area, but five years later, with animal rights groups becoming ever more troublesome, the nettle was grasped, and the resulting 1986 Animals (Scientific Procedures) Bill owed much to the work of this select committee.

The membership of this committee forms a good example of the blend of expertise the House can employ on a subject of this kind. The chairman was Lord Ashby, a Cambridge botanist, a life peer and former chairman of the Royal Commission on environmental pollution, a crossbencher who later moved to the SDP. Another member of the committee was Lord Adrian, a hereditary crossbench peer, who had been professor of cell physiology at Cambridge. Another member was the fifth Earl of Cranbrook, a Conservative hereditary peer, holder of a PhD in anatomy, who was a trustee of the British Museum, a member of the Royal Comission on environmental pollution, and of the Natural Environment Research Council; a peer who entered the Lords in 1978, and who succeeded a father (the fourth earl) who had also developed a reputation through his work in the House for animal welfare issues. Other members were: Lord McGregor of Durris, a life peer who held a chair in social institutions at London University; Lord Skelmersdale a hereditary peer, a keen amateur naturalist and president of the British Naturalists Association; Lord Newall, also a Conservative hereditary peer, well-known in the horse-racing world; and Lord Beaumont of Whitley, a Liberal life peer and ordained Anglican clergyman, who had a strong interest in 'green' issues generally. Both Lord Halsbury and Lord Houghton were also members of this select committee. On any reckoning it represented the mobilisation of considerable relevant expertise.

Two bills seeking to alter the law on charities were referred to a select committee in 1984, which decided neither were satisfactory, but under the chairmanship of Lord Brightman (a Lord of Appeal), the committee formulated a third bill which it recommended to the Lords, and which was passed in the 1984–5 session. The object of this legislation was to bring clarity and accountability to the bewildering world of small charities, tens of thousands of which had tiny annual incomes, produced no proper accounts, and in many cases had simply gone to sleep. The 1985 bill empowered tiny charities to spend their capital, and many other small charities to amalgamate. This was a subject which the House of Commons Expenditure Committee had reported on in 1975, as had a National Council for Social Services committee under the ubiquitous Lord Goodman. The Government had considered both these earlier reports, but announced in 1980 it would not introduce legislation. It was an area in which it was generally agreed something ought to be done, but deciding exactly what should be done was a very difficult matter. The Lords' select committee cleared the way for legislation.

In early 1987, the Infant Life (Preservation) Bill, introduced by the then Bishop of Birmingham, Dr Montefiore, was referred to a select committee. This issued an interim report based on the evidence it managed to take before the dissolution of Parliament. One of its early witnesses was Dr Montefiore, himself no longer a member of the House because he retired from his See soon after introducing the bill. The committee was re-appointed in Autumn 1987 at the instigation of Lord Houghton of Saverby, an opponent of the Bishop's bill.

Since 1970 four *ad hoc* committees investigating particular subjects have been established. Three of these were in the broad area of economic policy, the exception being the 1971–3 committee on Sport and Leisure chaired by the tenth Viscount Cobham, a former first-class county cricketer. A committee on commodity prices under Lord Roberthall — a professional economist — met forty-eight times during 1976 and 1977, producing a well-documented report illustrating the intractable nature of the difficulties involved in trying to get greater stability into commodity markets. In 1981–2 the Lords appointed a committee to examine unemployment, and in 1984 a committee to consider the causes and implications of the deficit in the balance of trade in manufactured goods.

This latter committee was prompted by the fact that in 1983 Britain had become, for the first time ever, a net importer of manufactured goods. It was chaired by Lord Aldington, a business man who had once been a Conservative minister, and among its members were two other former Conservative ministers, as well as Lord Ezra, former Chairman of the National Coal Board, Lord Beswick, a former Labour Minister and former Chairman of British Aerospace, and Lord Kearton, former Chairman of Courtaulds, of BNOC, and of the Industrial Reorganisation Corporation, 1966–70. The committee's report, published in October 1985, attracted much public attention because it sounded severe warnings about the economic, social and political crisis Britain would ultimately face unless the Government took urgent steps to alter the situation. Unprecedently the Secretary of State for Trade and Industry, the barrister Leon Brittan, issued an immediate statement rejecting the main findings of the committee. The House of Lords debated the report in December 1985, and it was widely cited over the following eighteen months in both Houses of Parliament and elsewhere. The Government's displeasure with the report was as real as the report's lucid and authoritative commentary on Britain's shrinking industrial base.

Conclusion

The reception given to this report may be taken as illustrative of the strengths — and weaknesses — of the House of Lords in regard to select committee work. The Lords can appoint highly talented and experienced members to a range of committees. Witnesses can be cross-examined in a more searching way than is usual in the Commons. Reports almost invariably score well for their rigour in analysis, the lucidity and force-fulness of their argument, and their generally well-researched and sure-footed flavour. The report on Overseas Trade apparently ran through five editions in two years (Silk 1987, p. 231). It was probably more widely read by undergraduates than any other recent select committee report. Indirectly it may well have had a considerable influence. But select committees in Britain in the 1980s which produce reports challenging fundamental government policies — on employment, overseas trade, entry to the EMS, or whatever — cannot be expected to have immediate impact. The Government may momentarily yelp in frustration or embarrassment, but no more. Nonetheless in the longer term they may contribute to a remoulding of informed public opinion.

On the other hand select committees which produce reports on complex issues, such as the tangled and outdated condition of the law on small charities, or how best to update the law on animal experiments, or how to standardise EC measurements of cereals, receive less publicity, but almost certainly achieve more of tangible consequence within the Executive in bringing about legislative change.

In conclusion to this whole chapter, it seems reasonable to argue that the House of Lords does a considerable amount of work of a relatively obscure kind for which MPs do not, in general, show great enthusiasm, for example, on private bills and in select committees on subjects which lack political kudos. The House of Lords has tended, in recent years, to develop activities in ways which enable it to play a complementary role to the Commons. This is a point taken up again in the final chapter.

9

WHAT ROLE FOR THE LORDS?

The main concern of this book has been to analyse the House of Lords as it existed and as it functioned in Britain in the 1980s. But it would be odd if such a study did not conclude by offering some consideration of the possible reform or abolition of the Lords. Such questions may have faded somewhat from public debate over the last few years, but their return to prominence cannot be indefinitely postponed. This final chapter takes up these matters, and in so doing offers a brief analysis of the various suggestions which have been made for reform of the Lords, as well as indicating some of the consequences which could follow abolition.

It is helpful to approach this whole subject by considering successively the functions, powers and composition of the House of Lords. That these three are interrelated, and ought to remain so, is obvious. But the general argument of this chapter will be that the functions and powers of the present House are a good deal more satisfactory than its composition. The discussion of functions will involve briefly reviewing and drawing some conclusions from earlier chapters of this book, and then indicating possible lines along which present functions could be extended. The discussion of powers will require some comparison between the rôle of the House of Lords under a Labour Government and its rôle under the Conservatives. The discussion of composition will include reference to schemes for reform.

The Functions of the House

If functions specifically are being discussed it is reasonable to speak of these as being threefold: the House of Lords has a legislative, a deliberative and a constitutional rôle. Any of these may involve power, but in practice the former two are discharged largely without the question of power arising, whereas the constitutional rôle clearly does involve the assertion of power.

The scrutiny and amendment of legislation remains the most important task of the Lords. This is primarily a revising rôle, but it is not simply a matter of affording opportunities for draftsmen to improve their handiwork.

It is also a question of making minor adjustments to legislation in response to anxieties and concerns which have surfaced in various ways during a bill's earlier legislative stages. Usually it is the give and take of the legislative process which produces as its end product a bill recognisably the same as the one first submitted to Parliament, but (at least in the case of major bills) different in many detailed ways. But major adjustments are also forced on governments. A very close observer spoke of his experience in the House of Lords in the mid-1980s as witnessing the Government moving from one trouble-spot to another and the Lords being on occasions an effective curb on government intentions; a remark borne out by the analysis presented in Chapter 6.

The fundamental forces which shape legislation lie well beyond the House of Lords. Their focus is primarily on the Cabinet and on Whitehall departments; in so far as they have a parliamentary focus it is on the House of Commons. But the House of Lords, like the Commons, does mull over the details of legislation, though each House does this in its own way. The Commons generally takes much more time than the Lords, a feature made possible by the former's widespread use of standing committees, though the effectiveness of these is often criticised (see Griffith, 1981). Debate in the Lords is usually less thorough; it must be kept concise because every stage of every bill (almost) is taken on the floor of the House. But since all major bills go through the Commons first this doesn't necessarily matter. Debate in the Lords can afford to concentrate more sharply on issues left outstanding by the Lower House. Of course in practice this is not always the case. Debate at times is repetitious, though again this may not be undesirable. If the executive appears to be contemplating giving ground, then arguments may need to be reiterated to encourage this process.

Debate in the Lords is less obviously partisan. The overall party political context is clear enough in the Upper House, but debate generally is freed from the incessant demands of party rivalry which dominate the Commons. Partisanship is not absent, but it is muted, and it is expressed differently in the Upper House.

On private members' bills the House of Lords has a creditable record of edging along discussion, especially on some issues which give rise to inhibitions among MPs and which governments dare not touch. Sometimes through this form of parliamentary private enterprise the Lords has helpfully had a cockshy at getting a difficult idea distilled into a viable piece of legislation.

Then there is a kind of underworld of parliamentary legislative activity discussed in Chapter 8, relatively obscure and yet by no means without importance. In these areas the Lords appears helpful in relieving the Commons of tasks which the Lower House has little time and probably little enthusiasm to sustain.

The deliberative work of the House of Lords is conducted partly in the chamber, and partly in committees. The work in the chamber is difficult to evaluate. What *is* the outcome of all those Wednesday debates with so many worthy speeches, conscientiously prepared (on the whole) and faithfully recorded in *Hansard* for a wider readership (but how wide?)? Sometimes they are fascinating, informed and highly persuasive; sometimes boring, irrelevant and even almost incoherent. But such qualities, like beauty itself, lie at least in part in the eye of the beholder. Significant perhaps is the simple fact that many very busy and accomplished people, presumably not on the whole short of things to do, participate in debates. Select committee work too has attracted many peers. A tradition of public service encourages such activities — perhaps the continuing strength of this tradition is a rather special British phenomenon, just as the House of Lords is unique among parliamentary chambers. At virtually no public expense the services of many experienced and talented individuals are mobilised for select committee work. Even if such activities don't have much apparent influence (and that depends on bodies besides the House of Lords), they can hardly be thought to do any harm. Some undoubtedly do have an influence upon government.

In regard to both legislative and deliberative work, the House of Lords essentially plays a complementary rôle to the Commons. Such complementarity is most obvious in relation to the newer parliamentary functions, notably work on European Community matters. In relation to more traditional tasks, such as the scrutiny of domestic statutory instruments and private bills, even the primary legislative process, reforms aimed at reshaping procedures to enhance complementarity (rather than the continuing formal duplication of rôles) could be considered.

Mention was made in Chapter 5 of the Lords select committee on practice and procedure which recommended select committees to consider Government legislation. (See also HL 141, 1976–7.) This proposal received a hasty burial when it was first made, but is worthy of re-examination. The committee recommended the establishment of a range of subject-based select committees, to which bills would be referred as soon as they had received second reading in the Commons. These committees would monitor the progress of a bill in the Lower House, publishing a report indicating time taken on different sections of the bill, ministerial undertakings given and other such information. Additionally, such committees would take evidence from interested parties, civil servants and others, in the same sort of way as the European Communities Committee takes evidence on draft legislation. Once a bill had reached the House of Lords, it could be referred to the select committee which had already been monitoring it (with the minister in charge and possibly some other peers added) at its committee stage. For bills introduced into the Lords both the above stages might be taken together in an extended committee stage.

Such committees would, in part, be doing the kind of work special standing committees (SSCs) in the Commons have undertaken since 1979 — on those rare occasions when the Government has permitted their establishment (see HC 49–I–II, 1984–5). It seems primarily to be executive hostility to such attempts to raise a little more of the legislative process above the waterline of public visibility which has so severely restricted the use of SSCs. But whilst one objection to their use in the Commons has been the time they take (and possible consequent delay in dealing with a bill), select committees on bills in the Lords could be at work while a bill was still before the Commons, and in this case no slippage in the legislative timetable need occur. The proposals made by the Lords select committee on practice and procedure were designed both to improve the quality of legislative scrutiny by the Upper House, and to alleviate the problems caused for the Upper House by the very uneven flow of legislative business. The experience of the Lords with select committees on private members' bills provides encouragement for such developments.

There may be further arguments for extending select committee work in the Lords. The departmental committees which have existed in the Commons since 1979 do not provide a very satisfactory means for the critical evaluation of a department's administrative performance. It is the very closeness of the linkage between the Government and the Commons which appears to handicap all party groups of MPs in regard to such work. Select committees formed in the Upper House are able to work in a noticeably more detached manner, and this is a feature of which greater use could be made.

The third function of the House of Lords is a constitutional one. This has not been given much prominence in this book. It is a much less clear rôle than that of revising legislation or deliberation. It also brings us inevitably to the discussion of power, so is best considered under that heading.

The Power of the House

The constitutional rôle is twofold. On the one hand the House of Lords has certain powers vested in it which, in theory at least, would enable it to prevent the subversion of some basic constitutional principles, notably any unilateral action by a majority party in the Commons to postpone a general election. In addition the power the House of Lords retains to delay any item of government legislation may also be thought of as a more general constitutional function. Both need to be considered here.

Under the Parliament Acts the House of Lords retains an absolute veto over any bill to extend the lifetime of a parliament. In 1915 and again in 1940 when the House of Commons passed bills to defer general elections then due, the House of Lords agreed to them, as did Opposition party leaders. The unsuitability of holding elections in wartime conditions was reason enough for their postponement. But if a government attempted so drastic a step without Opposition support, would the House of Lords in practice be able to exercise its veto? (And if the Government was a Conservative Government, would the House wish to exercise a veto?) No sure answer can be given to such questions, mainly because they presuppose a degree of ill-health in the body politic far beyond any malady recently experienced.

Again, it is conceivable that a government may wish to sack a judge, a procedure which at present would require a majority vote in both Houses. This, it can be argued, helps to sustain the independence of the judiciary (Crowther-Hunt, 1980). But, without being drawn too deeply into this area, it seems reasonable to suggest that the formal independence of the judiciary rests on more solid foundations than the continued existence of the House of Lords, and that the threats to judicial independence operate in a far more subtle way than through an open frontal assault by Parliament (consider for example decisions about the promotion of judges).

The constitutional rôle of the House of Lords in these areas may have a theoretical clarity, but in practice the circumstances involved appear so hypothetical that the ability of the Lords to take any effective action must also be described as hypothetical. The present basis on which the membership of the House is composed does little to enhance its suitability as a body capable of mounting some last-ditch defence of the Constitution, a point we will return to later in this chapter.

However, the constitutional rôle of the House of Lords must not be too narrowly defined. There is a sense in which, simply by being there, as part of a parliamentary process through which all legislation must pass, the Lords has a constitutional function. Bills cannot become the law of the land until the Upper House has given its approval, or until its disapproval has been overridden by a public, and very precise, procedure stipulated in the Parliament Acts.

The power to delay legislation may be used very sparingly but it remains an important part of the context within which the House of Lords carries out its functions. The way the power is understood has however altered drastically since it was first defined in the 1911 Parliament Act. At that time there was no suggestion that the Lords ought to refrain from using this power. Indeed the contrary was implied; the House of Lords would be neglecting its constitutional duty if it failed to impose delay on some bills of a highly controversial kind: and this the Lords did up to the First World War. But thereafter, for sixty years, the power to delay bills was unused, save, ironically, the delay imposed on the 1947 Parliament Bill, the measure which cut the Lord's power of delay from two years to one.

By the 1960s the House of Lords had not used its power for so long that the common understanding about the circumstances in which it might reasonably do so had changed. No longer was the exercise of power seen as a proper part of the discharge of the functions of the House of Lords in relation to the revision of controversial bills. Rather the use of delaying power by the Lords had come to be viewed as a kind of ultimate weapon to which the Lords might be driven in extreme circumstances. In 1967 Lord Carrington, Conservative leader in the Lords, argued that the House should not delay the London Government Bill (which postponed London borough elections) because it could only expect to use its delaying power once, and therefore the power should be reserved for a matter of great constitutional and national importance (HL Debs 16 February 1967, cols 419–24). Bee-like the House could sting once, then die, either through abolition or through having its remaining powers removed. It seemed as if a new convention of the constitution had been established reserving the Lords' power of delay to matters of fundamental constitutional importance.

But another aspect to the possession of this power was the simple fact that it enhanced the credibility and standing of the House of Lords as a revising body. When introducing the 1947 Parliament Bill, Herbert Morrison speaking for the Labour Government had emphasised this point, stating 'if the position were that the House of Lords sent their amendments to the Commons, but the Commons could indifferently ignore them and pass a bill into law without further ado, then the Lords would be entitled to say that there was no guarantee that any serious consideration would be given to their amendments, and that we might as well resort to single chamber government' (HC Debs, 10 November 1947, col. 38). The continued possession of some formal power was seen as necessary for the Lords to discharge its revising function adequately.

The corollary to this was that if the House of Lords felt its proposed changes to bills — any bills — were not being accorded sufficiently serious attention, it could threaten delay. In the highly confused and unprecedented parliamentary situation of the mid 1970s this is what happened. The Lords did use its power to delay two bills, not because the particular legislation objected to contained matters of great constitutional and national importance, but rather because it was exasperated at its treatment by a highly tenuous Commons majority. It is worth, for a moment, trying to describe the contrasting perspectives which the two major parties had on the exercise of power at that time.

The Conservatives saw a government with the most fragile possible Commons majority insisting on passing a mass of contentious legislation. In a formal sense the Labour Government had attained office quite legitimately, but unlike past governments with low majorities (such as 1950–1, 1964–6) it appeared in no way to moderate its legislative programme. In particular in 1976 five major bills were 'guillotined' in the Commons, and none of these reached the House of Lords until very late in the parliamentary session. The Lords scarcely had the time to revise these bills properly, but then such amendments as it did make were rapidly reversed in the Commons under a very tight allocation of time order. When the bill nationalising aerospace and shipbuilding was found to be hybrid in regard to ship repairing, the Government responded by putting down a motion setting aside the hybridity procedure in the Commons. How much undivided power was it proper for a Cabinet in control of a bare Commons majority to be able to enjoy? (Hailsham, 1976). Should not the House of Lords check the Government in some way and if it failed to do so, wasn't it acquiescing in the devaluation of its own rôle as a revising chamber?

To the Labour Government the matter had a very different appearance. The legislation it advanced had been included in its election manifesto; in particular ship-repairing was specifically referred to in both the 1974 manifestos. It may have had a low Commons majority, but it had nevertheless clearly won the October 1974 election, and that was what mattered. The hybridity issue was a procedural red herring, which had only arisen because the private firms involved had been so unco-operative in refusing to provide enough information about themselves. If the parliamentary wing of the Labour Party was to retain the co-operation of the trade union wing of the party, then this legislation had to be implemented. At least that was how it looked to the parliamentary leadership. The Lords was an anachronistic body which Labour had attempted — unsuccessfully — to reform. It was now quite wrong and completely irresponsible for the Conservative Opposition to use its built-in strength in the Upper House to overturn aspects of the Government's programme.

In the final debate on the Nationalisation Bill in 1976 both party leaders agreed that the matter of ship-repairing was not a great issue of principle. But while on the Labour side this point was emphasised so as to illustrate how foolish it would be to jeopardise the relationship between the two Houses (over a 'fragment of an industry'), Lord Carrington argued that this was exactly the sort of issue where the powers left with the Lords under the Parliament Acts ought to be used, and he quoted Herbert Morrison's statement (cited above) in support of this view; if the Lords were to perform a revising function effectively, then it would also be necessary from time to time at least to make use of its power (HL Debs, 22 November 1976, cols 1657–88).

This illustrates the ambiguity which surrounds the retention of power by the House of Lords. In so far as power is necessary for the Lords to act as a constitutional watchdog, then such power may be viewed as rather like the nuclear deterrent: to be kept in reserve, but only to be used once in extreme circumstances. In so far as power is necessary simply to ensure that adequate notice is taken of the Lords as a revising body, then a short delaying power is all that is necessary, long enough only to impose some awkwardness on the Government and perhaps partially to alert a slumbering public. This exercise of power should not give rise to any kind of constitutional crisis, though it is illustrative of a constitutional function possessed by the second chamber (see p. 134, Lord Boyd-Carpenter's comments on the British Nationality Bill). But many years of non-use of such power had created an assumption (encouraged by such statements as Lord Carrington's in 1967) that *any* exercise of power by the House of Lords must be a matter of supreme constitutional importance.

This analysis could be taken as indicating the desirability of keeping separate these two aspects of power, namely the power to ensure the Lords remains an effective revising body, and the power to defend important constitutional principles. The 1911 Parliament Act, by making special provision for any bill to extend the lifetime of a parliament, pointed the way to such a distinction. Defining precisely a category of subjects upon which the House of Lords retained a power of veto (or at least a strong power, appropriate to genuine constitutional issues) would be difficult, and may be tantamount to producing a written constitution. But it would be appropriate to try and recognise more explicitly the difference between these two kinds of power. While one — if it is to be retained at all — needs to be a strong power, the other — the power to ensure legislative revision is taken seriously — need only be a brief delaying power. The 1968 White Paper proposed a six-month delay from the date of disagreement between the two Houses, which would be quite long enough to be effective.

However in order for a second chamber to use such power realistically and effectively, its own legitimacy must be safeguarded. The present House of Lords shares in what Lord Hailsham described as the priceless advantage of immemorial antiquity which characterises the British Constitution. This undoubtedly — in the British context — confers upon the House of Lords an element of legitimacy. But institutions need to adapt to a changing environment. To some extent the Lords has done this, for example, through the Life Peerages Act. But has its adaptation been adequate? Discussion of this question takes us on to consider the composition of the House of Lords.

Composition

The argument thus far in this chapter has been that as regards both functions and powers, while present arrangements are not ideal, they are nevertheless satisfactory. The functions of the House of Lords could usefully be developed somewhat, and if a clearer understanding of the distinction between power to defend basic constitutional principles and power to ensure an effective revising rôle could be developed, then this would be helpful. But composition is a problem.

From a practical point of view the present mixture of hereditary and life peers may provide a body capable of performing most of the functions of the House adequately, at least under a Conservative Government. Though the membership favours the Conservative Party, there is no longer an overall party majority, and in any case there is enough independent-mindedness among peers for the House of Lords to be awkward enough, at times, to a Conservative Government. Legislation is revised and at least some constitutional excesses are checked (as, for example, the proposal for an interim body to replace the GLC in 1983). But under a Labour Government this is not the case. Because a Labour Government is defeated as a matter of routine in the Lords' division lobbies, the Commons also as a matter of routine is asked to cancel Lords' amendments. The revising function is less well discharged, resulting possibly in the House becoming factious and digging its heels in even on matters for which the Government can claim an electoral mandate (as in 1976), or perhaps being intimidated into not using its power to check the Government when some constitutional impropriety was being perpetrated (as in 1967).

This is the manifest consequence of the absurdity by which a parliamentary chamber contains a permanent built-in superiority for one party. But can the manner of composing the chamber be altered so as to avoid this?

There are three basic ways in which the House of Lords may be composed — inheritance, appointment and election. In effect the Lords has always been composed of a mixture of the first two methods, a combination of peers by succession and those themselves created hereditary or life peers, together with Lords Spiritual. The balance has recently moved in favour of appointed members, especially among the active element.

Little need be said as to inheritance. It may so happen that individuals of great ability or unusual experience arise through succession, but many others with neither of these attributes also inherit peerages. The great disadvantage of a House composed this way is that it reinforces the class division which remains one of the besetting weaknesses of British society. Abolishing hereditary membership of the Lords would on its own, of course, do precious little about this (one must keep a sense of proportion!), but the retention of this system of membership is indicative of an unwillingness seriously to tackle the legacy imposed by a class-based society and a class-based party system. But even those who repudiate the relevance of the above remarks must recognise that succession no longer establishes an acceptable claim to the legitimate exercise of power in a democratic society. Indeed it is the very recognition of this fact which has made the Lords so reluctant to use its remaining powers, and threatened it, at times, with extinction.

As to appointment, the drawback of the present method is the patronage power it allows a prime minister. The effectiveness of such patronage depends on the eagerness of recipients and potential recipients for the honour in question, but there seems little doubt that in recent years demand has been high. Any extension of the power of patronage would be unwelcome and ought to be resisted. The fact that the 1968 reform proposals, had they been implemented, would have resulted in a House composed entirely through the patronage of successive prime ministers was the greatest single reason for their demise. And that was before Mr Wilson's resignation honours list in 1976!

At present the only constraints upon a prime minister in regard to the exercise of this patronage are the honours scrutiny committee (with the right to veto obviously unsuitable candidates), possibly the monarch (who might in some circumstances conceivably resist some awards), and the more general constraint of convention by which a certain number of nominations must be invited from the leaders of opposition parties. Assuming that any reform would leave the Upper House still, in part, composed through appointment, a more formalised machinery for initiating suggestions should be composed, maybe an expanded honours scrutiny committee which would be obliged to report on the balance of party membership and the range of expertise and experience represented in, and omitted from, the House of Lords. Perhaps a Speaker's conference should be called to define a formula which prime ministers would be required to observe in making nominations. Beyond that would lie the possibility of creating a system of appointment by committee, but this could too easily degenerate into producing even more of the safe, unimaginative, dull appointments that critics claim the present system already achieves.

Another form of appointment sometimes advocated is to extend the ex officio principle already embodied in the House through the Bishops and the Law Lords. This sounds plausible, but at least two serious objections can be immediately mentioned. First, a serious difficulty arises in defining precisely what office-holders would qualify, and how any list agreed upon at one time could later be altered. Second, it is doubtful whether a House composed in this way would be other than highly fragmented. In any case the present House of Lords does, to a considerable degree, represent the community in its functional aspects, informally and in a rather random way. So too does the House of Commons. Most groups have their

spokesmen in Parliament already, and although these are merely spokesmen, this form of representation may be more suited to our parliamentary
system than a formal incorporation into Parliament of office-holders within
such groups.

The remaining method which could be used to compose the House of
Lords is some form of election. Most recent schemes of reform have
advocated a House at least in part elected. Sometimes indirect election has
been proposed but there have been few advocates of such a change, unless
it were carried through as part of a more sweeping reform, say one
introducing regional assemblies throughout the UK (Crowther-Hunt and
Peacock, 1973). Direct election has more frequently been suggested,
usually on the basis of proportional representation, with only part of the
House coming up for re-election at any one time. The Home Committee
recommended such a scheme (1978) as did a Labour MP in a Fabian
pamphlet (Bell, 1981). Election could of course be combined with
appointment and even inheritance. The Home Committee would have had
a House composed by all three methods for a transitional period, until
existing peers by succession died.

The obvious objection to election is that the Lords would become a rival
to the Commons. Election by some method quite different from that used
for the Lower House might only intensify rivalry because the reformed
second chamber could reasonably claim that its electoral legitimacy
(derived through a proportional system) was greater than that of the
Commons. Furthermore, any proposed reform would have to be accepted
by the Commons, and it is extremely difficult to see a Lower House so
jealous of its own position agreeing to such a change. The only likely basis
for such a reform would be the introduction of an accountable regional tier
of government. Perhaps the most one can say in 1987 is that if a devolution
of power to the regions ever does take place, then second chamber reform
ought to be included as part of a general new settlement.

While it is difficult to see a reform which involved an elected House
being introduced, other possible reforms are open to even greater
objections. Should the House of Lords, then, be left alone or abolished? In
1978 the Home Committee stated that to keep the status quo was 'not a
prudent policy. Indeed we are doubtful whether it is a policy at all.' That
was said in the wake of the conflicts of 1975–6, at a time when 'at best the
present House of Lords faces gradual but relentless atrophy' (ibid, paras 66
and 68). Matters look at least a little different in 1988. But the return of a
Labour Government could rapidly alter the picture again, making the
House of Lords, once more, seem very vulnerable.

Sometimes when abolition is advocated, replacement is intended; such is
the position of the Labour MP Stuart Bell in his somewhat misleadingly
entitled pamphlet How to Abolish the Lords (Bell, 1981). Against this, one

has to say that radical discontinuity of the kind that totally sweeps away one institution and replaces it with an entirely new body has not been characteristic of British constitutional developments, and where it has taken place (for example, in local government) it has not, on the whole, been successful. (This may be regrettable or it may be laudable, but that is beside the point.) Change that adapted the present House of Lords, perhaps quite radically as the Home Committee proposed, is both more realistic and more likely to endure.

Some who stress, and on the whole approve of, the gradual development and continuity of the Constitution have foreseen as part of this process the eventual abolition of the House of Lords through its own decay and collapse. Bagehot spoke of atrophy in the mid-nineteenth century, just as the Home Committee did in the late 1970s. Nevil Johnson, himself a member of the Home Committee, saw the House of Lords as so marginal as to be almost irrelevant (Johnson, 1977, p.43). But such decline to the point of possible collapse has, at least temporarily, been arrested. It is the 'Rise of the House of Lords' (to quote the title of a prescient article by a leading journalist, Rutherford, 1984) which has been characteristic of the 1980s. The House of Lords has become a good deal more important again in the whole business of government. Its collapse has at least been postponed!

If the House of Lords was abolished without replacement the most obvious immediate effect would be the loss of opportunities to improve legislation. It may be argued that reforms in Commons procedure and increased numbers of parliamentary draftsmen could reduce the need for the extra legislative stages provided by the Lords. But the House of Commons has shown itself much more concerned to preserve legislative procedures, which serve the purposes of traditional two-party conflict, than to introduce reforms to these procedures so that they serve the purpose of effective legislative scrutiny. Special standing committees have been virtually unused, and proposals designed to ensure that every part of a bill receives at least some time in standing committee have been eschewed in favour of continued use of the 'guillotine'. To abolish the Lords or even to allow it to collapse quietly, without ensuring some *quid pro quo* changes in the Commons would be foolish. If some legislation leaving the Commons now is unfit to be let loose on the public (Griffith, 1974, p. 231) this situation would only worsen.

Abolition may be advocated as part of a process involving the removal or diminution of every obstacle to the power wielded by a Commons majority. A concern for strong government may be seen as paramount over a concern to maintain parliamentary government; if so the second chamber should be removed and the Commons subdued and elective dictatorship allowed to flourish. The very lack of legitimacy of the present

House of Lords is a convenience to those so minded. Any reform which enhanced its legitimacy could be a set-back to their cause, and is accordingly resisted. But even the present House of Lords may prove much more difficult to abolish for all sorts of practical reasons (Crowther-Hunt, 1980) as well as more theoretical reasons (Mirfield, 1979). Awareness of this fact was no doubt responsible for the failure to include the Labour Party's 1977 Conference decision to abolish the House of Lords outright in its subsequent election manifestos.

Conclusion

The basis on which the House of Lords is composed remains unaltered because no sufficient agreement about an alternative basis has ever yet existed. This does not mean that the way in which the House of Lords is now composed commands any widespread support: it simply happens to be the status quo. The children of patronage mingle with the children of aristocrats, and neither has a more obvious claim than the other to be afforded places in a modern parliament.

Major obstacles lie in the way of introducing an elected second chamber. At least, that is how the matter looks in 1988. But it is inconceivable that the House in its present form should continue indefinitely. No doubt change will occur: it is usually a crisis which produces decisive constitutional change. It was a crisis which produced the 1911 Parliament Act, not the measured conclusions of the 'good and the great' at the Bryce Commission.

Meanwhile, the House has shown a remarkable resilience. It has adapted and expanded its activities. It has worked its way back from the margins of political life. It has, to a surprising extent, regained an importance within the whole business of government.

APPENDIX A

EXPENSES PAYMENTS FOR PEERS AND REMUNERATION FOR OFFICE HOLDERS IN THE HOUSE OF LORDS

Prior to 1946 no allowances of any kind were payable to peers in respect of their attendance at the House of Lords. Earlier generations had assumed peers were men of substance, unlikely to be concerned about such trifling matters as expenses payments. Ministers did receive salaries, but they were paid in respect of their ministerial office, on identical terms to the salaries paid to Commons' ministers.

The post-war Attlee Government introduced a travel allowance in 1946, to which was added in 1957 an expenses allowance. Both of these were subsequently adjusted and extended in scope. During this period the salaries of ministers in the two Houses began to diverge as Commons' ministers received an expenses allowance and then a parliamentary salary additional to their ministerial salary. Also a gradual increase took place in the number of office-holders in the House who became entitled to a salary. Each of these matters is briefly examined in this appendix.

A. Travel Allowances

In 1946 peers became entitled to claim for the cost of first-class rail travel between their nearest home station and London. An 'assiduity' rule only allowed claims from peers who attended over one-third of the sittings of the House (though in 1947 this was relaxed for peers who lived in Scotland). The object of this rule was to prevent casual attenders claiming for travel to London. However the rule came in for increasing criticism on the grounds that many peers who attended less than a third of the time did contribute significantly to the work of the Lords. It was eventually abolished in 1972.

Meanwhile, in 1961, a car mileage allowance had been introduced as an alternative to rail fares, limited at first to the cost of equivalent rail travel. The car allowance was gradually increased and in the 1970s became linked to similar allowances payable to civil servants. After the latter had become graduated according to car engine size, MPs decided to accept a steeply tiered allowance, but peers voted (by 128 to 64) not to do so; instead they kept a uniform allowance based on medium sized cars. Many peers believed that in so doing they were acting in a more responsible way than MPs (26 July 1984).

Gradually the basis of travel payments has altered from a system only offering help towards the rail fares of regular attenders to a system which basically pays the travel costs involved for any peer who attends the House of Lords.

B. The Attendance or Reimbursement of Expenses Allowance

The introduction of an expenses allowance in 1957 was open to criticism on three grounds. First, it was officially described as a 'daily attendance allowance' which implied that it could be claimed simply on the ground of attendance, whereas the intention was that only out-of-pocket expenses directly incurred in attendance should be payable. In 1981 it was officially renamed a 'reimbursement of expenses allowance'.

Second, the definition of expenses which could legitimately be claimed was left vague, deliberately so it would seem, in 1957, but never properly clarified until 1975, in which year the Top Salaries Review Board found 'a great deal of confusion' among peers about the expenses to which they were entitled. A third, and related point, was that from the outset it was made clear that peers would not have to produce any evidence about their actual expenditures; the Leader of the Commons, R. A. Butler, thought such procedures would be 'undignified' for those he termed 'our distinguished brethren in another place' (HC Debs, 9 July 1957, col. 231–2).

The upper limit of the allowance was initially set at three guineas per day (£3.15), then raised to four and a half guineas (£4.72) in 1964 following the Lawrence Committee Report (Cmnd 2516). Thereafter, by resolution of the House the sum increased in 1970 to £6.50 and by stages to £13.50 in 1975.

The Top Salaries Review Body (TSRB) made the first thorough examination of the whole subject in 1975 (Cmnd 6749). A survey of peers found that 82 per cent of those eligible to claim expenses did do so, and that 55 per cent thought the permitted maximum inadequate. In its report the TSRB recommended that four separate headings of permissible expenditure be identified, namely overnight accommodation, day subsistence, secretarial expenses, and finally — on the grounds that 'a revising chamber should be a well-briefed chamber' — the purchase of journals, subscriptions to bodies relevant to a peer's work in the House of Lords and similar expenditure.

If implemented in full the recommendation of this report would have taken the maximum daily allowance from £13.50 to £24.50. The Labour Government decided it could not do this because of its newly introduced pay policy; this was a curious decision given the emphasis that had always been placed on the fact that the peers' allowance was merely for expenses and not in any sense remuneration. The then prevailing £13.50 allowance did however cover all the expenses recommended by the TSRB except for overnight accommodation, so the effect of the Government's decision was to discriminate against peers living at a distance from London. For peers obliged to stay overnight in London a maximum of £16.50 was allowed from March 1977.

In 1979 the TSRB recommended that the fourth element in the allowance (as recommended in 1975) should be merged with the third, creating in effect a secretarial and research allowance; this was to meet objections to the four-element system which it had been suggested peers would find difficult to operate (Cmnd 7598). At the same time it recommended a maximum of £36 for peers requiring overnight accommodation, £17.50 for others, and this was accepted in full by the newly elected Conservative Government.

In 1982–3 the TSRB again made a full investigation of the expense allowance system (Cmnd 8881). A survey showed highest dissatisfaction with the allowance system among the most regular attending peers, but the Review Body felt unable to recommend remuneration as such for any group of peers. However, substantial rises were agreed, taking the daily allowance to £33 for those not requiring overnight accommodation and to £73 for those in need of such accommodation (HL Debs, 25 July 1983, col. 1370–4). Since 1984 these allowances have been linked to changes in civil servants' pay and expenses, which has obviated the need for any public announcement about increases being made in the Lords (HL Debs, 26 July 1984, col. 401–6). However annual adjustments have been made: from 1 August 1987 peers could claim up to £57 for overnight accommodation; up to £20 for day subsistence and incidental travel; and up to £22 for secretarial expenses.

In 1987 the TSRB made a full inquiry into MPs' and peers' secretarial costs. This followed a Commons vote in which, to the anger of the Government, MPs awarded themselves a 52 per cent increase in their secretarial expenses allowance, at the same time as peers accepted a much more modest increase. A survey showed once again that it was the active peers who felt most keenly the inadequacy of the allowance. As stated in Chapter 4 the report of the Review Body (Cmd 131) particularly singled out the more or less full-time backbench peers and the Opposition frontbench spokesmen as most in need of additional help. This matter was pending in Summer 1987 (see HL Debs, 23 July 1987, cols 1529–47).

C. Salaries Payable to Ministers in the Lords

Ministers in both Houses received identical salaries until 1946 (and by modern standards these were generous salaries — that for a senior minister was fixed at £5,000 in 1830, and remained at this level until 1964). In 1946 ministers in the Commons became entitled to receive £500 of an MP's salary to cover the costs of constituency representation; subsequently this was increased, and in 1972 a parliamentary salary for Commons ministers was introduced. As a result the total salaries of junior ministers in the Lords (as well as of Lords-in-Waiting) fell considerably below those of Commons ministers, and lower even than the salaries of back-bench MPs. This state of affairs continued throughout the 1970s, because, though regarded as anomalous by the TSRB in 1976, the Labour Government was unwilling to rectify the matter lest this appear to breach its incomes policy. (By 1979 MPs were paid £6,897, junior ministers in the Lords £6,622, and Lords-in-Waiting £5,522.)

The TSRB emphasised, in 1976 and again in 1979, that higher ministerial salaries for peers could only be justified if their ministerial responsibilities were greater than those of Commons ministers. This it had not found to be the case. However, Lords ministers did become entitled during the 1970s to a limited secretarial allowance for their parliamentary work, and also to a London salary supplement.

In the early 1980s the financial position of junior members of the Government front-bench in the Lords attracted some attention, with questions being asked in the House (see 7 July 1980, col. 880; 12 March 1981, col. 379). In addition to increasing all salaries substantially in 1980, the Government decided, in 1981, to override the TSRB recommendation and pay ministers in the Lords higher ministerial salaries than their Commons counterparts. This decision received support in 1983 when management consultants commissioned by the TSRB examined the jobs concerned and recommended higher pay for Lords' ministers on the grounds that they did have to do more work (though not necessarily more important work) than Commons ministers (see pp. 68–9). By 1987 Lords-in-Waiting received salaries £3,000 ahead of those paid to back-bench MPs, with junior ministers receiving £3,000 more again. While the relative pay of Lords' ministers has improved greatly, their salaries remain modest by comparison with those payable elsewhere in the public sector (let alone at senior levels in the private sector). Cabinet ministers in the Lords received £36,390 in 1987, ministers of state £30,640, and Lords-in-Waiting £21,570. For comparison's sake the standard rate for a permanent secretary was £62,100 and for a senior principal just over £23,000.

D. Office-Holders

If we exclude government ministers (including the Lord Chancellor), prior to 1965 only one peer received a salary because of the office he held in the House of Lords, namely the Lord Chairman of Committees, whose salary has been long-standing, and was linked to that of his opposite number in the Commons, Chairman of Ways and Means. In 1974 the salaried post of Principal Deputy Chairman of Committees was created (see Chapter 4).

In 1965 remuneration for the Leader of the Opposition and the Opposition Chief Whip was introduced. At first the Opposition leader was paid £2,000 (compared with £3,250 for MPs). By 1979 this was £4,403, still well behind the MPs' salary, but the TSRB in its report that year stated that the post had 'hitherto been seriously undervalued'. From 1980 the salaries payable to the Opposition leader and Chief Whip moved ahead rapidly, the former rising by 1987 to over £24,000.

Conclusion

Since 1980 both the allowances which peers may claim and the salaries paid to those who hold offices have improved very markedly. Nonetheless, the whole expense allowance system remains unsatisfactory because it fails to differentiate between peers whose commitments to the House and whose contributions to the work of the House, vary enormously. However, the introduction of salaries for peers, or even some narrowly defined category of peers, such as Opposition front-bench members, remains problematical. A more satisfactory system of recompensing peers is unlikely to be achieved until some fundamental reform of the composition of the House of Lords is brought about.

APPENDIX B

PEERAGES DISCLAIMED, 1963–87

Tony Benn MP	Viscount Stansgate	1963
John Grigg	Lord Altrincham	1963
Sir Alec Douglas-Home	Earl of Home	1963
(Lord Home of the Hirsel since 1974)		
Quentin Hogg	Viscount Hailsham	1963
(Lord Hailsham of Saint Marylebone since 1970)		
Charles Fitzroy	Lord Southampton	1964
William Collier	Lord Monkswell	1964
Sir Max Aitken	Lord Beaverbrook	1964
Victor Montagu	Earl of Sandwich	1964
Sir Hugh Fraser	Lord Fraser of Allander	1966
Mr Anthony Lambton MP	Earl of Durham	1970
(also known as Viscount Lambton, MP)		
Dr Alan Sanderson	Lord Sanderson of Ayot	1971
Charles Reith	Lord Reith	1972
Arthur Silkin	Lord Silkin	1972
George Archibald	Lord Archibald	1975
T. O. Lewis	Lord Merthyr	1977

Three of the above disclaimers had died by 1987. These were William Collier in 1984, Sir Max Aitken in 1985, and Sir Hugh Fraser in 1987. The heirs to the Monkswell and Beaverbrook peerages both decided to take up their peerages, and both became active members of the House of Lords, Lord Monkswell on the Labour benches and Lord Beaverbrook on the Conservative side. Sir Hugh Fraser left no heirs, so the peerage he had disclaimed became extinct upon his death.

APPENDIX C

DEBATES AND SELECT COMMITTEE REPORTS
ON TELEVISING THE HOUSE OF LORDS

On 15 June 1966 the House debated and approved a motion moved by Lord Egremont, which welcomed 'the televising of some of its proceedings as an additional means of demonstrating its usefulness in giving a lead to public opinion'.

On 21 July 1966 the House agreed to establish a select committee to consider how to put this resolution into effect. This issued three reports, and on its own recommendation had referred to it the subject of sound broadcasting (HL 190, 1966–7, HL 284, 966–7 and HL 27, 1967–8). Following a three-day closed circuit experiment in televising debates conducted in February 1968, a full review was made by the same select committee (HL 159, 1967–8). This included detailed recommendations for a public experiment in televising the House. The report was debated by the House on 20 March 1969 and well received, but no further experiment was held.

From 1978 sound broadcasting from the House was introduced, as also from the House of Commons.

In December 1983 the Lords debated a motion moved by a former Leader of the House, Lord Soames, which stated that 'this House endorses its decision of 15 June 1966 in favour of the public televising of some of its proceedings for an experimental period and instructs the sound broadcasting committee to consider and report how this decision should be implemented'. The resolution was carried by 74 votes to 24 (HL Debs, 8 December 1983, cols 1189–253). The select committee on sound broadcasting reported in August 1984, stating how such an experiment could be conducted (HL 299, 1983–4). The Lords agreed to this report after debate in November 1984 (HL Debs, 27 November 1984, col. 764–860). A six-month experiment took place from January 1985, and in July the Lords agreed to extend the experiment on a motion moved by Lord Soames and carried by 135 votes to 52 (HL Debs, 22 July 1985, col. 991–1046).

In April 1986 the select committee on televising the House of Lords made a full report on the fifteen-month experiment, recommending that the proceedings of the House should be permanently televised (HL 102,

1985–6). This was debated by the Lords on 12 May 1986 (HL Debs, col. 963–1005), and without a division the Lords agreed to the select committee's proposals.

PRINCIPAL SOURCES

A. The main official sources used in this work have been:

House of Lords Hansard, cited in text as HL Debs, followed by date and column number, e.g. HL Debs, 26 October 1984, col. 343.

House of Commons Hansard cited as HC Debs, and then as above.

Journals of the House of Lords (published sessionally).

House of Lords Committee Reports, cited as HL followed by number and session in which published, e.g. HL 31 (1986–7).

House of Commons Committee Reports (references given in the same way as those for House of Lords Reports).

The Standing Orders of the House of Lords Relating to Public Business, 1984 edition (SOs).

The Companion to the Standing Orders, 1984 edition (companion).

Command Papers, Cmnd, Cd, Cmd, followed by number and year of publication.

The following official sources should be particularly mentioned:

HL 9 (1987–8)	Report by the Group on the Working of the House.
Cd 9038 (1918)	Report of the Conference on Reform of the Second Chamber, Chairman Lord Bryce (Bryce Commission).
Cmnd 7380 (1948)	Parliament Bill, 1947. Agreed Statement on Conclusion of Conference of Party Leaders.
Cmnd 3799 (1968)	House of Lords Reform.
HL 141 (1976–7)	First Report of the Select Committee of the House of Lords on Practice and Procedure.

All the above are published by Her Majesty's Stationery Office.

B. The major reference works used have been:

Who's Who, Dod's Parliamentary Companion, Whitaker's Almanac and *Keesing's Contemporary Archives.* The edition of *Erskine May's Parliamentary Practice* used and cited has been the 20th, edited by Sir Charles Gordon, published in 1983 by Butterworth.

C. Information has been supplied by the House of Lords' Information Office, the office of the Leader of the House and Chief Whip, and by the whips' offices of the other parties.

D. Interviews were held with some 45 peers, especially in 1984, but also intermittently before and since.

E. Major works on the House of Lords. Particular mention should be made of the following:

Bromhead, P.A.   (1958) *The House of Lords and Contemporary Politics, 1911–57*, Routledge and Kegan Paul.

Morgan, Janet   (1975) *The House of Lords and the Labour Government 1964–70*, Oxford University Press.

Baldwin, Nicholas (1985) *The House of Lords*, unpublished PhD Thesis, Exeter University.

BIBLIOGRAPHY

Bagehot, W. (1867 1st edn and 1963 edn) *The English Constitution*, Fontana.

Baldwin, Nicholas (1985) *The House of Lords*, unpublished PhD thesis, Exeter University.

Bates, St. John (1985) 'Select Committees in the House of Lords', in G. Drewry (ed.) *The New Select Committees*, Oxford University Press.

Beith, A. (1981) 'Prayers Unanswered: Parliamentary Scrutiny of Statutory Instruments', *Parliamentary Affairs*, Vol. XXXIV, No. 2, pp. 165–73.

Bell, S. (1981) *How to Abolish the Lords*, Fabian Tract No. 476.

Beloff, N. (1976) *Freedom under Foot*, Temple Smith.

Blewett, N. (1972) *The Peers, the Parties and the People*, Macmillan.

Blom-Cooper, L. and Drewry, G. (1972) *Final Appeal: A Study of the House of Lords in its Judicial Capacity*, Oxford University Press.

Borthwick, R. (1973) 'Public Bill Committees in the House of Lords', *Parliamentary Affairs*, Vol. XXVI, No. 4, pp. 440–53.

Boyd-Carpenter, J. (Lord) (1980) *Way of Life*, Sidgwick and Jackson.

Braham, S. (1986) *A Hard Core of Wind; Inside the Lords*, Val Publishing.

Bromhead, P. A. (1958) *The House of Lords and Contemporary Politics, 1911–57*, Routledge and Kegan Paul.

Bromhead, P. A. and Shell, D. R. (1967) 'The Lords and their House', *Parliamentary Affairs*, Vol. XX, No. 4, pp. 337–49.

Bruce-Gardyne, J. (Lord) (1980) 'Late Nights on the Ermined Treadmill', *Sunday Telegraph*.

Butler, D. (1976) 'The Australian Crisis of 1975' *Parliamentary Affairs*, Vol. XXIX, No. 2, pp. 201–10.

Butt, R. (1978) 'The Case for a Stronger Second Chamber', in J. P. Mackintosh, (ed.), *People and Parliament*, Saxon House (for Hansard Society).

Chester, D. N. and Bowring, N. (1962) *Questions in Parliament*, Oxford University Press.

Crick, B. (1st edn 1964, 2nd edn 1968) *Reform of Parliament*, Weidenfeld and Nicolson.

Crossman, R. H. S. (1975 and 1976) *Diaries of a Cabinet Minister*, Vol. 1 and Vol. 2, Jonathan Cape.

Crowther-Hunt, Norman (Lord) (4 December 1980) 'Labour's Threat to the Lords', *The Listener*.

Crowther-Hunt, Norman (Lord) and Peacock, Prof. A. (1973) *Royal Commission on the Constitution, Memorandum of Dissent*, Cmnd 5460–II.

Devlin, Lord (Patrick) (1956) *Trial by Jury*, Stevens.

Devlin, Lord (Patrick) (1965) *The Enforcement of Morals,* Oxford University Press.

Drewry, G. and Burton, I. (1980) *Legislation and Public Policy: Public Bills in the 1970–74 Parliament*, Macmillan.

Drewry, G. and Brock, J. (1971) 'Prelates in Parliament', *Parliamentary Affairs*, Vol. XXIV, No. 3, pp. 222–50.
Drewry, G. and Brock, J. (1983) *The Impact of Women on the House of Lords*, Centre for the Study of Public Policy, University of Strathclyde.

Franklin, M. (1986) 'MPs' Objections to Televising Parliament' *Parliamentary Affairs*, Vol. 39, No. 3.

Gaitskell, H. (1983) *The Diary of Hugh Gaitskell 1945–56*, ed. by Philip M. Williams, Jonathan Cape.
Ganz, G. (1987) *Quasi-Legislation*, Street and Maxwell.
Gordon, Sir Charles (ed.) (1983) *Erskine May's Parliamentary Practice*, 20th edn, Butterworth.
Grantham, C. and Hodgson, C. M. (1985) 'Structural Changes: The Use of Committees' in P. Norton, *Parliament in the 1980s*, Basil Blackwell.
Griffith, J. A. G. (1974) *The Parliamentary Scrutiny of Government Bills*, George Allen and Unwin.
Griffith, J. A. G. (1981) 'Standing Committees in the Commons' in M. Ryle and S. A. Walkland (eds.) *The Commons Today*, Fontana.

Hailsham, Lord (1976) 'Elective Dictatorship', BBC.
Heffer, E. S. (1973) *The Class Struggle in Parliament*, Collins.
Hindell, K. and Simms, M. (1971) *Abortion Law Reformed*, Owen.
Home, Lord (1978) *Report of the Review Committee on the Second Chamber*, Conservative Political Centre.

Johnson, N. (1977) *In Search of the Constitution*, Pergamon Press.
Jones, G. W. (1966) 'A Forgotten Right Discovered', *Parliamentary Affairs*, Vol. XIX, No. 3, pp. 363–72.
Judge, D. (ed.) (1983) *The Politics of Parliamentary Reform*, Heinemann.

Kolinsky, M. (1975) 'Parliamentary Scrutiny of European Legislation', *Government and Opposition*, Vol. 10, No. 1, pp. 46–69.

Laski, H. (1938) *Parliamentary Government in England*, George Allen and Unwin.
Le May, G. (1979) *The Victorian Constitution: Conventions, Usages and Contingencies*, Duckworth.
Livingstone, K. (1987) *If Voting Changed Anything, They'd Abolish It*, Collins.
Longford, Lord (F. Pakenham) (1974) *The Grain of Wheat*, Collins.

Mirfield, P. (1979) 'Can the House of Lords be Lawfully Abolished?', *Law Quarterly Review*.
Moran, M. (1977) *Politics of Industrial Relations*, Macmillan.
Morgan, J. (1975) *The House of Lords and the Labour Government*, Oxford University Press.

Northfield, Lord (Donald Chapman) (1978) 'Reforming Procedure in the House of Lords', in D. Butler and A. Halsey (eds.), *Policy and Politics*, Macmillan.
Norton, P. (ed.) (1985) *Parliament in the 1980s*, Basil Blackwell.

Powell, J. Enoch and Wallis, K. (1968) *The House of Lords in the Middle Ages*, Weidenfeld and Nicolson.
Punnett, R. M. (1973), *Front Bench Opposition*, Heinemann.

Redcliffe-Maud, John (Lord) (1981) *Experiences of an Optimist*, Hamish Hamilton.
Rhodes-James, R. (1986) *Anthony Eden*, Weidenfeld and Nicolson.
Richards, P. (1963) *Patronage and British Government*, George Allen and Unwin.
Richards, P. (1970) *Parliament and Conscience*, George Allen and Unwin.
Roth, A. (1972) *Lord on the Board*, Parliamentary Profile Services.
Roth, A. (1977) *Sir Harold Wilson*, MacDonald and Jane's.
Roth, A. (1986) 'Mrs. Thatcher's other Chamber', *New Statesman*, 11 July 1986.
Rutherford, M. (1984) 'The Rise of the House of Lords', *Financial Times*, 23 March 1984.

Shell, D. R. (1983) 'The House of Lords', in D. Judge (ed.), *The Politics of Parliamentary Reform*, Heinemann.
Shell, D. R. (1985) 'The House of Lords and the Thatcher Government', *Parliamentary Affairs*, Vol. 38, No. 1, pp. 16–32.
Silk, P. (1987) *How Parliament Works*, Longman.
Stewart, M. (1980) *Life and Labour*, Sidgwick and Jackson.
Strang, William (Lord) (1956) *Home and Abroad*, Deutsch.

Theakston, K. (1987) *Junior Ministers in British Government*, Basil Blackwell.

Vincent, J. (1966) 'The House of Lords', *Parliamentary Affairs*, Vol. XIX, No. 4, pp. 475–85.

Walker, J. (1987) *The Queen Has Been Pleased*, Sphere Books.
Weston, C. C. (1965) *English Constitutional Theory and the House of Lords, 1556–1822*, Routledge and Kegan Paul.
Weston, C. C. (1986) 'Salisbury and the Lords, 1868-1895', in C. Jones and D. L. Jones (eds) *Peers, Politics and Power, 1603–1911*, Hambledon Press.
Whale, John (1985) 'Bishops in the Lords', *The Listener*, 8 August 1985.
Wilson, H. (1971) *The Labour Government, 1964–70: A Personal Record*, Weidenfeld and Nicolson.
Windlesham, Lord (1975) 'The House of Lords: A Study of Influence Replacing Power', *Politics in Practice*, Cape.

INDEX

DATE DUE

APR 0 9 2012	
JUN 7 2012	
JUN 1 1 2012	

JUN 10